A Vicar in Victorian Norfolk

A Vicar in Victorian Norfolk

The Life and Times of
Benjamin Armstrong (1817–1890)

Susanna Wade Martins

THE BOYDELL PRESS

First published 2018
The Boydell Press, Woodbridge

ISBN 978 1 78327 330 0

The Boydell Press is an imprint of Boydell & Brewer Ltd
PO Box 9, Woodbridge, Suffolk IP12 3DF, UK
and of Boydell & Brewer Inc.
668 Mt Hope Avenue, Rochester, NY 14620–2731, USA
website: www.boydellandbrewer.com

A CIP catalogue record for this book is available
from the British Library

The publisher has no responsibility for the continued existence or accuracy of
URLs for external or third-party internet websites referred to in this book, and
does not guarantee that any content on such websites is, or will remain, accurate
or appropriate

This publication is printed on acid-free paper

Printed and bound in Great Britain by TJ International Ltd, Padstow, Cornwall

Contents

Illustrations

The author and publishers are grateful to all the institutions and individuals listed for permission to reproduce the materials in which they hold copyright. Every effort has been made to trace the copyright holders; apologies are offered for any omission, and the publishers will be pleased to add any necessary acknowledgement in subsequent editions.

Acknowledgements

This book could not have been written without the generosity of Benjamin Armstrong's great-grandsons, Christopher and David Armstrong. Christopher trusted me with the eleven volumes of Benjamin's diary and David shared with me his work on family history. Both Christopher and David searched out family photographs, many of which appear in the book.

The Dereham Antiquarian Society and particularly its secretary, Sue Walker-White, have also been very helpful in seeking out and providing further illustrative material.

David Neave kindly sent me a copy of his publication on Armstrong's time at Crowle.

As ever, the Norfolk Record Office has been very supportive, pointing me in the right direction for documents. The librarian and archivist at Norwich Cathedral Library helped me find my way through the antiquarian books which would have been part of Armstrong's library.

The anonymous reader's comments were extremely useful and pointed out areas where expansion and further explanation were needed. Errors that remain are entirely my responsibility.

I am grateful to the Rt Revd Graham James, Bishop of Norwich, for reading the manuscript and writing the foreword, and to my editor Caroline Palmer for her encouragement.

My husband Peter has been extremely supportive and together we have explored the places with which Armstrong was associated, including the back streets of Dereham. All the modern photographs were taken by him.

Foreword

by the Rt Revd Graham James, Bishop of Norwich

I was a curate in Peterborough in the mid-1970s when I first discovered Benjamin Armstrong's diaries. Scouring a second-hand bookshop I found the extracts chosen by his grandson Herbert, vicar of St Margaret's, King's Lynn (now King's Lynn Minster), during the Second World War. This selection, published in 1963, contained a masterly introduction by Owen Chadwick, placing Armstrong within the context of the Victorian church and wider society.

Susanna Wade Martins has further enlarged our understanding of the diarist by writing as full a biography as the sources permit. Armstrong deserves to be remembered both for his own qualities and as a representative of many clergy of his generation who exhibited a new pastoral zeal alongside a desire for the highest standards in public worship. It was a new age of spiritual seriousness in the Church of England. Armstrong did not seek novelty but the recovery of the Catholic and sacramental character of his church expressed in the beauty of holiness and service to the poor.

Four decades ago I was immediately drawn to Armstrong. He was the sort of priest I admired. His commitment to daily public worship was one shared in my council estate parish, where there was a Eucharist every day, something Armstrong would have barely imagined possible. He had served in Dereham for fourteen years before even introducing a weekly service of Holy Communion. It was upon the dedication and vision of Victorian clergy like Armstrong that the twentieth-century Church of England was built.

Prior to discovering Armstrong I had already read the diaries of another Norfolk clergyman, James Woodforde of Weston Longville.

I felt no connection with Woodforde at all. He seemed not merely a remote figure (though he was both in time and social circumstance) but someone who did not exercise a ministry remotely akin to my own. Armstrong, writing only half a century after Woodforde, inhabited a world I recognised. It's a lesson in the rapidity of change in the Church of England in the nineteenth century.

Clerical diarists are not a scarce breed. Woodforde, Witts, Kilvert and others were mostly rural clergymen. Armstrong is different. He may not have been a city priest, but Dereham was a relatively populous and growing market town parish. He did not need to write a diary to fill his time. His was no leisured life. Neither was his diary an exercise in introspection nor even a spiritual journal. It was very much a record of daily life, carefully preserved for posterity but perhaps occasionally therapeutic as he records what he thinks of those who oppose his ministry or his frustrations with members of his family, especially his sister and her husband.

Susanna Wade Martins enables us to discover dimensions of Armstrong's life which make him the more fascinating. He would have preferred a career in the Army but finance and circumstance dictated otherwise. His vocation (and his Catholic churchmanship) came later, not least as a result of the reading he was expected to do for his ordination examinations and the company of those he met along the way. Coming as he did from a family wealthy enough to travel, his experience of the Roman Catholic Church in continental Europe (he spent two months in Paris when he was 23 before travelling through Belgium, Germany and Holland) spoke to his natural aesthetic sense. In continental Catholicism he admired the use of churches for prayer every day of the week, and their ordered liturgy. This experience seems to have shaped his mind and thinking for the rest of his life. When in London he would seek out the most advanced Anglo-Catholic churches in which to worship. In time he became chairman of the Norwich Diocesan branch of the English Church Union, which was uncompromising in its support of the Anglo-Catholic cause.

Yet in his parish, as the author describes so well, Armstrong was not revolutionary but gradually reshaped both the interior of his church, the worship which went on within it and the ministry exercised in the town. Armstrong visited all his parishioners and was diligent in going to the homes of the poor and the sick even if he found it hard to bridge the social chasm. His commitment to education is reflected in the priority given to his work in schools. He wasn't the sort of ritualistic slum priest Anglo-Catholicism produced in the cities – his temperament and culture somehow didn't permit it – but there seems no indication that he was other than respected and appreciated by the population he served. There is, though, a rather sad entry in his diary in 1880, when the father of one of the children in the church school came to see him to thank him for the education his son had received. Armstrong comments 'this is recorded as being almost the only instance of any expression of gratitude ever met with'. That may have been the well-known Norfolk reserve at work, but it also suggests a continuing social gulf between parson and people that even an assiduous pastoral ministry could not overcome. It may also reflect two other features which this biography reveals – Armstrong's lack of a sense of humour and his pomposity: the two are frequently connected.

Susanna Wade Martins comments on the hauteur Armstrong sometimes adopts, both in relation to his dealings with his contemporaries (the lesser gentry bored him) and his wife and family. Nellie, his wife, is socially well connected, but his compliments are occasionally patronising and feel routine rather than heartfelt. Undoubtedly his favourite child was their eldest, Helen, a close and lifelong companion.

Given the way in which Armstrong records so many issues in church and state from his vantage point in Norfolk, it is surprising, as the author notes, that there is no reference to Darwin and the publication of *Origin of Species* and the debate on the origins of life, whereas ritualist controversies or the reverberations of the Crimean War gain ready attention. One wonders whether what we think of now as the most significant conflicts of the Victorian age did not appear so at the time.

Armstrong never served under a Bishop of Norwich sympathetic to his churchmanship. Samuel Hinds, who instituted him with 'hard dry indifference', was not sympathetic to any of his clergy, so Armstrong could scarcely feel victimised. John Pelham, his successor, was a low church Evangelical also theologically opposed to the positions Armstrong took. Nevertheless he was pastorally effective. Armstrong found him hospitable and largely supportive of his ministry. What Armstrong would make of the Diocese of Norwich today with a Bishop of Catholic churchmanship, let alone a Cathedral with a strong sacramental tradition and using incense so frequently, one wonders. I'm sure he would not expect to see a female dean, however. It's a reminder that tradition develops and that, to use the words of Cardinal Newman, 'to live is to change'. Armstrong saw many changes in his long and well-recorded life. Susanna Wade Martins reveals his qualities and recognises his shortcomings while understanding that he was one of a great swathe of similarly minded clergy who changed the Church of England for good – by improving its pastoral ministry, and in a lasting way.

+ Graham Norvic:
January 2018

Author's Note

The following abbreviations have been used:

CMS	Church Missionary Society
ECU	English Church Union
LAO	Lincolnshire Archives Office
NNAS	Norfolk and Norwich Archaeological Society
NRO	Norfolk Records Office
PP	Parliamentary Papers
SPAB	Society for the Protection of Ancient Buildings
SPCK	Society for the Propagation of Christian Knowledge
SPG	Society for the Propagation of the Gospel

Dates of entries in the diaries are given in brackets (D/M/Y). The early entries (pre-1842) where Armstrong appears to be summarising previous journals are often undated.

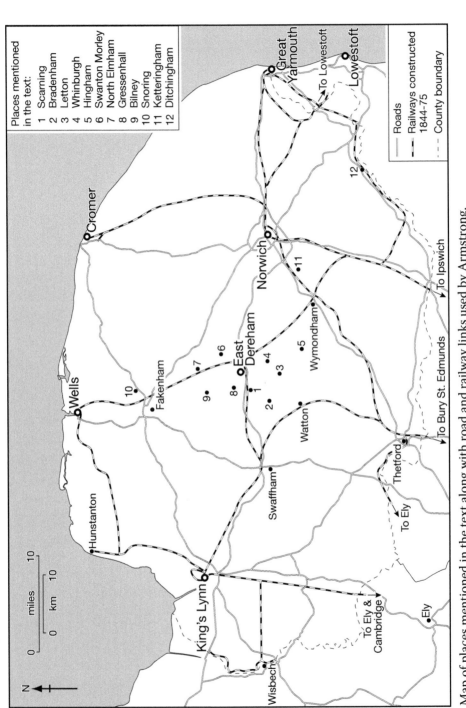

Map of places mentioned in the text along with road and railway links used by Armstrong.

Places mentioned in the text:

1 Scarning
2 Bradenham
3 Letton
4 Whinburgh
5 Hingham
6 Swanton Morley
7 North Elmham
8 Gressenhall
9 Bilney
10 Snoring
11 Ketteringham
12 Ditchingham

Roads
Railways constructed 1844–75
County boundary

Introduction

When the Revd Benjamin Armstrong sat at his desk in his study in the fenland parish of Crowle to summarise his early journals before beginning one which he would write nearly every day from 1842 to 1887, he was part of a tradition of clergy diarists. These diaries are now seen as an important corrective to the previous tendency to write the history of the church from the top down, concentrating on the theologians in Oxford and Cambridge, the Ecclesiastical Commissions and the reforming bishops both in the House of Lords and their dioceses. The parson, along with the squire, if he were resident, was likely to be the most educated and influential person in his rural parish. It was the clergyman who would be the face of the established church to his parishioners and on him rested the responsibility for the ensuring the influence of the church and implementing reforms at grass-roots level. This was especially true of the Victorian Anglican church, with its supporters of high and low church practices and the conflicts between science and literal interpretations of the Bible. The famous and influential players have dominated the pages of the standard histories. While 'thought of prelates, politicians and dons provides a valuable insight into the minds of those shaping opinion, it avoids the question of how (or even if) their ideas were assimilated in the country at large'.[1] What Armstrong's diaries have allowed us to do is to see how these major controversies were played out at parish level; they add a further dimension to the increasing, but still limited, number of studies in which the clergy and their parishioners are placed centre-stage.

The earliest histories of the Victorian church were written from the high church standpoint, filtering events through the eyes of a few Oxford men. As early as 1891 the Anglo-Catholic R.W. Church published *The Oxford Movement: Twelve Years, 1833–1841*, in which the supporters of the high church are credited with saving the church from decline. The Evangelicals also offered their distinctive interpretation, the most influential being G.R. Ballentine's *A History of the Evangelical Party in the Church of England* (1908). While Owen Chadwick's authoritative two-volume *The Victorian Church* (1966 and 1970) devotes a chapter to the 'Country Parson', scholars have continued to concentrate on conflicts within the church, the role of church leaders and government reforms.[2]

The first book looking at the clergy of this period themselves appeared in 1953 (C.K. Francis Brown, *A History of the English Clergy, 1800–1900*); in 1960, Diana McClatchey's *Oxfordshire Clergy, 1777–1869* still relied heavily on diocesan sources such as Visitation Records, as well as Bishop Wilberforce's Diocesan Books. The mid-century journals of such men as Edward Elton in the Oxfordshire village of Wheatley show how much an energetic parson could contribute to the improvement of the lives and spiritual condition of his parish.[3] There followed several books in the 1970s and 1980s continuing this interest in the clergy as a group. Anthony Russell and Rosemary O'Day considered how far a 'career' in the church could be seen as a 'profession' in the Victorian period, as other professions were increasingly becoming recognised.[4] Brian Heeney studied the many text books for young curates that were being produced in mid-Victorian England as an indication of what was expected of the ideal parson,[5] while Alan Haig considered the training available for aspiring clergymen, both in the universities and new colleges.[6] All these books looked at the way clergy were trained and operated as a profession rather than as individuals. Frances Knight attempted in her book to look at the church from grass roots upwards, not only considering the work and personal piety of the incumbents, but also those of their parishioners. This pioneering approach heralded an increasing interest in the clergy themselves, of which *The Victorian Parson* by Barry Turner (2015) is the most recent example, and one in which the use of clerical diaries is important. As interest is moving towards the individual clergy and their influence amongst their parishioners, the value of their diaries becomes increasingly recognised.

The clergy formed an important strand of society in Victorian England, particularly in the countryside, where, alongside the squire and the large farmers, they could exercise tight control over village affairs. In a small market town, they would share this influence with a group of leading tradesmen and professionals, but their control was nonetheless considerable. The Revd Benjamin J. Armstrong, the subject of this biography, was no exception, and it is the existence of his diaries which have made this study possible.

Benjamin Armstrong was ordained in 1841 and remained a serving priest until 1888, his incumbency covering years of tremendous change in the Church of England. Much of that time, from 1850 to 1888, was spent in the market town of East Dereham in central Norfolk. Partly as a result of recently opened railway connections, the town saw its population rise by a third during these years, and new industries using coal and steam were rapidly developing. Newcomers, 'part dissenting and part antagonistic to any form of Christianity' (16/5/74), with new skills were joining the indigenous population and changing the character of the town. These economic, social and ecclesiastical changes are all recorded in detail in eleven volumes of closely, but clearly written prose against the background of a family and personal life with its moments of tragedy and upheaval. It is both the continuous run of this record, covering nearly fifty years, and its background of religious, economic and social change, in addition to family concerns, that make these diaries so important.

The clergy as diary-writers

The clergy as a group were men who had time and the literary ability to keep diaries. The most famous Norfolk journal is the seventeen volumes written by Parson Woodforde, the final ten volumes describing his time as vicar of Weston Longville, not far from Dereham in Norfolk, from 1776 to1807.[7] Those of William Holland and John Skinner are well-known Georgian Somerset examples.[8] Holland's journal covers the years of the Napoleonic Wars and he was well aware of the distress rising war-time food prices were causing the poor, and took his parochial duties seriously. He had little time for those who neglected their parishes, 'instigated by vanity and not a true zeal for religion'.[9] He was a man of strong convictions, with a hatred of democrats, Methodists and Catholics. His diaries describe his parishioners, his family and his travels. He took regular services at several parishes, most of which were well attended, but gives no hint of the form these services took. He was entirely isolated from the wider church. Skinner's diaries cover the ten years before Queen Victoria's reign and describe some of the traditions of this earlier period. It was the existence of the village band that drew people to church, although Skinner himself would have preferred a choir of schoolgirls, but again he recorded little about the services themselves. Water streamed through the roof of his chancel, a state of affairs which was typical of many Georgian churches. He was an enthusiastic amateur archaeologist, and as well as his academic studies, his diaries describe writing sermons, visits to the sick and family worries. His increasing paranoia and belief that the Methodists were about to take over the world led to his suicide.

The diary of the Revd Francis Edward Witts covers the years 1820–1854. He succeeded his uncle as vicar of Upper Slaughter (Gloucestershire) and he was typical of the wealthy clergy who did not rely on their parish for an income. The ninety notebooks of his diary described both village life and his frequent visits to Bath. He was a magistrate (parson-magistrates were men of whom Armstrong disapproved) and chairman of the local Board of Guardians from 1836. He was very much a member of Gloucestershire rural society and a practical farmer, but, like many clergy, he disapproved of his fellow parsons hunting. His diaries describe his visits to the sick, but other than this there is little in the published extracts about his work or family life.[10]

The best-known of published Victorian diaries is that of the Revd Robert Francis Kilvert. Three notebooks of a much larger collection survive covering the years 1870–1879.[11] They contain lyrical descriptions of nature and anecdotes about people. They are the work of a man with a watchful eye and clear style. He was well aware of the poverty and squalor in which many of his parishioners lived and did what he could to help them while not in any way questioning the standards, values and attitudes of society which allowed these conditions to exist. He described country society as 'cumbrous, stiff, vulgarly extravagant, artificial and unnatural', comparing it with the simplicity and openness of the French (30/9/70), but there is little in his diaries about his clerical duties. He visited the poor and the children in the school. He mentioned writing sermons and taking two services on a Sunday. He was not a supporter of the ritual of high church services, although an anthem was sung on Easter Day.

The diaries of the Revd John Egerton, curate and then vicar of Burwash (Sussex) from 1857 to 1888, provide a full picture of rural life in what appears to have been a lawless and rowdy village.[12] He typified the professional attitude towards their parochial work which was emerging amongst the Victorian clergy and was deeply involved with the school. He visited his parishioners regularly, giving small doles to those who, often through no fault of their own, were left destitute. Unlike others, such as Skinner, he was on good terms with the dissenters, even taking the chair at a 'Tea meeting on behalf of a little meeting room', which he 'enjoyed heartily'.[13] He was aware of the hardships suffered by farm labourers and noted when wages were raised or reduced. He was sympathetic towards their trade union and preached a sermon for them. 'I tried with God's help to hold the balance even and to keep the peace.' He believed their movement must be based on justice and counselled arbitration.[14] He also understood the problems for farmers brought about by the agricultural depression of the 1870s and he reduced tithes accordingly, 'not wanting to be the only person in the parish not suffering'.[15] The main emphasis in the diaries is on the lives of the ordinary people of his parish, and his observations led to the publication of a book, *Sussex Folk and Sussex Ways*, in 1884. There is little about his family, and the religious controversies of the period are only briefly mentioned. He chose to obey the law and not go down the road of the ritualists. He wore a surplice to preach and had an anthem sung at Easter, but 'weekday services are not to our taste'.[16]

As well as these published diaries there are no doubt many others, some waiting to be discovered in record offices and family collections. Already known are those of Francis Massingbred in the Lincolnshire Archives Office (LAO MSS/8/1) and of a neighbouring clergyman, John Rashdall, in the Bodleian Library (Bodl MSEng. Misc e, 351), both of which describe their sense of isolation, and their fits of depression, self-doubt and spiritual unease.[17] McClatchey makes use of the diaries of Edward Elton of Wheatley and Charles Jerram of Witney, who admits the problem 'of having to say so much the same thing to so many persons, or to the same person day after day'.[18] Armstrong's diaries are unique both for the long period and the range of topics covered. Church and town affairs are described and they provide a vivid picture of the family and social life of the Victorian comfortably-off.

The Victorian church

Unlike the other diarists already mentioned, Armstrong devoted much space to the affairs and controversies of the Victorian church and they show how these arguments impacted on worship in a small Norfolk town well away from the main centres of debate. Armstrong entered the church at a time when the high church ideas of a small group of clergymen in Oxford were attempting to move the Anglican church nearer to its Catholic roots. Those such as Armstrong, who sympathised with what came to be known as the Oxford Movement, were labelled as tractarians, ritualists or high church.

The diaries cover a period when Christianity was coming to be increasingly marginalised in the formal life of the nation. Changes in the law show a trend towards a tolerant religious pluralism. From 1828 non-Anglicans were able to sit in the House of Commons, which meant that the debating of church matters in the House became a nonsense, and during Victoria's reign Parliament gradually lost interest in ecclesiastical affairs. The 1837 Civil Registration Act made the state responsible for the registration of births, and the Civil Marriage Act of the same year meant that marriages did not have to take place in a church. The Civil Graveyards and Cemeteries Acts of 1852 and 1853 removed the necessity for the church to be involved in the registration of deaths. In 1854 non-Anglicans were able to take BA university degrees, and from 1871 more advanced qualifications were open to them. The universities of Oxford and Cambridge ceased to be dominated by the clergy, as academics came to include non-ordained professors of science and the humanities. From 1870 the church's hold over education was being reduced with the introduction of Board Schools supported by a local rate. The increase in scientific knowledge and particularly the arguments over Darwinianism rocked certain parts of the established church, but surprisingly received no mention in Armstrong's diaries. It led to the growth of 'Christian Liberalism', whereby the moral aspects of the Christian faith came to be emphasised above doctrinal arguments and over the literal interpretation of the creation as described in Genesis and the miracles performed by Christ. The publication of some of these more liberal views in a series of articles by both Oxbridge theologians and beneficed clergy in a book entitled *Essays and Reviews* in 1860 was received by a storm of protest by many of the traditional clergy, Armstrong among them.

Of more practical significance to the church in Armstrong's time were the arguments between those supporting high and low church forms of service and the place of ritual in worship. Armstrong favoured a high church service and gradually introduced more ritual at Dereham, beginning by restoring the chancel and increasing the importance of the sacraments, particularly the frequency of services of Holy Communion. The choral element of the service became more important and finally both choir and the priest wore surplices. All these changes are recorded in the diary. The problem was that the *Book of Common Prayer*, introduced after the restoration of Charles II, relied heavily on the theology and wording of Thomas Cranmer, writing in the more extreme Protestant years of Edward VI and laying down a specific rubric enforcing a simple service. For instance, candles should not be lit on the altar (described as a 'Table' in the Prayer Book) purely for decoration, only if they were needed for light. The Table should be covered by a 'fair white linen cloth' and not an embroidered altar frontal. While these distinctions may now seem trivial, to the Victorians they mattered a great deal. The position at which the priest stood while celebrating Communion was also controversial. The Prayer Book stated that he should stand to the north of the altar, while the high church clergy wished to face east towards the altar they venerated, but with their backs to the congregation. Those influenced by the Oxford Movement and the spirit of the Gothic revival wished to return church services to some of the splendour of the medieval church and were prepared to fight for the right to depart from the strict requirements of the Prayer Book. When in London Armstrong would attend churches such as St Alban's, Holborn, known for their high church practices, and when visiting other churches would comment on the indications that their priests were high or low church, such as the number of candles on the altar. Because the 1662 Prayer Book had been agreed by Parliament, only Parliament could authorise changes to it and any deviation could be regarded as breaking the law. Armstrong followed the progress of cases, through first the church and finally civil courts, of priests who had introduced rituals forbidden by the Prayer Book which resulted in several priests being sent to prison.

Both the archbishops of Canterbury and the bishops in Norwich during this period were supporters of the simpler low church forms of service. Archbishop Sumner took up his post at Canterbury in 1848 and remained there until his death in 1862. He was opposed to the tractarians, who he felt were undermining the Protestant church, and instead openly supported the Evangelical wing with its roots in the parish of Clapham. He thus had many tensions within the church to cope with, as well as the re-establishment of a Roman Catholic hierarchy in Britain in 1850. In spite of Sumner's own convictions, he handled all these crises in a statesman-like way.[19] Considering Armstrong's high church views, it is not surprising that when in 1853 he went with his father to hear Sumner speak at the London Mansion House, he described him as 'vapid' (16/6/53). Sumner was succeeded by Charles Longley, whose main achievement was the calling of the first Lambeth Conference to which bishops from the world-wide Anglican Church were invited. Longley was more sympathetic to the high church priests and set up a Commission on Ritual.[20]

He was followed after only six years by Archbishop Tait. Queen Victoria is said to have tried to influence the debate by saying to her new archbishop, 'something must be done about ritualism'. Disraeli's cabinet was divided and Tait hoped to resolve the arguments by introducing into the House of Lords, as a Private Members' Bill, the Public Worship Regulation Act. This aimed at limiting the growing ritualism in the church. It was passed in 1874 with few amendments. Judges appointed by the two archbishops, rather than the bishops themselves, as in the original bill, were to hear complaints from parishes.[21] In the event the bill proved impossible to enforce and very soon became obsolete. On Tait's death, Armstrong wrote that in spite of his Presbyterian tendencies, 'he was tolerant and remarkable for his common sense' (3/12/82). He was followed by Edward Benson, whose efforts to set up a House of Laymen would have been approved by Armstrong.

An important consideration for the high church clergyman was the physical state of his church. On his youthful travels Armstrong had been struck by the ornamentation of continental Catholic churches and particularly by their stained-glass windows. His diary describes his efforts to beautify his church in Dereham, beginning with the chancel and eventually, in his final years, getting rid of the box pews and the first-floor galleries, which got in the way of his ambition to return to the medieval appearance of the building.

Armstrong's diaries

Beyond the confines of the church and church politics, Armstrong was very much involved with the affairs of the town, and his diary describes his work on various local government boards concerned with public health, street lighting and the running of a Literary Institute. He was, however, never a Poor Law Guardian and felt being a magistrate was not compatible with his perceived role as a friend of the poor. All of his activities for the welfare of the town are recorded in detail. He also supported concerts, the Oddfellows Friendly Society and the Rifle Volunteers. He was a familiar figure around the town and at public occasions. The diary gives a vivid picture of mid-Victorian town life through the eyes of an active member of local society. It also describes the many changes that were taking place through his lifetime with the growth of industries and factory employment, attracting more families to the town. In 1874 he visited a boot and shoe factory in Church Street which he described as 'quite a new feature in our town'. It employed fifty people and he was amazed that a pair of boots could be made from the uncut skin to completion in two hours (16/5/74).

While Armstrong's prose and descriptions of landscapes and the natural world do not share the literary bent of Kilvert's style, he was certainly capable of portraying a character and a scene in a few masterly chosen words. After a funeral where the young widow's grief was 'very affecting', his 'sententious and matter-of-fact' clerk, Mr Philo, declared 'that such noisy mourners speedily marry again' (13/7/54). Country walks with his eldest daughter, Helen, are also described. One after-noon they walked to the neighbouring parish of Hoe for which he also had responsibility, 'lingering to gather the numerous wild flowers which grow on Norfolk banks. – birds singing, leaves coming out, grass green, lazy cattle wending their way along – altogether a day that made one thankful one's lot was cast in the country' (14/5/54).

A duty that he took very seriously was that of regularly visiting all the poor in the town, so he probably knew more about their living conditions than most of his social equals. However, even he found the group difficult to relate to, describing them as 'heavy and dull'. He recorded his concern and urged farmers to pay a fair wage and to encourage children to attend school, all attitudes typical of the time. Private philanthropy and paternalism rather than government interference was required. The social order had to be upheld and he greeted with horror the 1884 extension of the franchise which gave the labouring class the vote. This led at the next election to Joseph Arch, 'the demagogue and agitator and deceiver of labourers' replacing C.S. Read, tenant farmer and an acquaintance of Armstrong's, as the local MP (9/12/86).

His relationship with the local non-conformist (or 'dissenting') ministers was mostly cordial, and he was happy to work with them on civic matters, for instance sitting with them on the committee of the Literary Institute. However, he was never prepared to accept their validity as ministers of religion. In his eyes, the Church of England was instituted by God, while the dissenters' ministers and 'meeting houses' (he could never bring himself to call them chapels) were created by man.

The eleven volumes of Benjamin Armstrong's diaries are therefore of unique importance. They cover without a break the entire period of his ministry, giving an insight into the ecclesiastical divisions within the Church of England from the point of view of a serving parish priest rather than the major players in the disputes. This is alongside a detailed description of his day-to-day work amongst the poor and at school in a class-ridden society which he is happy to accept as the norm. His time at Dereham was a period of great change in market towns, and the diary also provides a vignette of small-town life alongside that of the local gentry in the surrounding countryside. He remarked that the worlds of the town professionals and tradesmen and those of the country squire and farmer were too far apart for them to be able to mix socially.

A further strand covers Armstrong's home life and again gives us a glimpse of a typical middle-class family: its hopes and fears, its pleasures, the tensions within it and its moments of tragedy are all vividly and personally portrayed, providing a grass-roots history to which we can truly relate.

Inevitably, the main source of information for this biography has been Armstrong's own writings. However, where possible sources such as local newspapers and directories, parliamentary commissions and censuses as well as material available about the Norfolk clergy and their churches in the Norfolk Record Office have been consulted to provide a context for the often turbulent times through which Armstrong lived.

Notes

1 F. Knight, *The Nineteenth Century Church and English Society*, 1995, ix.
2 Ibid., ch. 1.
3 D. McClatchey, *Oxfordshire Clergy, 1777–1869*, 1960, 93–4.
4 R. O'Day, 'The Clerical Renaissance in Victorian England', in G. Parsons (ed.), *Religion in Victorian Britain*, vol. 1, *Traditions*, 1988, 185–212; A. Russell, *The Clerical Profession*, 1980.
5 B. Heeney, *A Different Kind of Gentleman: Parish Clergy as Professional Men in Early and Mid-Victorian England*, 1976.
6 A. Haig. *The Victorian Clergy*, 1984.
7 R.L. Winstanley, P. James and H. Richards (eds), *The Diaries of James Woodforde*, 1981–2000.
8 J. Ayers (ed.), *Paupers and Pig Killers: The Diary of William Holland, 1799–1818*, 1984; J. Skinner, *Journal of a Somerset Rector, 1803–1834*, 1984.
9 Ayers 1984, 45.
10 D. Verey (ed.), *The Diary of a Cotswold Parson, 1783–1854*, 1979.
11 W. Plomer (ed.), *Kilvert's Diary, 1870–1879*, abridged edition, 1944.
12 R. Wells (ed.), *Victorian Village: The Diaries of the Reverend John Coker Egerton of Burwash, 1857–1888*, 1992.
13 Ibid., 101.
14 Ibid., 174.
15 Ibid., 204.
16 Ibid., 262.
17 Ibid., 142.
18 McClatchey 1960, 95; W.O. Hassall (ed.), *Wheatley Records, 956–1956*, Oxfordshire Record Society 37, 1956.
19 N. Scotland, 'Sumner, John Bird, 1780–1862', *Oxford Dictionary of National Biography*, vol. 53, 2004, 330–2.
20 J.C. Garrard, 'Longley, Charles Thomas, 1794–1868', *Oxford Dictionary of National Biography*, vol. 34, 2004, 401.
21 G.I.T. Machin, *Politics and Churches in Great Britain*, 1987, 70–1.

I
The Early Years

One

Early Life

Many would smile and ask what there be in the unobtrusive and secluded life of a parish priest to interest anyone but himself.[1]

With these words a young parson, Benjamin Armstrong, writing in 1842, began a journal which was to run to eleven volumes, and which he wrote in a clear hand nearly every day until shortly before his death in 1890. It reveals to us an intelligent, lively man with a wide range of interests, living through a period of religious turmoil and social change. His influence may well not have extended far beyond the mid-Norfolk market town of East Dereham, his parish for over thirty years, but the value of the diaries lies in the insight this record provides into the life of a hard-working and deeply committed priest, as well as the changing religious practices of the time and the growing community which he served.

In an idle moment in 1842, 'mainly for pleasure', the 25-year-old vicar, then at Crowle St Oswald in north-west Lincolnshire, took up his pen to summarise his earlier diaries before destroying them and beginning in earnest to keep a daily journal. He had been married six months to 'an elegant, amiable and devoted' wife. His younger sister Annie was also happily married with a baby, and his parents were in good health and living in Islington. He described his hobbies as being 'mainly my profession'. This included church architecture, visiting the poor and sick and teaching poor children. 'The composition of a sermon (I always write my own) affords me the greatest delight.' However, the diaries show that throughout his life, he took a great interest in music, art and travel, all of which can be traced back to his early years. One pastime which he rather reluctantly gave up when he became a clergyman was field sports, from shooting rats as they scattered when a corn rick was taken down, to fox and stag hunting with the 'foremost nobles of the land'. In later life we see him shooting and fishing and taking his son to watch a fox hunt, although no longer riding to hounds himself. The ancient church in the small market town on a main road and not far from the canal suited his inclination towards a high church Anglo-Catholic form of worship, which, as we will see, he gradually introduced in Dereham.

Childhood and early education

Armstrong's summary reveals that he was born in November 1817 in a house on the Old Kent Road. He was the first child of his young parents (his father was married in 1814 at the age of 21 to his 19-year-old wife). His sister was born three years later. His father worked in the family oil business based at Hatton Wall. The firm's fortunes had prospered when it had gained the contract for installing and then supplying the whale oil for London's street lights. Profits from the business were extensively invested in London freehold property. Later his father was to build a fine house nearby in Hatton Gardens, 'notwithstanding that the neighbourhood was bad', which would be the family home as Benjamin and Annie grew up. His earliest memories were of riding to school perched in front of his father on his horse and of his indulgent grandmothers 'of moderate, but independent means', who supplied the children with toys and money.

His love of travel began at a young age when his grandfather moved to Jersey, probably to escape creditors, and the family spent summer holidays there. The sea crossing could be rough and hazardous and remained fixed in the young child's memory. On one occasion the holiday was extended to include a trip to Cherbourg and the Loire valley, where he first visited a convent.

His early years were spent in London, and throughout his life Armstrong continued to enjoy the city's exhibitions, theatres and concerts, as well as its churches. However, in 1830 his parents bought a 'commodious cottage', Elmfield Lodge, near Uxbridge, at Southall Green, where an increasing amount of time was spent. Here Armstrong developed a taste for country life. There was 'a garden to tend, a canal to fish in and a pony to ride': all interests that would remain with him

1 Elmfield Lodge, Southall, where Armstrong spent much of his youth.

17

for the rest of his life. Cows and poultry were kept, as well as three spaniels. It was a 'second paradise'. He would go back to London with his father for the week, attending school firstly in Kensington and then in Holborn, before returning to the country for the weekend.

After an idyllic couple of summers, in the autumn of 1831, he was sent to a boarding school in Ealing, going home on alternate Sundays. The 120 boys there were intent on bullying the newcomer and the enforcing of a harsh fagging system. After a few weeks of misery he gained the respect of the other pupils by showing himself to be an excellent boxer, and the following three years passed 'pleasantly enough'. The school must have been very typical of its time and had gained an excellent reputation. It was run by two masters, 'who examined only in classics and preferred their horses to teaching', and six assistants. The day was long, with lessons starting at seven. There were nine classes and the education was 'good', particularly in classics, at which Armstrong excelled. His interest in the theatre developed and he took part in school plays. There was also time for fishing and he became a very good angler.

The Armstrongs' friendship with the Duncombe family had begun when Armstrong senior had been a sponsor for Tom Duncombe, from the Yorkshire branch of the family, helping him to gain a seat in Parliament representing Finsbury. Tom's later radical views and support of the Chartists would not have been supported by Armstrong's family, but Benjamin became a firm friend of William Duncombe from the age of 12 and spent time on the Duncombes' Hertfordshire estate of Lagley in Northchurch, near Berkhamsted ('a lovely spot'), where he learnt to fish and shoot and went hunting, as well as visiting Ascot for the races.

He left school in the summer of 1834 at the age of 17, with a good grounding in the classics and a love of literature and the arts, but, by his own admission, little mathematical ability. The question of a suitable profession now arose. The typical choices available were the law, the church, the army or joining his father's business. His preference would probably have been the army, but as he was an only son, the option of long periods overseas, probably in the disease-ridden West Indies, was rejected. Much later, in 1855, he was to write 'Were I a few years younger and single I would prefer the army to other professions: its regularity, exactness, foreign travel, and leisure for literary and artistic purposes' (12/1/55). He had no business ability, and anyway his father

2 Lagley, North-
church, the home of the
Duncombe family.

19

had already taken on a partner to whom in 1835 he handed over the business, he 'being naturally averse to trade'. This left the church as a likely choice.

None of the various books published about this time on how to choose a career for one's son suggested that a sense of vocation was required to join the church; rather, after a spell at university, 'There should be no difficulty whatever in the purchase, through the medium of any of the clerical agents the presentation of a living. ... one of £300 a year, with an incumbent over sixty might be had for less than £1,000.'[2] The candidate should be 'carefully nurtured, bred as a gentleman and educated as a scholar'. As a profession it was no more time-serving or selfish than most others. However, it would not be an attractive profession to someone who was not rich but ambitious, while it could suit a rich man who was not ambitious.[3]

Armstrong's main objection to the church was that he would have to spend several more years 'shackled' to examinations and further education. There is little indication at this stage that he felt a religious 'calling'. He mentions in his diary his grandfather, who 'had strong, but peculiar religious impressions' (5/5/57). He learnt Hebrew from a Jewish teacher so that he could read the Old Testament in the original language. He was an early riser, drank only water and was a vegetarian. Armstrong's immediate family were regular attenders at the local Anglican church at Norwood. The clergyman was said to be 'good' and the church full. However, neither he nor his sister had been confirmed and both had been baptised at private ceremonies at home of which there was no record, suggesting that their church-going was little more than a social formality. A final decision as to what profession to pursue was put off and it was decided that Armstrong would spend a year at the newly founded (1831) Anglican King's College, London, which would prepare him for a place at an Oxford or Cambridge college. Meanwhile the summer of 1834 was spent pleasantly enough at Southall in rural activities such as supervising haymaking. William Duncombe senior and his children, William and Ann, became frequent visitors to Southall. There were picnics, 'gypsy parties', pony rides and sightseeing. Before starting at King's, Armstrong spent time with the Duncombes at Lagley. There was plenty of shooting, sometimes involving trespassing and encounters with gamekeepers.

Armstrong was back in London in time for the beginning of the academic year and lectures in divinity, classics and mathematics. The teaching was far less rigorous than it had been at school, with lectures rather than lessons and plenty of time for the theatre and parties during the week, and weekends at Southall and the chase. It was also at this time that Armstrong first fell in love with a house guest at Southall, described in later diaries as his 'first love', Miss Harriett Parker. However, the romance was short-lived and the young lady in question soon married and was later to ask Armstrong for the loan of some sermons for her husband, the Revd Robert James of Southleigh, Devon. What with all these distractions, his achievements at King's were only second rate, and further tutoring would be needed if he were going to gain a university place. After a summer of country pursuits and a tour of the midland counties with his father, Armstrong settled down in October 1835 to a regular course of mainly classical reading with Mr Rodwell, an Anglo-Catholic priest and incumbent in the London parish of Saffron Hill. By now he was fairly settled on entering the church as a profession, a decision which may well have been influenced by Rodwell. To this end he was confirmed in June 1836 at Christchurch, Newgate and was struck by the beauty and solemnity of the service. Although there was still time for the theatre, parties and visits to galleries, 'I was now completely given over to my books' and 'writing long dissertations on sundry rusty subjects' such as the establishment of the church and keeping dissenters out of the universities (they were refused entry until 1854). Evenings were spent with a new friend, Captain Swann. With him, he took up the habit of smoking while arguing into the small hours against Swann's liberal and 'low church' ideas. At the same time he wrote in his diary, 'I did not take up any views in regard to the controversy between Romanists and dissenters until I began to read for holy orders', although his evenings spent in discussion with Captain Swann would suggest otherwise. He certainly disapproved of a friend from Jersey who was staying. She was a dissenter who prayed for 'our clergyman's dark and unconverted soul because he did not preach to please her'.

It was at this time that the family gave up their London house and instead enlarged that at Southall to suit their needs. A painting of the 1890s shows a substantial three-storey gentleman's residence. The arrival of a railway line to London in the 1850s meant it was possible to travel up to town every day. This was a change of which Armstrong did not entirely approve. 'The rusticity of the village gave way to a London-out-of-town character.' However, there was still plenty of opportunity for field sports and country pursuits. It was not until 1856 that he travelled on this line himself, a mode of transport that he thoroughly enjoyed.

A time of church reform

Armstrong would be entering the church at a time of great change within the establishment. Some of the institutional failings of the church were being reformed under Robert Peel. The lack of parsons on the ground, the need to build them houses and the need to bring the poorest livings up to a level to provide a reasonable stipend were all addressed, if somewhat belatedly, after Peel's Ecclesiastical Commission of 1835 resulted in Acts in 1836 and 1838. Bishops' stipends were fixed and made more equitable, and two new dioceses were created in the industrial areas, while those of Bangor and St Asaph, and Gloucester and Bristol, were merged. Savings meant that poor livings could be supported and new parishes created in cities. No more than two livings were to be held by one parson and their combined income should not be more than £1,000, the distance between the two should not be more than 10 miles and the incumbent should be resident in one of them.

It was not only the administration of the church that was being reformed at this time, but also the theology and the form of worship. Both were the subject of lively and sometimes divisive debate. The Oxford Movement, with which Armstrong sympathised, originated with a small group of academics in Oxford in the 1830s, of whom Keble, Pusey and Newman were the most important. In 1833 John Keble, Professor of Poetry, gave the Assize Sermon in which he attacked plans to remove eight bishoprics in the Irish church. Although these were mainly wealthy sinecures, and thus ripe for reform, and the savings from them would go to augment the stipends of the poorest clergy, it was the principle of Parliament legislating for the church which he regarded as sacrilege. The cause was then taken up by John Newman who published a series of tracts aligning the Church of England closer to Roman Catholic practices. He called for the restoration of ancient rituals, led by priests whose authority stemmed directly from Christ's apostles (apostolic succession) and who had the power of absolution. The enemy was 'liberalism', which for Newman stood for atheism, immorality and democracy. Instead, Newman emphasised in the published *Tracts for the Times* the importance of the sacraments and the liturgy as well as the authority of the church and bishops. A restored church and ritualistic service filled with spectacle and music was the key to the appreciation of higher things.[4] Ritual and the sacraments should be central to church worship. The *Tracts*, short, direct and easily understood booklets, particularly appealed to young clergy struggling in often isolated parishes. Their positions were given greater recognition as Newman sought to 'magnify' their office.

At the other end of the spectrum and equally influential was the Evangelical movement originating in the late eighteenth century as the Clapham Sect, founded in the 1790s, which included bankers and barristers as well as clergymen such as John Venn, vicar of Great Dunham in Norfolk from 1783, who moved to Clapham ten years later. The movement emphasised personal piety and a sense of mission, bringing literacy and morality to the poor. Bridging the gap and encouraging pastoral revival was the charming, energetic and sociable Samuel Wilberforce, third son of the anti-slavery campaigner William, who was brought up in a strongly Evangelical environment. Later, as Bishop of Oxford from 1845 to 1869 and of Winchester from 1869 to 1873, he was political and pragmatic in his efforts at reform. His fame stems partly from the fact that his achievements were recorded in great detail by his son Reginald. He should be seen as one of several reforming bishops, who include Kaye in Lincoln and Stanley in Norwich.[5] Although he leaned towards the high church, he knew what was achievable, realising that the Catholic views of the Oxford Movement would never be acceptable to many of his clergy.[6] His Diocese Books show that he kept in close contact with his clergy and wrote to those who were not providing all the church services they should.[7] He then followed up his correspondence with regular visits to them.[8] He advocated a simpler service in which the sermon and spiritual teaching dominated over ritual. Within his two dioceses he demonstrated what a conscientious and pastoral bishop might achieve, encouraging in his clergy a 'pastoral ideal'.[9] He is best remembered for his opposition to Darwin and Huxley in the debates over the *Origin of Species* in 1859–60. One of his main achievements was the founding of Cuddesdon College near Oxford as a training college for the clergy.[10] He was careful not to be labelled as belonging to either of the church factions, and if in later years he moved towards the high church he was never tempted to follow his three brothers, who converted to Rome. Armstrong noted his death in July 1873 when he was thrown from his horse, quoting the *Times*'s description of him as the 'greatest monument of the English Church' (19/7/73).

Armstrong's student life

Armstrong began his university education at Caius College, Cambridge in October 1837. His original intention had been to go to Jesus College, but Mr Rodwell was friendly with the tutor at Caius and so his plans changed. In spite of his determination not to live beyond his means; a resolution which he was able to keep throughout his student days, he still managed to enjoy life to the full. As his mathematical ability was limited he chose to read for an ordinary rather than an honours degree, allowing him more spare time, which he occupied with reading and also a little drawing. Students were expected to attend chapel once every day and twice on Sunday (Armstrong thought the service was read too fast). There were daily lectures on the classics, the gospels and Latin composition. These were over by midday and the rest of the day was his own. As well as visiting the museums and the botanical gardens, he had time for shooting, rowing on the Cam, going to the races in Newmarket and Royston, as well as wine and supper parties. College feasts were regular events. On Sundays he also went to the University church and on Saturday to the chapel at Trinity, where an anthem was sung. The introduction of sung services was something he was to encourage as a minister. His friend William Duncombe soon joined him at Cambridge, but without the same resolve to avoid debt. Armstrong was determined to keep on good terms with his tutors, one of whom was high and the other low church. The prospect of his first-year classics examinations worried him greatly, but they were passed and university life continued.

The year 1837 saw the death of William IV and the accession of Queen Victoria and Armstrong went with his father to see the late king's lying-in-state. Throughout his life he was to take a close interest in national affairs and wished where possible to be an eyewitness to signif-icant events. The following year he watched new queen's coronation procession. Meanwhile his father was made a magistrate for the County of Middlesex and the rising population of Southall meant that a new chapel there 'annexed to the Church of England' but of a low church leaning, was to be built. Armstrong went to the ceremonial laying of the foundation stone, but found the 'anti-high church spectacle' so alien to his own beliefs that 'from that day I began to view the low church party with disgust'.

In his second year Armstrong determined to take one day a week for recreation. This included his usual pursuits of rowing and shooting, as well as attending some very rowdy parties at which windows were broken and church bells rung, resulting in headaches the next day. Duncombe was responsible for holding some of the larger parties, and his behaviour was so bad that he was rusticated in the spring term. In spite of his rather boisterous social life, Armstrong passed his second-year examination, gaining a First for his translation. In the summer he went on a family holiday to Ramsgate, where he tried sea bathing and bought a fine Irish hunter to replace his pony, which had been hit by a train. This was not the only incident recorded in which a train was involved. Armstrong was out hunting with the Queen's Staghounds in January 1839 and the hunt was in hot pursuit when faced by the Great Western railway line. Most of the riders diverted across the railway bridge, but the hotheads, who included Armstrong and Duncombe, rode straight across the line. One of the riders fell, his horse was killed and a train derailed.

By his third year Armstrong was taking a more serious attitude to his studies and attended divinity lectures. Every candidate for ordina-tion had to have a certificate confirming that he had attended twenty. It was at this time that the controversy over the Oxford *Tracts* was at its height. Armstrong read them and while accepting that they recom-mended a more ritualistic form of worship, he could not agree that they promoted 'popery'. 'From this time I never spoke in favour of the *Tracts* – I never joined the hue and cry that was now being made against them.' His last term was devoted to study as he concentrated on obtaining his degree. He was tired of parties such as those instigated by his friend William Duncombe and instead preferred to spend the evening with a few friends. He left university 'out of debt, on good terms with my tutors, my friends and myself'.

Armstrong's university career appears typical of his times. During his first two years he entered into all aspects of student life. There is no sign of the serious-minded cleric he later became. By the third year he was set to enter the church but was careful not to get involved in arguments over religious practice. However, his support for the high church movement was already clear, as was the direction in which he would lead any parish where he became incumbent.

The young clergyman

The first step towards entering the church was to find a curacy, and Armstrong was anxious for a rural one. He preferred rural life and he liked the country clergy, 'who knew their flock by name'. His father was more ambitious for him and thought a position in London would be a better career choice than 'burying himself in the country'. He was offered two London curacies: 'Two more miserable localities could not have fallen my lot.' One, Saffron Hill, involved joining his old tutor, Mr Rodwell, and was seen as the lesser of the two evils, particularly as he did not have to take up his position until after his ordination. Armstrong was lucky to have a choice of parishes to go to. The rapid expansion of Oxford and Cambridge universities, combined with the expectation that ordination would almost automatically follow, meant curacies could be difficult to find.[11]

Ordination took some time, and Armstrong described the initial process in his diary. Unusually for the time, he was from a business and London background (his father had been made a Deputy Lieutenant of Middlesex in 1839, and in 1842 was to be a director of Amicable Life Insurance Company). Armstrong wrote to the Bishop of London (the architect of many of Peel's reforms) for an interview which was fixed for 5 May 1841. On arrival at the appointed time, he was kept waiting two hours before being ushered into Bishop Blomfield's study. For the meeting Armstrong needed testimonials from his college and his prospective parish, evidence that he had studied divinity at university and that he had a curacy to go to. After some initial questions, including his age, the bishop replied that he was too young. Although he could become a deacon at 23 years old (the age he would have reached in November 1840), to be ordained as a priest he would have to be at least 24, and it seems that the Bishop of London preferred deacons also to have reached this age. He was given a long reading list of theological books and asked to return in October, when he would be examined.

There then followed a gap of about four months in which he went on an extended continental tour with his father. He visited churches, which were always open, and was impressed by the profusion of rich stained glass, 'which is the perfection of church architecture', and the ritual of the services with their processions and priests dressed in surplices and capes, to which the English church compared unfavourably. At home, in contrast, the church buildings 'were closed all the long week through, and our dandy and secularised clergy and our high-backed well-stuffed dozing pews ...which deprived the poor of their undoubted right to a seat in the parish church'. After two months in Paris, where they visited numerous theatres and art exhibitions, they spent a month in Brussels before travelling through Germany and back through Holland.

When he returned to London, Armstrong again visited the bishop and took the examinations, which lasted four days with seven papers in all, each with twelve questions. He passed and was commended by the bishop 'upon an excellent paper on the subject of sanctification'. He was given more books to read and his ordination was fixed for the summer of 1841. As well as becoming familiar with the Greek New Testament, he would need to tackle a reading list including works on the disagreements between Romanists, dissenters and the Church of England. He spent a few days a week studying in London and the rest of the time at Southall, enjoying the hunting and field sports. Following further examinations and tests to ensure his acceptance of the Thirty-Nine Articles of the Church of England and the Book of Common Prayer, neither changed since the 1660s, he was ready for ordination as deacon, which took place in St Paul's Cathedral on Trinity Sunday (6 June) 1841.

The service was a moving and impressive one, attended by his parents and friends. If his decision to enter the church was very much a second choice after the army, once made, he took his Apostolic Commission to 'Preach and administer the Sacraments' seriously. He had studied hard and prepared himself prayerfully for ordination. He was humbled by the fact that that among the forty young men with whom he was ordained, there were some 'who would go to distant lands, never to return again'. For instance, of Armstrong's first five curates in Dereham, two went abroad, one to India and the other to New Zealand.

Armstrong's experiences seeking ordination were rather different from those of William Andrew in Norwich ten years earlier and demonstrate the contrast between the reforming Bishop Blomfield of London and the old-style 87-year-old Bishop of Norwich, Dr Bathurst of pre-reform days. Andrew's background too was an urban one, and it was only through an inheritance that he was able to go to university. Before being ordained, Andrew had to find a position and was introduced to the vicar of Cromer, who was seeking a curate. The examination by the bishop consisted of two written examinations and an interview. This was conducted by the chaplain, who simply demanded the rewriting of his Latin essay before saying 'you will present yourself for ordination tomorrow'.[12] As bishops became younger they took a closer interest in the men they ordained. As in Armstrong's case, they conducted the interview and examinations themselves and used them to test the orthodoxy as well as the knowledge of candidates. The reforming Bishop Kaye of Lincoln in the 1830s could require written examination papers 'chiefly doctrinal' which would then be discussed with the bishop. The whole process took three days.[13]

Armstrong then took up his position as curate at St Peter's, Saffron Hill. The church, designed by Charles Barry and built between 1830 and 1832 in a brick mock-Tudor style, was one of the new churches serving the fast-growing population of this part of London. With a stipend of only £100, a year he needed financial support from his father. He found himself lodgings adjacent to his new parish near the old family home, at 36 Hatton Gardens, where he took part of the house for 52 guineas a year and furnished it. Saffron Hill had already been made infamous as the setting for Fagin's den in Dickens's *Oliver Twist*, published in 1838. He described the 'narrow and dismal alleys' leading off Saffron Hill, where filthy shops sold the silk handkerchiefs provided by the pickpockets. The densely populated area (nearly 10,000 inhabitants in 1841) was notorious for its criminal gangs and it is not surprising that Armstrong disliked the work and the surroundings, which were a world apart from rural Southall. There was the constant visiting of the poor in the 'sickly dens' of the parish. He respected Mr Rodwell, 'a pious and learned man but afraid to speak out'. Keeping his diverse congregation happy was difficult. Many in the congregation had a 'dissenting spirit' and Armstrong fell out with some of the congregation when he objected to prayers being spontaneous rather than those laid down in the Book of Common Prayer. He took morning and evening services as well as week-day ones. Mr Rodwell could not be persuaded to have part of the service sung rather than said. Many in the parish were Jewish or Roman Catholic, and so had little time for the church. Although there was much about the work and the dismal surroundings he disliked, he found satisfaction in the writing of sermons, ensuring that most of what he said was original, rather than borrowed from the many books available to help the parson. His time in Saffron Hill coincided with the work of the Scottish Presbyterian Mr Andrew Proven, who, horrified with the conditions that he found there, opened a Ragged School in November 1841 in nearby Field Lane. His school was much resented and had to be moved several times as windows were broken and the schoolroom trashed. Finally, Proven managed to establish it on a permanent footing, and, wanting to be free of any denominational organisation, he founded the Ragged School Union, which attracted the interest of Lord Shaftesbury, who visited Field Lane many times. Proven's Union later became the Shaftesbury Society.[14] It is surely significant that this initiative was not mentioned by Armstrong in his diary, although he does mention the church-controlled National School, supported by John Martin, 'a regular puritan'. We know that he regarded the education of the poor as central to the role of the parson, and yet the appalling conditions under which the Ragged Schools operated outside the influence of the established church were something he could not have coped with. Saffron Hill was certainly not his sort of parish and he did not have the missionary zeal needed to work there. Armstrong's time at Saffron Hill could well have been isolated and lonely, but he was friendly with the curate, Mr Jones, at the neighbouring 'high church' St Alban's in Holborn. They had many discussions about the role of the church in society. Jones saw its moral importance as cementing the link between church and state, while Armstrong's beliefs emphasised the spiritual element.

A joyous occasion was the marriage, on 5 August 1841 at Norwood church, of his sister to the eminent London surgeon and public health reformer John Challice, at which he officiated. Armstrong's initial reaction to news of the betrothal was muted, but when he learnt that John Challice's father had been a clergyman and that Challice himself had a good practice, and moved in 'a gentlemanly sphere', added to the fact that he had not heard any slander attached to him, he relented. John had in fact published books on how to avoid cholera, was the first Medical Officer of Health in Bermondsey and continued to be active in public health debates. However, in future years he was to prove hopeless with money, making several very unwise investments and frequently needing bailing out. Shortly after this Armstrong's parents let the Southall house and moved to Hyde Park, where Annie and John joined them.

Although his clerical duties allowed little time for recreation, Armstrong did manage to visit both Southall and his friend William Duncombe at Northchurch, where he fell in love with Duncombe's eldest sister, Ann (Nellie). They had known each other for many years, but only now did their friendship blossom. He described her as 'young, pretty, accomplished, well-off and descended from a good family' (Lord Feversham of Duncombe Park, near York). Here, as in the case of John Challice, the importance of a gentrified background was all-important. He proposed, was accepted and both families were happy. Christmas was spent at Southall and Northchurch, where he participated in hunting. Field sports, particularly hunting, had been one of his greatest pleasures, but it was regarded with disapproval by the clergy. In later years Armstrong noted in his diary, 'I was once a keen sportsman in my little way, but I gradually saw that such pleasures are incompatible with our sacred calling, and so first shooting and then hunting were abandoned.' However, he did continue to enjoy fishing (11/5/55). In Anthony Trollope's novel *Framley Parsonage*, it was hunting and the purchase of expensive horses which nearly led to the downfall of the young parson, Mark Robarts. The Revd William Andrew of Ketteringham, Norfolk, noted in his diary with disapproval that he had seen 'two clergymen shooting with Sir John' (his patron, Sir John Boileau).[15]

On 22 May 1842 Armstrong passed the final hurdle, when after passing more examinations, aimed at 'drawing out the additional knowledge supposed to be acquired during a year or so of clerical life',[16] he was ordained as a priest. The welcome opportunity to get away from the hated Saffron Hill arose when the incumbent at Northchurch was looking for a short-term replacement. Not surprisingly Armstrong jumped at the opportunity to be near his betrothed and was given leave to take up the post. The early summer passed with time for long walks and sketching parties with Ann, as well as fishing trips and visits to Ascot with her brother William.

The business of negotiating a marriage settlement was left to the fathers of the happy couple. If they were to marry it was clear that Armstrong would need a parish and there was some difficulty in persuading William Duncombe to help. With a view to providing a living for his son, William, Anne's father bought the patronage of Crowle, a living worth about £777 a year, from the existing incumbent and patron, Godfrey Egremont. Egremont had been non-resident for nearly forty years, moving away in 1804, claiming that the damp climate was detrimental to the health of his wife and daughter. In 1813 he had added the living of Welton-le-Wold, worth £600 a year, to his responsibilities, but chose to live in Louth. When the reforming Bishop Kaye of Lincoln reprimanded him for 'being in the insidious position of a pluralist with two good livings and resident in neither' he claimed poverty as a result of bank failures and mismanagement of his affairs.[17] On 6 June 1842, Egremont died, leaving the living vacant, and Armstrong went to see it with his future father-in-law. It was agreed that Armstrong should have the living, but only until such time as young William was ordained and ready to take it up. This at least provided a temporary solution and allowed Anne and Benjamin to marry.

First incumbency

The small town of Crowle was on the Isle of Axholme, a flat plain set amid the Lincolnshire fens and described by Armstrong as a 'miserably dull place' and the town the 'dullest place I ever saw'. The church was 'miserably deserted' and the parish had been neglected for twenty-five years, owing, in Armstrong's opinion, to the inefficiency of the curate and the non-residence of the incumbent. In contrast, four dissenting chapels, Methodist, Baptist, Calvinist and 'ranters' (Primitive Methodist), were flourishing. He was shocked by the immorality of the place. However, the position would allow him to get married with a substantial stipend plus the income from 500 acres commuted at the time of enclosure in lieu of tithes. On 16 August 1842, he was instituted by the Bishop of

Lincoln and on 20 August he was married in Northchurch. The bride was dressed in snowy white and looked beautiful, the church paths were strewn with flowers and afterwards the schoolboys gave three cheers. There followed a grand ball at the Duncombe family home at Lagley and a honeymoon of three weeks on the Isle of Wight while Crowle vicarage was made ready for them. They visited all the tourist spots, admired the donkey wheel in Carisbrook Castle, the Needles, Freshwater Bay and the church there, which had recently been restored, the multi-coloured layered rocks at Hurne Bay, and Shanklin, Ventnor and Ryde. They returned to Crowle, where they were welcomed to the vicarage, their 'new and distant home', by Armstrong senior. The vicarage itself was a large and rambling building opposite the church.

It is quite clear that although it had allowed him to marry and provide a home and income for his wife, Armstrong disliked Crowle almost as much as Saffron Hill. He felt very far from family and friends, the flat landscape and town he found unattractive and the people were 'awkward, viscous and seem only cut out for these desolate and neglected parts'. However, this did not prevent him entering his new life with enthusiasm. No sooner was he established than he set about visiting his congregation and the revival of church life began.

How was Armstrong, straight from university and a short curacy in London, prepared for the work of a parish priest? There were few theological colleges before 1840 and these provided a way into the church for only a minority of clergy. His university studies and reading for the bishop's examinations may have made Armstrong familiar with the original New Testament in Greek and some of the controversies facing the church at the time but were of little practical value. A young priest could feel very alone in taking responsibility for his first parish. *The Ecclesiastical Gazette*, founded in 1838, and the *Clerical Journal*, begun in 1853, helped to keep the clergy in touch and so less isolated. The lack of any proper training for many young clergymen began to be remedied through the appearance of textbooks in the 1850s and 1860s, such as R.W. Evans's *The Bishopric of Souls* in 1841 and J.J. Blunt's *The Duties of a Parish Priest* in 1856. Armstrong read Blunt's book on holiday in Ireland shortly after its publication. He could not agree with the author that more good was done through the sermon than through personal visiting, on which Armstrong always laid great stress. Some of these

3 Crowle rectory, the first home of Armstrong and his wife, Nellie.

books were little more than reference books explaining the statutory duties of the parson, while others assumed most parishes were rural and that the clergyman would be the best-informed person within his community. His congregation would all be rustics, and he would spend most of his time reading. The sermon would be his most important means of influence at a service attended by most of the village. Politics should not be introduced and precise obedience to the Prayer Book was expected. It was his duty to know every person in his parish and to oversee the village school.[18] Several years later, in 1857, when instructing his new curate, Armstrong described the duty of the priest as 'the Church, the School and the Cottage'. These were the priorities stressed by men such as Samuel Wilberforce, picked up in later textbooks, and clearly were his in Crowle.

The two areas where most effort was required were counteracting the effects of many years of maladministration and the restoration of the neglected church. In a letter to the bishop he described the poor state of religion and morality, the large number of dissenters as well as atheists, who 'omit no opportunity of <u>disseminating</u> infidelity'. This view is upheld by a request sent to the SPCK in the curate, James Johnson's time for help in establishing a parochial library to counteract the effects of 'socialists' within the parish. The 'notorious freethinker' Richard Carlisle had visited the town and reports on popular lectures on socialism in 1839 had appeared in the *Doncaster Chronicle*.[19] Armstrong acknowledged that Johnson had undertaken the whole work of the parish for twenty-three years and one of his first acts as vicar was to raise the curate's stipend from £80 to £120 a year to help him support his thirteen children. However, Armstrong was not impressed by his abilities and asked the bishop if there was any chance of finding Johnson his own living, which 'would render him independent of any superior'.[20] The previous incumbent had left much of the parish work to him, but he could not preach a sermon and 'rattled over the prayers at railway speed'.

Whether James Johnson had been as inefficient as Armstrong portrayed him in the diary is unclear. In a letter to his reforming bishop, John Kaye, in 1840 Johnson had asked permission to begin an afternoon service in a building in the canal-side hamlet of Eastoft within the parish. Up to that date there had been three Sunday services in Crowle, but he intended reducing this to one morning and one evening, allowing him to go to Eastoft in the afternoon.[21] This does not sound like the request of an inadequate clergyman. The most likely cause of the rift was that Johnson had been used to going his own way and did not take kindly to the arrival of a resident parson above him. Finally, following active opposition from Mrs Johnson, Armstrong dismissed him. This move was not universally popular with the congregation, who wrote to the bishop to complain, describing Armstrong as an 'unprincipled Vicar, a man who from his haughty overbearing behaviour, and his dangerous Romish doctrines, we can never tolerate'.[22] The charge of 'Romish doctrines' was investigated by the rural dean, who reported that they were 'without foundation'. Armstrong was certainly high church, but never a supporter of Rome.

The parish covered 7,000 acres, much of it fens that had been reclaimed by Vermuyden in the seventeenth century. The population in 1841 was 2,395, 300 of whom lived in the canal-side hamlet of Eastoft, three and a half miles from the church. It was described in directories of the time as 'a small but thriving market town' with a large central Market Place where markets were held on alternate Mondays. The main crops in the parish were potatoes and hemp, which provided the raw materials for a domestic sack and rope industry. Four corn mills ground the local cereal crops. There were five inns, several around the Market Place, and housing stretching along the surrounding roads. The church itself was a stone building dating back to Norman times, with a fine Norman doorway and Saxon cross used as a lintel over the tower arch. The north aisle had been rebuilt in the 1790s, but since then little had been done. A major concern of the high church clergy was the state of church buildings, which in many cases had suffered from a century or more of neglect. Armstrong complained of the plain interior, 'like a meeting house', with the chancel unused. There was a gallery and a variety of pews. The three-decker pulpit dominated over the 'filthy Communion table' propped up on bricks. There was no font and instead a basin on a washstand was used for baptisms and the chalice and other Communion plate was of pewter. 'I am ashamed of my church', he wrote, and undertook some improvements, 'but there is no capability of doing much'. He restored the chancel arch and his mother-in law, Mrs Duncombe, worked a fine altar cloth. He put a stove in the chancel

4 St Oswald's, Crowle. The chancel was restored by William Duncombe, Armstrong's successor.

to help dry the walls and the Sunday School was held there. Much remained to be done and the chancel was rebuilt by William Duncombe in 1856.

No sooner had Armstrong settled in than he introduced a second Sunday service in the afternoon, with a sermon attended by a 'highly respectful audience'. Armstrong quoted the local paper describing the service as using 'the beautiful prayers of the Church of England and a talented sermon'. His sermon was on the theme 'feed my sheep' and 'the true spirit of Christianity breathed through the whole of the discourse'. He took great care with all his sermons to ensure they were well understood, and he soon came to believe that he was 'well-liked'.

He soon set about visiting all those in the parish and inundating the place with tracts while also selling bibles at half-price. As well as introducing an afternoon service in the parish church, he found a suitable room and started one in Eastoft, something which Johnson claimed also to have done. The major achievement, in which his new wife played no small part, was the establishment of Sunday School, which was soon attended by 170 children, instructed by a paid master and mistress helped by volunteers. This flurry of activity did not meet with universal approval. Trees that were planted in the churchyard were uprooted, and both the Baptist and Methodist ministers 'indulged in considerable invective when they saw their congregations diminished'.

All this must have been very dispiriting, but within a year Armstrong was able to write in his diary that the congregation and the school were thriving. A red-letter day was when the bishop came to take a confirmation service. The good behaviour of 300 young people was commented on, but it is not clear how many were candidates for confirmation. Mission services were regularly taken in a barn at Eastoft. In 1855, well after Armstrong had left Crowle, Lady Strickland, of a family with Yorkshire estates but with no known connections with Crowle, built a small church at Eastoft as well as a parsonage house, endowed a small school and provided a stipend for a curate.[23] Armstrong noted in his diary what a help it would be for the present incumbent, his friend William Duncombe. He was soon accepted by local society and his wife's connection to Lord Feversham may well have increased his social standing. There were dinner parties and other social gatherings and he soon met with the local clergy. All except one of the parishes in the local area now had a resident clergyman, where until recently there had only been one. There were also visits to Hull, Doncaster and Lincoln to provide entertainment. His parents came for a fortnight in August and visits were made to the local towns as well as to York, where the Minster was much admired. With a curate left in charge, it must have been a relief to return to his familiar haunts in the south for Christmas, which was spent in Northchurch and London. He preached in his previous parishes. At St Peter's in Saffron Hill he dressed in the high church fashion, wearing a surplice, 'which would not have found favour with the congregation'. There were also days of hunting ('I could not resist the opportunity').

In July 1843 he also published a book of six lectures he had given in the town supporting the high church stance on the integrity of the Book of Common Prayer and explaining its origins. The lectures, said to be in a 'pure and classical style', were well received and Armstrong quotes at length in his diary from favourable reviews of the book in the local press.[24]

We see here that in spite of the fact that Armstrong did not like Crowle, and knowing that he would not be there long, he still conscientiously set about improving the church and the standard of church services, visiting parishioners and providing a Sunday School – all which he felt were the core duties of a clergyman. Once the decision to enter the church had been made, he determined to fulfil the role in an exemplary way and soon became an active advocate of the high church movement.

However, by the autumn of 1843 William Duncombe was established as curate in Whitby, where Armstrong visited him for a few days of salmon fishing and grouse shooting. It was clear that he would soon be ready to take on the living of Crowle, so another parish would have to be found for Armstrong. His father felt that some financial help should be forthcoming from William's father as part of his daughter's marriage settlement, and in January 1844 visited William Duncombe senior at Lagley 'to induce him to fulfil his promise' to help. Although other members of the Duncombe family supported Armstrong's father 'in this act of justice', he was not to be persuaded,[25] and in the end Armstrong senior spent the not inconsiderable sum of £4,000 on buying the advowson of Little Stanmore-with-Whitchurch in Middlesex from the sisters of the previous vicar, Maria and Sophia Mutter. To do this he had to mortgage eight of his London properties, and relations with the Duncombe family were strained for several years. The parish was a country one, but not far from London, Northchurch or Southall. Proximity to their families would be more to the young couple's taste. They had felt isolated while living in Lincolnshire but a rural parish would suit them well. Before they left Crowle their first child, a daughter, Helen Ann, was born on 16 January 1844 and on 4 February, after barely two years in Crowle, Armstrong was installed in his new parish. After the installation he returned to Crowle to christen his daughter with both his own parents and the Duncombe family present.

Little Stanmore-with-Whitchurch days

Little is known of Armstrong's time at Stanmore, except that it was a happy six years. The main drawback was the vicarage at the gates of the church. It was old and dilapidated and so far less comfortable than that in Crowle. However, according to Armstrong's father's journal, he spent time and money on improving it for the young family.

The contrast between the market town of Crowle with its ancient church dating back to Saxon times and the scattered parish of Little Stanmore and Whitchurch clustered along the Roman road from London to St Albans with its church of St Lawrence isolated on the Whitchurch Road could not have been greater. Adjacent to the church was Canons Park, previously the seat of the Dukes of Chandos. James Brydges, later the 1st Duke (died 1744), amassed a huge fortune as the Duke of Marlborough's paymaster general and with it built a fine and lavishly appointed mansion. Money was lost in the South Sea Bubble and family debts mounted, not helped by the behaviour of his son, the 2nd Duke. Finally, between 1747 and 1753, the entire contents of the house were sold and as a buyer could not be found for the house, it was demolished to be replaced later by a new mansion. All that remains of the 1st Duke's building work is the church. While the medieval tower still stands, an unaisled nave was designed by John James in 1714. Despite its plain brick Queen Anne exterior, the interior was highly decorated, with paintings showing the nativity and a *pietà* by the Venetian artist Antonio Bellucci. The walls were painted in grey monochrome with classical-style figures representing the gospel writers and the Three Virtues in separate classical niches in grey relief, attributed stylistically to Francesco Slater. The vaulted ceiling was also painted, giving the appearance of an Italianate baroque interior, by Louis Laguerre, a prolific decorator of grand houses at the time, whose work can be seen at Blenheim, Chatsworth and elsewhere. The woodwork was by Grinling Gibbons, one of the many craftsmen and artists who worked on the house.[26] A distinctive feature of the church was the grand ducal pew forming the west gallery, again with a painted ceiling by Bellucci, and its own fireplace, no doubt occupied by the Duke when his protégé Handel played the fine organ placed behind the altar. A painting of the church, executed shortly before Armstrong arrived, probably in the time of the Revd George Mutter, shows the three-decker pulpit and box pews, which still remain and are typical of early eighteenth-century church design.

By Armstrong's time Canons House had been rebuilt and was the home of Lady Plumer, widow of Sir Thomas, who had bought the estate in 1814 and who became his friend and supporter of his high church practices. Presumably she and her family occupied the ducal pew. By 1848 the classical style of the church was deeply unfashionable and the Bishop of London described it as 'A Heathen Temple' when he installed Armstrong to the parish. The thinking of the time was that Gothic was the purest form for church architecture and Armstrong therefore regarded the style of the classical St Lawrence's as 'debased'. However, he reluctantly admitted its 'richness required some notice' and gave it the 'appearance of Rome rather than the generality of Anglican places of worship'. He found a well-maintained, albeit classical, building a great relief after the dampness and dereliction of Crowle. His enthusiasm for the place and its history resulted in a second publication: a twenty-page pamphlet on the history of Little Stanmore in which he described the heyday of Canons Park.[27]

Armstrong's residence in Little Stanmore from 1844 to 1850 coincided with the time of most heated argument between the two wings of the Church of England. John Henry Newman had left Oxford and his position at the university church in 1842, moving to his other parish in nearby Littlemore with a small group of followers, where they lived a semi-monastic life. In 1843 he resigned his Oxford parish and finally,

5a, b   St Lawrence's, Little Stanmore-with-Whitchurch. All but the tower was rebuilt to a design of John James in 1714. The classical interior would not have been to Armstrong's taste.

in 1845, he made the decisive break and was accepted into the Roman Catholic Church. Armstrong was distressed that several of his friends followed Newman to Rome: John Julius Plumer, a fellow of Balliol and son of Lady Plumer, became a Roman Catholic in 1846.[28] It is not surprising therefore that the controversy dominated his thinking at the time and his thoughts fill many diary pages. Although he was distressed by the loss of many able men, he was never tempted to follow them. Like another of Lady Plumer's sons, Charles John, rector of nearby Elstree, and later of Ilford in Sussex, he supported the high church movement, but remained loyal to the Church of England. The ritual of the Roman Catholic church and its emphasis on the sacraments were aspects that he admired, but there were other doctrinal positions with which he disagreed. The many pages of his diary at this time devoted to religious matters and the strength of his sense of vocation show that even if a career in the church was a second choice over one in the army he had now become fully committed to his calling.

According to his monument in the porch of the church, the previous incumbent, George Mutter, preached 'two sermons every Sabbath to a numerous congregation'. However, Armstrong felt that this could be improved upon and once established in the parish set to work to build a regular pattern of services and increase his congregation. Under Mutter, there had been six communion services a year with an average attendance of twenty-five. Armstrong increased this to a monthly service and attendance increased to forty, with as many as sixty on major festivals. In spite of the fact that the church was isolated, the average attendance at Sunday services increased from 150 to 300.

Although the major arguments about church ritual did not erupt until the 1850s, disagreements over the wearing of surplices, the use of Gregorian chant and a greater emphasis on the sacraments over preaching were already beginning to surface. At Armstrong's installation the Bishop of London had made clear his preference for his clergy wearing a surplice to preach, and the baptism of infants before a congregation, something which Armstrong performed when he christened his second daughter, Louisa Marion (born in 1848), during the afternoon service. Several of his neighbours were also high church, but some were attracted to the services at St Margaret's, Edgware, which was in fact nearer for many of his parishioners and where the style of worship was more 'Calvinistic'.

While he always preached in a surplice, used the old Gregorian music, kept saints' days and taught the controversial doctrine of apostolic succession, he knew that the most important duty of a parish priest was the 'personal guiding of souls'. 'This is the true work of a priest, and nothing external, however beautiful, perfect or grand ought to keep that fact in the background.' In this he could agree with his 'Calvinistic brethren'. He much admired his neighbour in Harrow, Mr Munroe, a man of 'great piety and zeal', who lived a self-denying life, took a daily service, led a 'brotherhood in a monastic building of his own founding' and set up a 'college for labourers'.

While only about a dozen of his congregation were fully committed to the religious life that he himself followed, with daily family prayers, Armstrong himself found the greatest spiritual comfort from the 'mid-day office, a sanctuary from the world's turmoil'. The fact that the same words were being used at the same time by Anglicans everywhere gave him comfort and he printed off the first prayer of the office and distributed it to his congregation, many of whom used it. Under his encouragement the congregation doubled in number. Confirmations took place regularly and Armstrong took particular pride in the fact that on the third occasion, forty-five were confirmed, most of whom came to the Communion service the following Sunday, bringing the numbers up to sixty-two. Weekday services were introduced. Schools, parish charities and allotments were flourishing. Every family was visited four times a year, although he found that home visits were not always the best way to give spiritual guidance. They were 'quite inadequate to meet the proposed end ... the kettle boils over, the baby screams or Tom comes home wet and hungry from his work'. He would far rather his parishioners could be persuaded to come to the confessional. In an unusually outspoken passage in the journal, which one would associate more with the 'ranters' he so much despised, he wrote 'We know the disease is raging among them, the canker of concealed sin eating into and consuming their souls and yet we must not personally prescribe for them.'

A less attractive side of Armstrong's character which is revealed in his diary is his self-righteous and smug attitude. While he thanks

God continually for his 'uninterrupted happiness and prosperity', his belief in the superiority of the established church over other denominations meant he saw himself as having God-given authority over the pastoral as well as spiritual affairs of his parishioners. This was typical of clergymen of the time and in a deferential age was still acceptable to contemporary society.

Armstrong's work in his first two parishes show him as one of a new young generation of clergy leaving the universities with strong social consciences and religious convictions, whose aims, as articulated by Armstrong, were 'the glory of God and the Salvation of souls' and who were to be responsible for the revival of the church during Victoria's reign. His education had been a good one and typical of that followed by his contemporaries entering the church. He had obtained a university degree. He had been expected to prepare himself seriously for ordination and had experienced a variety of parishes as both curate and parson before he embarked on what was to be a lifelong vocation in the small Norfolk market town of East Dereham.

Notes

1   Armstrong summarised his diary entries before 1842 in the first part of his new journal and entries remain undated until 1852 so no specific references are given for these early years.
2   J.C. Hudson, *The Parents' Handbook*, 1842, quoted in A. Haig, *The Victorian Clergy*, 1984, 8–9.
3   H. Byerley Thompson, *The Church as a Profession*, 1854, and J.F. Stevens in *The Cornhill Magazine* 9 (1864), both quoted in Haig 1984, 9–10.
4   R. Lee, *Rural Society and the Anglican Clergy 1815–1914*, 2006, 199.
5   F. Knight, *The Nineteenth-Century Church and English Society*, 1995, 16.
6   D. Bowen, *The Idea of the Victorian Church*, 1968, 29–33.
7   D. McClatchey, *Oxfordshire Clergy, 1777–1869*, 1960, 83.
8   Haig 1984, 180.
9   G. Parsons, 'Reform, Revival and Realignment', in G. Parsons (ed.), *Religion in Victorian Britain*, vol. 1, *Traditions*, 1988, 14–66, 26.
10 B. Turner, *The Victorian Parson*, 2015, 50–1.
11 Knight 1995, 107.
12 O. Chadwick, *Victorian Miniature*, 1960, 20.
13 Knight 1995, 113.
14 See www.fieldlane.org.uk.
15 Chadwick 1960, 95.
16 J.H. Blunt, *The Book of Church Law*, 8th edn, 1899, 210.
17 Cited in D. Neave, *Armstrong's Crowle Journal, 1842–1844*, 1986; Lincoln-

shire Archive Office (LAO), Correspondence of Bishop Kay B5/4/48/7/6.

18 Owen Chadwick, *The Victorian Church*, vol. 1, 1966, 172.

19 Cited in Neave 1986; LAO, B5/4/122/4 4/1/1838; *Doncaster Chronicle*, 5 January 1839.

20 R.W. Ambler (ed.), *Lincolnshire Parish Correspondence of John Kaye, Bishop of Lincoln 1827–53*, Lincoln Record Society 94, 2006, 256.

21 Ibid., 255.

22 Cited in Neave 1986; LAO, Correspondence of Bishop Kay B5/4/18/1.

23 W. White, *Lincolnshire Directory*, 3rd edn, 1872, 442.

24 B. Armstrong, *Six Lectures on the Morning Services of the Church*, 1843.

25 The diary of Armstrong senior, 1 January 1844. I am grateful to Christopher Armstrong for this information.

26 N. Pevsner, *The Buildings of England: Middlesex*, 1951, 148; *St Lawrence, Whitchurch, Little Stanmore: A Short Guide*, 2010.

27 B. Armstrong, *A History of Little Stanmore*, 1847.

28 P. Maurice, *Postscript to the Popery of Oxford: The Number of the Name of the Beast*, 1851.

Two

The Move to Dereham

Happy as he was in Little Stanmore-with-Whitchurch, Armstrong was looking for a larger parish and thus 'a larger sphere of duty'. The small market town of East Dereham in central Norfolk was suitable for a variety of reasons. Early in 1850 he visited the town with his father and together they decided that it would be a desirable move. Not only was it a larger parish than Little Stanmore with a population of 4,000, but the vicarage was better, the glebe extended to 50 acres and the living was worth more. The annual income from the living (£480) plus the vicarial tithes (£432) would bring his income up to a respectable sum approaching £1,000 a year.[1]

The process of finding a living usually involved recommendation by a patron. Nationally, in 1866 over half of the 6,235 livings in private patronage had been obtained by purchase or as gifts from family members. In at least 1,290 of those livings, the incumbent was likely to be a family member of the patron, as the patron and the parson had the same name.[2] The influential Norfolk families who held the patronage of several parishes would receive a stream of letters from curates or their friends and relations looking for positions. Private patrons were particularly numerous in Norfolk, a county where the local squirearchy was very influential. In 1835 a total of 162 patrons controlled 288 livings.[3] William Andrew was presented with the living of Ketteringham from the sister of the absentee squire and patron, Miss Atkyns, through the efforts of a friend of his wife. The Atkyns family were members of the minor gentry with only the one living at their disposal, but the eleven most powerful members of the aristocracy controlled five or more livings in 1830 and Lord Suffield owned as many as eleven. No members of his family at this date were clergymen, so none of his appointments were to relations, but eight of the eleven were held in plurality. The most valuable, that of Blickling, was held by the Revd Mr J.D. Churchill, who held three others. Thomas William Coke (Lord Leicester from 1834) owned nine, but only one, that of Tittleshall, was worth more than £500 and this was held by his brother-in-law, the Revd Mr E.S. Keppel, who also held a living in the gift of his father, giving him an income of £1,337 a year. Of the eighty benefices controlled by these eleven families, twenty-four were held by relations or those connected to the family by marriage and all but thirteen were held in plurality.[4] Where the candidate for a living was not a relative, the next consideration might be his politics, but as the number of those eligible to vote was increased from 1832, this became less important. As the century progressed patrons were being encouraged to choose the man the bishop considered best for the parish, rather than to assist the patron's family and friends.[5]

Patronage of parishes was not only in the long-standing gift of the landed aristocracy, but changed hands at auctions; something criticised by the antiquarian rector, Augustus Jessopp.[6] We have seen that Armstrong's father spent £4,000 to buy him the living of Little Stanmore. That of Wortham, across the border in Suffolk and one of the richest in the county, had been bought by John Cobbold of the Ipswich brewing family at a London auction in 1819. He then gave it to his clerical son, Richard, as a wedding present. When the elderly rector died in 1824, Richard installed himself there, and remained for forty-nine years.[7]

Those incumbents who were not related to their patron very often took a deferential interest in the family in the 'great house'. George Crabbe collected newspaper cuttings about the weddings, funerals and visits of the Prince of Wales to his patron, Lord Walsingham. His antiquarian leanings meant that he traced the history of the family's coat of arms and he recorded with pride that his article on one of Lord Walsingham's ancestors, Robert De Grey, had been published in *Norfolk Archaeology*.[8]

In Armstrong's case, the patron was the sinecure rector of Dereham, William Wollaston. The Wollaston family had begun their association with the church in Dereham in 1761, when Francis Wollaston had become rector after his father bought him the living. When he moved on to a richer living at Chiselhurst, he kept the Dereham rectory, but appointed a vicar to do the work. This began the line of sinecure rectors, entitled to the great tithes of the parish, but did not commit them to

6 Young Benjamin Armstrong shortly after his arrival in Dereham. 'Photography is a good cure for vanity', he wrote in 1856.

any parochial responsibility. The system was abolished under Peel's church reforms of the 1830s. In 1806 Charles Hyde Wollaston had been installed as vicar by his grandfather and held the position of vicar for over forty years. In contrast to the glowing eulogy on his memorial tablet in the church, Charles was extremely unpopular in Dereham and latterly at least had taken little interest in the parish. When he died in 1850 the position of sinecure rector passed to his son, William, who, although he had taken holy orders, did not wish to take on the responsibilities of rector, so instead chose to appoint a vicar to act on his behalf. No doubt Armstrong and his father had been keeping an eye out for such an opportunity and Benjamin was duly appointed.

In September that year Armstrong was accepted as vicar in the parish which he was to serve for over thirty years. He was much touched by the many gifts that were presented to him by the parishioners of Little Stanmore-with-Whitchurch, among them sofa cushions, a new cassock and silver inkstands, to which almost all the families in the parish, rich and poor, had contributed. He recorded with pride the inscription on the inkstand: 'Presented to the Revd B.J. Armstrong with the affectionate regard and esteem of his parishioners on the occasion of his leaving the Incumbency of Whitchurch'. As well as this there was a French clock, a sermon case and a richly bound prayer book.

On 14 September 1850 Armstrong boarded the train in London and set off to Norwich to be installed by the bishop as vicar of Dereham, and as he travelled he watched the houses of the great city of London give way to the flat Essex countryside. Passing through Cambridge he remembered fondly his student days and was inspired by the sight of Ely Cathedral standing up above the fenland landscape. From the fens the train entered the barren heathlands of the Brecks and he cast his sportsman's eye across the famous sporting estates with their plentiful game. Beyond Thetford the soils became more fertile and the train passed through rich farmland before reaching Norwich. His installation would not take place until the next day, so he had time to wander around the city and take in its 'numerous gothic churches and quaint monastic streets, its towering castle and beautiful cathedral'. The streets he found bustling with activity. The cheerfulness of its well-dressed inhabitants was a contrast to the 'dullness which hangs over many cathedral cities'. He was going to feel at home here. The cathedral itself he thought 'somewhat small', but he was impressed by its great antiquity, Norman arches and 'entrancingly elegant' spire. The service was 'tolerably performed' and he was impressed by the high altar and the bishop's throne behind (14/9/50).

Bishop Samuel Hinds had only recently replaced Edward Stanley (1837–49) as Bishop of Norwich. He in turn had replaced one of the longest-serving and only nonagenarian bishops, Henry Bathurst (1805–37). A genial card-playing Whig, Bishop Bathurst spent much of his later life in Bath. He was a bad administrator and his idleness was notorious amongst his contemporaries.[9] It was during his time that Norwich was known as the 'Dead See'.[10] Edward Stanley, on the other hand, was one of the new group of bishops following the ecclesiastical reforms of 1835–6. Born in 1779, he was an intellectual with literary and scientific pursuits which led him to be president of the Linnean Society from 1839 to 1849 and a patron of Ipswich Museum. Before moving to Norwich he had held the family living at Alderley in Cheshire, where he found a neglected parish whose former rector could boast of never having entered a sick person's cottage. There he remained for thirty-three years, 'a lively and humane pastor',[11] before moving to Norwich as bishop, and soon became a reformer, both of the administrative system and of the regulation of the clergy. He was particularly concerned with the provision of education and refused to join the clamour against dissenters. At his inaugural service before the mayor and leading citizens, he gave priority to providing seating for 1,200 charity-school children.[12] Ordinations and confirmations were held more regularly, parsonages were built and the rules on plurality were enforced. The result was, as elsewhere, a great improvement in the efficiency of the clergy and a general raising of standards. After his death, a huge commemorative west window by George Hedgeland was installed in the cathedral in 1854.[13]

His successor, Samuel Hinds (1849–57), was less effective. An Oxford intellectual, in 1850 he chaired the University Commission into the 'Discipline, studies and revenues of Oxford University'. This suggested democratic reforms in governance similar to those in German universities, some of which were implemented in 1854. This belief in consultation is shown when he called the first 'convocation of clergy' in the diocese for many years, but he was also described as 'learned and dry', giving little support to his clergy.[14] At the time of Hind's resignation through ill health, Armstrong was told by the archdeacon that he was 'shattered in body and mind'. His marriage to someone (his cook) 'beneath him in life' and whom he did not wish to introduce to society 'may have accounted for his coldness and desire to shun everyone' (26/5/57). He was against the high church Oxford Movement, diocesan synods and any involvement of the clergy in the running of the diocese,[15] though as mentioned above he did call a significant convocation of clergy. His low church beliefs meant that Armstrong had a poor opinion of him. At the installation ceremony he showed a 'hard, dry indifference which was like iron on my soul' (15/9/50). After this rather disheartening ceremony Armstrong went by train to Dereham, where he was 'inducted into the temporalities' of the living and next day read the service. He would not preach his first sermon until he had finally moved in. Hind's successor, John Pelham (1857–93), was seen as a 'stream of living water after years of drought'.[16]

Dereham in 1850

So what sort of a place was Dereham in the mid-nineteenth century? George Borrow, writing of his birthplace in *Lavengro*, published in 1859, looked back thirty years and described it as 'pretty quiet, Dereham, thou pattern of an English country town, with thy clean but narrow streets branching out from thy modest market place, with thine old-fashioned houses with here and there a roof of venerable thatch ... thy one-half aristocratic mansion'.[17] By this he meant the eighteenth-century Hill House, just off the Market Place, which had been the home of the antiquarian John Fenn. By Armstrong's day it belonged to Mrs Gooch, 'a respected parishioner' who was a frequent dinner guest at the vicarage. Paving and draining the town had begun in the eighteenth century and Borrow's view of the cleanliness of the streets was echoed in the early volumes of White's *Directory*, where it is described as 'one of the most improving towns in the county' with 'a spacious market place and several long streets lined with modern houses and well-stocked shops'.[18] The cleanliness of the town may well have been exaggerated, as Armstrong was to find when serving on the Sanitary Board for the town. While the main streets were paved and drained, conditions in the

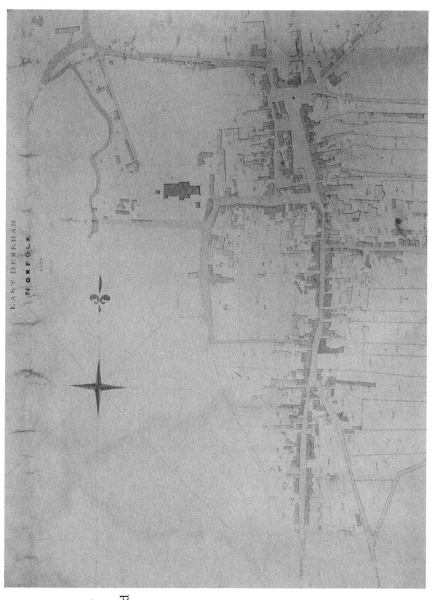

7   Dereham as shown on the tithe map of 1840 shortly before Armstrong moved to the town and before the arrival of the railway as. Most of the houses were tightly packed around and near the Market Place as well as along Church Street towards the church to the west (north is to the right of the map). (*Norfolk Record Office, DN/TA/267*)

53

8a, b   Two of the finest houses in Victorian Dereham. Hill House (a), at the north end of the Market Place, was the home of Mrs Gooch, and Moorgate (b), on the outskirts of the town, the home of the sinecure rector, Mr Wollaston, and later his relation, Mr Hyde. Hyde was the people's churchwarden, with whom Armstrong 'differed widely in religion and politics'. On his death in 1873, Armstrong wrote 'His capacity for business ensured for him a certain respect, even where he was far from being loved.'

many yards behind were very different. In 1840 houses were concentrated around the Market Place and down Church Street towards the church, south along the High Street and on towards South Green. At the west end of the Market Place a few houses strayed down Swaffham Hill and to the east there were a few houses on Quebec Road, but there was really very little building beyond the centre of the town.[19] As an agricultural county Norfolk supported many bustling market towns, all about 10 miles apart, where farmers could go once a week to sell animals and produce and conduct their business. Other than the major centres of Norwich, Yarmouth and Kings Lynn, only Wymondham, to the southwest of Norwich, had a population to match the 4,000 recorded in the 1841 census for Dereham. This figure was set to rise to over 5,000 during Armstrong's time in the town. In 1853 Armstrong commented on the 'numerous new houses built in Dereham in this last year' (18/8/53). Much of this increase can be attributed to the arrival of the railway in 1846, and between 1841 and 1851 the population rose by over 500. The railway, on which Armstrong was to be a regular traveller, provided several trains a day to Norwich and from there on to London and elsewhere. The original proposal had been for a station near the Market Place at the top of Church Street,[20] but it was finally built on the edge of the town, which soon became the centre of a new industrial area with maltings and granaries springing up, as well as a steam saw mill, brewers, a sack factory, four large iron foundries and engineering firms. A whole new area of terraced houses developed nearby, as well as larger detached and semi-detached villas for the better-off along roads leading away from the centre.

William Wollaston, the sinecure rector, had taken holy orders against his wishes and so was rarely seen in Dereham. The abolition of sinecure rectors meant that Wollaston would be the last holder of the position. From it he took the rectorial (great) tithes, valued at £710 a year,[21] as well as some of the income from the church estate. Over the years that Armstrong was vicar, their relationship was cordial. He gave generously to the poor and helped restore the church and build the school. He preached in the church several times a year, as well as giving the occasional party with his wife at Moorgate, his fine Georgian house on South Green, to which he invited the vicar and churchwardens. Although his wife lived at Moorgate, for much of the time he was not resident, but lived at the spa of Clifton, near Bristol, 'on account of an unhappy incompatibility of temperament existing between them'.[22] Mrs Wollaston, a clergyman's daughter, regularly give dinner parties at which the Armstrongs were frequent guests. Benjamin was a regular visitor, particularly during Mrs Wollaston's final illness in the spring of 1856. When she was obviously not going to recover he sent for her husband, who arrived before she died at the end of April.

Although the railway had brought new industries to the town, its business was still firmly rooted in the countryside. It was described as 'The Garden of Norfolk'[23] and as late as 1880 market gardens, nurseries and orchards were to be found not far from the centre.[24] The windmill off Norwich Road was built in 1836 for processing local grain. A second post mill had stood at the top of Quebec Road since the eighteenth century and appears in early photographs of the town. Pigs, corn and provisions produced in the many market gardens within the parish were all sold at the weekly market, while sheep and cattle fairs were held in July and September. Several Georgian brick houses stood near the marketplace, as did the Assembly Rooms, built in 1756, with a fine first-floor ballroom and wrought-iron balcony looking across the market, an indication of an earlier wealth. A gas works near the Quebec Road windmill provided gas throughout the town, which by 1850 had fifty street lights. However, the residents had to wait until 1881 before they had a piped water supply provided from an ornate brick water tower.[25]

On leaving his vicarage and walking through the churchyard, Armstrong would have reached the bottom of Church Street, where a row of thatched cottages had survived an earlier fire that had devastated the town. This small, low row housed seven families in 1851, one of which was a cabinet maker with a workshop backing on to the churchyard. On the corner opposite was the home of his clerk, George Philo, probably the son of the James Philo described in *Lavengro* who had died in 1829. In spite of becoming blind, George remained in post for all of Armstrong's time as vicar, dying, aged 85, only a week before his employer. The busy street contained tradesmen of all sorts, as well as a coffee house and the White Lion and Crown public houses. Here Armstrong would also have found an ironmonger, a blacksmith, a wheelwright, tailor, dressmaker/milliner, straw-bonnet maker, grocer, butcher, book binder and umbrella maker. He would have no need to venture further to post a letter, as Sarah Bone, the post mistress, was also in Church Street. Behind the street were several yards of small houses clustered closely together and mostly inhabited by poorer people, many of them unskilled labourers. The houses in Perry's, Whitethorn and Browne's yards were the homes of large families, the heads of whom were variously a groom, an ostler and labourers, while women took in washing, were dressmakers, seamstresses and charwomen. More shops and yards were to be found around the marketplace and up the High Street. A tea and coffee dealer, a glass and earthenware shop, two chemists, basket and shoe makers, several solicitors and banks and Dr Hastings the physician, were all to be found round the marketplace, as was a tailor employing seven men in the workrooms behind his shop. In Theatre Street was a machine maker with his fourteen men and four boys. The 1881 census records Jarrods Yard with three houses off the Market Place, while Barwells Court, School Yard and Smith's Yard were on the opposite side off Quebec Street, all full of small cottages teeming with children, whom Armstrong would endeavour to get into school.

Beyond this crowded centre an area of modern housing was beginning to develop by 1850. While the 1851 census lists labourers and laundresses in the yards behind the main streets, professional people such as solicitors, bank managers and those of private means were found in the newly developed areas on the edge of town.

Nearby mansions included Quebec Hall, built by a prosperous brewer in 1759, but by 1850 owned by a branch of the Lee-Warner family of Walsingham. Its home farm of 393 acres was let to a tenant. Dillington Hall was further afield, the home of the Long family until 1863, when it was bought by a Mr Everington, son of a London shawl manufacturer. The home farm of 278 acres was often also let. These two were the largest farms, but Watering Farm and others on the Yaxham Road and at Northmoor and Etling Green were all over 100 acres. Other farms varied from 5 to 80 acres.

The Corn Hall, opened in 1856, gave farmers somewhere to haggle over grain prices other than the many local pubs, nineteen of which are listed in the local directory. A theatre was built in 1815 and provided regular entertainment and both the Corn Hall and Assembly Rooms were used for a wide range of social events. The Friday market brought the town to life and Armstrong would regularly be interrupted in his study by a string of visitors. The town also supported at least four thriving chapels, and the arrival of a new parson must have been of general interest to both church- and chapel-goers. Armstrong was instrumental in founding a Mechanics' Institute (1854), which held lectures in the Assembly Rooms and by 1864 had a library of 1,000 books and 'a weekly-supplied newsroom'.[26] A Rifle Volunteers unit was established in 1860, with about seventy members. Armstrong, an enthusiastic supporter, was appointed their chaplain and frequently went on 'camp' with them in the grounds of the various Norfolk gentry and aristocratic houses.

The social standing of a town could well be enhanced by having a race course, and races were held regularly on commons in Swaffham, Fakenham and Dereham during the nineteenth century. The railway allowed for large attendances and there are reports in the press of meetings in the 1850s and 1860s. It was certainly a sport that Armstrong had enjoyed in his youth and would have enjoyed as a spectator, but there is no mention of his attending in the diaries. He may well have thought it did not become his status as a clergyman. While returning form a meeting of parsons in Fakenham in June 1867 he passed 'several people in Waggons' returning from the races which 'had been got up in Dereham and in which (as usual here) one of the running horses broke its leg and was killed on the spot' (12/6/67).

Set slightly apart from the marketplace was the huge church and to the south was the brick vicarage, a solid late Georgian structure built by Armstrong's predecessor and set within its own extensive grounds. Armstrong regarded it as too small for his increasing family, but there was plenty of scope for enlargement. It had 'a repose and character about it which renders it an appropriate residence for an ecclesiastic and a gentleman'. The church Armstrong thought 'magnificent', with its two towers, one at the intersection of the nave and transepts and one with eight bells standing separately in the church yard. It had a wide nave and the high roof was supported by 'clustered pillars'. There were four side chapels, galleries on three sides, seats of carved oak, a superb font and a brass eagle lectern. In his diary, Armstrong wrote of the honour which he felt in his promotion to Dereham and the increased responsibility which it would entail.

The nearest market town to Dereham was Swaffham with its high

9 Dereham vicarage, the home of Armstrong and his family for thirty-eight years. Two bays were added to the existing three-bay building in 1852.

10 St Nicholas's, Dereham, from a line block by Whimper, 1854.

church vicar, the Revd Salisbury Everard, who was to become a friend of Armstrong's. Although it contained many fine houses around the marketplace lived in by gentry and 'opulent people', Armstrong regarded it a 'declining and dull place' which had not taken advantage of the railway in the way that Dereham had (16/3/57).

Other denominations

Much of the pressure for reform of the church had come from the perceived threat posed by the dramatic rise of the Methodist movement. However, it was left to each diocese to implement change, and it was the early years of Victoria's reign that saw a group of reforming bishops making changes on the ground. By this time, however, the Methodists were there to stay and the relationship between Norfolk clergy and their dissenting neighbours was mostly one of toleration. Comments such as that of the Revd William Upjohn of Field Dalling in a Visitation return of 1845, that dissenters were 'the great pest of my parish', are rare.[27] Only occasionally, as in Swaffham, did parsons insist that all children in the school attend Anglican services. More typical was an attitude of respect and tolerance, which was partly because many dissenters sometimes attended church, particularly for baptisms and burials. Armstrong commented on his arrival in Dereham that 'dissent is by no means as influential at Dereham', although there were several chapels. The oldest was the Congregational (Independent) chapel, built in 1815 and expanded in 1820. This simple building was replaced in 1873/4 by a much grander edifice designed by the well-known Norwich architect William Boardman, on the site of the house of the poet William Cowper. The original Methodist chapel, built in 1824, was demolished in 1880 and replaced by a fine gothic-style building, again designed by Boardman. The Baptist chapel had been built just before Armstrong arrived in Dereham in 1849 and was a large classical building with galleries to seat a sizeable congregation. Armstrong was happy to baptise the children of dissenters, one of whom commented to him 'I ossus say begin and end with the church whatever you do between-whiles' (7/4/62).

There were limits as to how far cooperation should go. 'No-one can act with more charity personally towards dissenters than myself',

Armstrong wrote rather patronisingly, but this should not include sharing a platform with them at meetings such as those of the Bible Society. Of the two missionary societies, the Church Missionary Society (CMS) was generally supported by the dissenters and the Society for the Propagation of the Gospel (SPG) by the Anglicans, with Armstrong frequently chairing their meetings. Armstrong occasionally went to the CMS to show there was no ill feeling. However, he was fervently against Sir Samuel Morton Peto's Burial Bill (introduced in 1862), which would have allowed dissenting clergy to officiate in the churchyard at funerals, 'which is of course, only a prelude to their officiating in our Churches – Impudence can go no further' (12/6/62). Armstrong's view that the dissenters held little sway in the town is not supported by the religious census of 1851, not mentioned in the diary but undertaken shortly after his arrival in Dereham, which recorded numbers at the various services available in the town one Sunday in March. The congregation at the parish church was by far the largest, with 900 at the morning service, including Sunday School children, and 1,500 in the afternoon. There were 2,000 sittings, 1,000 of which were not allocated to particular families, accommodated not only in the nave and aisles, but also in galleries over the two aisles and at the west end. However, the Primitive and Wesleyan Methodists, Particular Baptists, Independents and Mormons also all had substantial congregations, totalling over 700, morning and evening.[28]

Mormons were spreading fast in the county. The first missionaries had arrived in Liverpool from America in 1830 and a peak in their influence was reached by mid-century. In 1851 there were thirteen Mormon congregations in Norfolk, including two in Dereham, one in the old workhouse and the other in Baxter Row. Together, according to the 1851 census, they attracted over fifty to their morning and evening services.[29] Although they are hardly mentioned by Armstrong, he does describe his encounter with an elder at Northall Green:

> In a certain cottage (on Northall Green) I was expostulating with the inmate on the absurdity of Mormonism to which she was addicted herself, when a fine tall young fellow entered the room and with a good-natured and amiable smile, said 'Well sister, how are you?' He was dressed in a green shooting coat, pink check shirt open at the

throat, and had a carpet bag slung over his shoulder by means of a stick. What was my surprise to discover that this truly unecclesiastical character was a veritable Mormon Elder. (3/3/54)

Further conversation revealed that the young man worked over a quarter of Norfolk, where there were 250 converts. He lived an itinerant life, trusting on the charity of church members.

Armstrong arrived in Dereham at the height of the controversy resulting from the creation by Pope Pius IX of a hierarchy of Roman Catholic bishops within the United Kingdom. Nicholas Wiseman, newly created a cardinal and appointed Archbishop of Westminster, was the head of this hierarchy. Although none of the new bishoprics received titles used by Church of England bishops, Protestant fears were aroused, a theme that was taken up by the press amid fears of Romish plots and foreign influences. Armstrong was part of the high church wing of the Church of England and regarded it as a member of the 'catholic' (i.e. 'universal') church, whilst always describing Roman Catholics as 'Romanists', many of whose beliefs he could not support. Many Anglican bishops issued protests and Blomfield urged his clergy to preach sermons on the subject. Guy Fawkes Night provided the opportunity for burning effigies of the pope and Wiseman, but in fact there was little violence.[30] Armstrong saw this as 'schismatic', 'uneucumenical' and something to be resisted, whilst sparking a lively correspondence in the local press. It was to be some years before there was a Catholic presence in Dereham.

Armstrong's years in Dereham were to see the church building restored, congregations increasing and more ritual introduced into services. The school prospered and there were many improvements in the town, often initiated by Armstrong himself. With his growing family, he became very much part of the social scene, entertaining at home and dining regularly with the local townspeople and gentry.

Notes

1   W. White, *Norfolk Directory*, 1864, 936.
2   B. Turner, *The Victorian Parson*, 2015, 148–9, quoting E. Bartrum, *Promotion of Merit Essential to the Progress of the Church*, 1866.
3   PP 1835 XXII.

4   P. Virgin, *The Church in the Age of Negligence*, 1989, 174–8.
5   F. Knight, *The Nineteenth-Century Church and English Society*, 1995, 159.
6   A. Jessopp, *Trials of a Country Parson*, 1894, xvii.
7   D. Dymond (ed.), *Parson and People in a Suffolk Village: Richard Cobbold's Wortham, 1824–77*, 2007, 3–4.
8   NRO, PD532/32.
9   D. Owen, 'The Cathedral 1840–1945', in I. Atherton, E. Fernie, C. Harper-Bill and H. Smith (eds), *Norwich Cathedral: Church, City and Diocese, 1096–1996*, 1996, 583.
10 R.G. Wilson, 'The Cathedral in the Georgian Period', in Atherton *et al.* (eds), 1996, 583.
11 Owen 1996, 615; O. Chadwick, *The Victorian Church*, vol. 1, 1966, 125–6.
12 Turner 2015, 51.
13 D. King, 'The Panel Paintings and Stained Glass', in Atherton *et al.* (eds), 1996, 428.
14 Chadwick 1966, 480.
15 O. Chadwick, 'Introduction', in H.B.J. Armstrong (ed.), *Armstrong's Norfolk Diary: Further Passages from the Diary of the Reverend Benjamin John Armstrong, Vicar of East Dereham, 1850–88*, 1963, 13–14.
16 Chadwick 1966, 475.
17 G. Borrow, *Lavengro*, 1896 Macmillan edn, 20.
18 White 1864, 803
19 NRO, 1839 tithe map, DN/TA/267.
20 W. White, *Norfolk Directory*, 1845, 308.
21 White 1864, 936.
22 Chadwick 1963, 11.
23 White 1845, 310.
24 OS 25 inch map XLIX.13 (1882–3).
25 N. Pevsner and R. Wilson, *The Buildings of England: North-West and South Norfolk*, 1999, 286–96.
26 White 1864, 309.
27 NRO, DN/VIS 49/7, quoted in R. Lee, *Rural Society and the Anglican Clergy, 1815–1914: Encountering and managing the Poor*, 2006, 60.
28 J. Ede and N. Virgo, *Religious Worship in Norfolk: The 1851 Census of Accommodation and Attendance at Worship*, Norfolk Record Society 62, 1998, 243.
29 Ibid.
30 G. Parsons, 'Victorian Roman Catholicism', in G. Parsons (ed.), *Religion in Victorian Britain*, vol. 1, *Traditions*, 1988, 148–9.

II
Public Life

Three
The Norfolk Clergy

I love the church too well to pretend that they [the clergy] reach the standards of their high calling or worthy of their vocation. There are good and true amongst them, but I am dealing with majorities and not exceptions.[1]

Let England's priests have their due: they are a faulty set in some respects, but only of common flesh and blood, like us all; but the land would be badly off without them: Britain would miss her church, if that church fell. God save it! God also reform it![2]

So wrote two observers of the clergy, one a Norfolk woman and the other the daughter of a Yorkshire clergyman. To these opinions can be added that of Armstrong:

It is often thought that the life of a country parson is one of perfect ease and freedom from care ... having no enemies and beloved by all.... Such are the characteristics of the class described by novelists ... but I am certain that no pastor of a country town desirous of doing the Church's work ought to expect this enviable freedom from trial. (4/9/55)

Who were the Norfolk clergy?

Aged 33 when he was appointed to Dereham, Armstrong was one of a large group of young men entering the ministry at the time. Reporting in 1835 on the age of the clergy, the Ecclesiastical Commission noted that while the largest number of incumbents in the Norwich diocese (fifty) were in the age group 60–65, there was also a significant group of younger men, with forty-five being under 30 and forty-three being between 31 and 35.[3] The years 1800–30 saw a huge expansion of Oxford and Cambridge universities, creating a pool of potential graduate clergymen and producing throughout Victoria's reign about 600 ordinands a year. As a result, nationally by 1840 the majority of parsons were aged under 45. For the first time since the Reformation the church was served by a majority of young and enthusiastic clergy.[4] To quote Charlotte Brontë describing in the first paragraph of *Shirley* the situation in the 1840s, 'They [the curates] are young enough to be very active and ought to be doing a great deal of good.' By the 1850s the profession was therefore predominantly a young one.

Once appointed to a parish, many clergymen remained there for the rest of their active lives. Armstrong stayed for thirty-eight years, resigning only as his health failed and retiring to a small house in Dereham where he died, aged 73, in 1890. However, there were several incumbents in Norfolk who served rather longer. The Revd Phillip Chandler of Lammas was installed in 1764 and was still there seventy years later.[5] Perhaps the longest-serving incumbent was the Revd Bartholomew Edward, the rector of Ashill, who was born the son of a rector in Hethersett in 1789 and secured his status amongst the gentry by a marrying a daughter of John Custance of Weston Hall.[6] Ordained by Bishop Bathurst in 1812, in 1813 he was appointed to Ashill, where he remained for seventy-six years, dying just before his hundredth birthday in 1889. He had no curate until he was 88 and continued taking services and preaching until shortly before his death.[7] Another long-lived but less exemplary clergyman was Dr Miles Beevor, who became vicar of Ketteringham in 1786 and remained there for thirty-nine years until 1835. During that time he held two other livings where he resided, and divided his time between politics and hunting. He came to Ketteringham only to perform his duty, and if there was no congregation waiting he locked the church and rode home. The normal congregation was four, 'the cobwebs gathered and the fabric began to decay. Sometime between 1814 and 1835 a whole tomb standing in the chancel vanished.'[8] George Crabbe, a relation of the poet, was rector of Merton for thirty-three years and on his death at the age of 65 he was described as 'taking the keenest interest in all that concerned the parish, the hall and the neighbourhood'.[9] Arthur Roberts remained at Woodrising from 1831 until his death in 1886 and while there published seventeen volumes of village sermons.[10] The fact that once installed, the incumbent had the freehold for life discouraged moving and this was not necessarily good for the parish. The Revd Augustus Jessopp of Scarning argued that a change in this situation was long overdue. A long tenure could lead to an 'absence of fresh interest and the invigorating stimulus of a new career'. There was a 'loss of old fire and force and efficiency'.[11]

Throughout Victoria's reign, the two most influential families in a rural parish were likely to be those of squire and clergyman, and in the many villages without a resident or dominate landowner, the parson might reign supreme. What sort of person was he likely to be? The Ecclesiastical Commission of 1835 collected a wealth of statistical information about the make-up of the clergy from which to start answering this question. Of the 300 or so Norfolk clergymen, the largest number (67) of those whose backgrounds we know came from clerical families, 44 from the professions, 42 were the sons of the landed gentry and 31 came from the peerage.[12] These would be the sort of backgrounds that could afford to support a son through one of the universities. Compared with the law, the army or medicine, the church was a cheap profession to enter, providing an elegant, leisured and gentlemanly lifestyle.

By far the majority of parishes were still rural, and incumbents shared a common aspiration and culture with the gentry classes. This unity of interest was not only the result of social but also of educational background. As noted above, in the 1830s and 1840s, the bulk of new ordinands came from Oxford and Cambridge. A typical country parson was therefore an educated and well-connected gentleman who cared about the spiritual health of his flock, tried to improve their church attendance, resisted non-conformity and played a pivotal role in developing education and the care of the poor.[13]

The years post 1850 saw university education become more secular. The colleges could no longer be seen as Anglican seminaries and some of the tutors were even declared atheists. The new theological colleges filled the gap. The earliest was St Bees in Chester diocese, founded in 1816. More influential was Cuddesdon, founded in 1854 by Samuel Wilberforce next to his Oxfordshire episcopal palace. By 1877 there were diocesan colleges in Lichfield, Salisbury, Lincoln, Truro, Chichester and Gloucestershire.[14] Although the courses were much like those at one of the universities, with lectures on the Bible and early church history, the tone was more serious. Smoking was banned as 'a habit repugnant to the formation of clerical character'.[15] Armstrong's lively student days and his enjoyment of a smoke in later life would have been frowned upon. The seminarians generally preferred urban livings, while the university men continued to make up the bulk of rural clergy.

Clergy income

One of the reforms following the findings of the Ecclesiastical Commission was the restricting of the holding of more than one benefice (plurality). The main reason for clergy taking multiple livings was that many were poorly endowed. In 1830 16 per cent of English benefices were endowed with less than £100, while something between £300 and £400 per annum was seen as the amount needed to maintain a respectable middle-class life. In Norfolk 158 parishes were endowed with less than £300.[16] The problems which this created were recognised by the Ecclesiastical Commission and gradually these very poor benefices were augmented, partly from funds provided by Queen Anne's Bounty. The 1838 Pluralities Act stipulated that no clergyman should hold more than two livings and that they should not be more than 10 miles apart. However, before this rule could be enforced there needed to be suitable parsonages in every parish. The 1835 returns showed that nationally nearly 3,000 parishes had no parsonage and many more were 'unfit to live in'. If a house did exist, but was occupied by a poorly paid curate only on the night before he was due to take a service, there was no incentive to keep it in good order and so it fell into decay.[17] Some limited improvement had taken place when Gilbert's Act of 1776 had empowered Queen Anne's Bounty to make loans for building and repairs to parsonages. The 1838 Act went further and clause 62 empowered bishops to demand that parsonages should be built or repaired on all livings worth more than £1,000. The responsibility for this lay with the incumbent, who could take out a loan which should be repaid over thirty years by the incumbent and his successors, something that could lead to real hardship. William Andrew arrived to take up his position at Ketteringham to find there was no house for him and eventually he had to buy one for himself in the nearby village of Hethersett. When Bishop Stanley arrived in Norwich in

1837 he set about enforcing residence. In 1843 the Revd John Bluck of Walsoken, a living worth £300 year,[18] was brought before the Consistory Court because he had not been resident in his parish for three months. For this he was deprived of a quarter of his annual income.[19] Gradually the non-resident parson who hunted with the gentry and was only interested in rent from his glebe and collecting tithes from his parishioners was replaced by a high-minded parson living in the heart of his village.

The value of endowments and therefore of stipends had much to do with history, but little with the needs of the parishes. As late as the 1890s many Norfolk stipends were still very low. Both Andrew and Armstrong had considerable private incomes. Andrew's stipend was as little as £200 a year[20] and Jessopp estimated that 'not 5% of clergy are living on income from their benefices'.[21] Out of their income the clergy were expected to pay a curate if they had one and also to set an example of charitable giving. In some parishes the contents of the offertory box would be distributed to the poor rather than kept for church work. In 1820, the rector of North Barsham, who lived in style at Cranmer House near Fakenham, gave a shilling after the service to all the poor who attended. He noted that, perhaps not surprisingly, 'some attend who are not of this parish'.[22] The nature of a country parish meant that the parson needed to keep a pony and trap and the more wealthy might keep riding-horses and even go hunting, although this was generally disapproved of. Most of the rural clergy would have regarded themselves as belonging to the 'gentry' class, but at the same time their calling meant they spent much of the time mixing with their social inferiors. The lifestyle of a gentleman did not always sit easily with what was expected of a clergyman. Armstrong gave up field sports when he became a priest but continued to enjoy fishing (23/5/55). Books of advice to clergy maintained that the minister's demeanor should be solemn and he should cultivate a gravity of manner. In society, especially, this should be borne in mind.[23]

An indication of the clergy's social position in the nineteenth century was the number of servants kept, and censuses suggest that although the standing of the clergy generally rose during the century, the Norfolk clergy were on the same level as substantial farmers rather than the great house. Few kept butlers or footmen.[24] In 1854 Armstrong was worried about his finances and feared he would have to part with his footman: 'The increased taxation we will have on account of the [Crimean] war, demand some retrenchment. I fear I must cease having a footman in the house, any inconvenience being preferable to the wretched conviction that one is living beyond one's income' (18/5/54). Rectories too reflected social status. On the whole they were in the second rank of parochial properties, below the manor house but above most farm houses,[25] although as we shall see there were some notable exceptions.

The contradiction between the poverty and simplicity of Christ's life and the need to maintain the trappings of his position in society was a moral problem that was faced by the Lincolnshire parson Francis Massingberd. A New Year's resolution in 1841 was to reduce his 'establishment' and

> to submit to the humiliation of having no man servant in ye house etc. – *Humiliation?* Think of Christ! But it will help us pay off debts, and restore or rebuild Driby church and pay curate – and will answer other good purposes of self-denial. Dear wife quite willing.[26]

The gulf between the richest and the poorest clergy was great. While in Norfolk over one hundred parishes were worth less than £300, thirty were valued at over £1,000.[27] The injustice of this was highlighted by Victorian novelists such as Anthony Trollope. In his novel *Framley Parsonage*, the Rev. Mark Robarts received £900 a year (roughly the same sum as Armstrong) on which he could live comfortably, although fine horses were beyond his means, while his neighbour received only £130 and lived in poverty, leading to loneliness and despair. Richard Jefferies, whose essays are based on life in the Wiltshire countryside in the 1870s, described a country parson living in a substantial and well-furnished house which gave the appearance of wealth while in fact he was extremely poor, with a wife who tried to make ends meet by keeping goats, cows and then bees.[28]

There were various ways in which clergy could augment their incomes, the most usual being taking in pupils, which was a sort of 'cottage industry' that some parsons found profitable. An advertisement in the *Norfolk Chronicle* is typical:

> The Rev. T.C. Haddon, incumbent at Tunstead wishes to receive into his family a few little boys to educate with his own son, now eight years old.

The boys would be prepared for entry into a public school.[29] For a year or so between school and university some parents who could afford it sent their sons to live in a vicarage and polish up their classics with a learned vicar before going to Oxford or Cambridge. Most parsonages were large enough to house several boarders, and with their knowledge of the classics, the clergy were in a position to coach boys for Oxbridge. This form of tutoring decreased towards the end of the century as education became more technical and complex.

The Revd Joseph Brereton went further. His concern was the education of the sons of the middle classes, and particularly for farmers' sons who lived too far away from market towns to make the daily journey to schools there. Before he succeeded his father as rector of the Norfolk parish of Massingham in 1870, he was based in Devon, where in 1861 he established a 'County School' in West Buckland, now West Buckland School. This was a fee-paying boarding school aiming to educate the sons of farmers. Once in Norfolk he was instrumental in setting up the Norfolk County School Association with Lord Leicester as president and the Bishop of Norwich one of the trustees. Brereton was the chairman of the directors. He began in 1871 by opening a small school in Massingham with seven boys, later described in the County School magazines as the 'Massingham seven'. The number soon rose to thirty and three masters were employed. It was this core of pupils that moved in 1874 to the purpose-built 'County School' near North Elmham. Brereton remained an active director until the school was finally forced to close because of a lack of pupils in 1893.[30]

Armstrong's neighbours

Soon after his arrival in Dereham Armstrong wrote in his diary an assessment of his fellow clergymen, whom he described as 'numerous and opulent', having much in common with their eighteenth-century predecessors such as Parson Woodforde of Weston Longville.

> Indifference is the prevailing feeling among them, and the farm, the Petty Sessions or the [Poor Law] Union Board are their occupations. They live like educated and well-disposed country gentlemen, and seem to have no taste for the 'work of the ministry' and scarcely a

recognition of their high office in the guidance of souls. (undated; 1851, vol. 1)

Thomas Howe (1770–1848) of Morningthorpe and Fritton would probably have fitted Armstrong's first description. He was a landowner in his own right. His estate was small and somewhat impoverished and he took an active interest in the farming there and on the glebe, keeping a detailed day-to-day diary from 1803 to 1827.[31] When he died in 1848, his nephew inherited and found the estate very run-down. He also provided a not very flattering description of his uncle. Although 'of clear and sound understanding, he was not trained or invigorated in the pursuit of the serious branches of learning'. His taste was for 'the lighter kind of literature'. He had taken holy orders at an early age 'rather with a view to a maintenance than as a serious profession (a practice too common in the eighteenth-century Anglican church)'. He was an attentive if not 'zealous' priest with 'no ambition for distinction in the pulpit'.[32]

Armstrong may have had men like Howe in mind when he criti-cised those who spent their time 'on the farm, the bench and buying railway shares', none of which were the 'true work of a priest'. In spite of the improvements that Armstrong began to see, there were still those whom he described as 'Trifling, dandified, morning-calling priests, more interested in the small gentry (than their parishioners)' (2/1/55). He claimed that the clergy of north Norfolk were fifty years behind the rest, and parishes remained many years in the same hands (18/1/70). Where local clergy were incumbents of small parishes and at a certain time of life, they were often more out of touch with new ways and style of services than younger men (20/4/65). Instead they should be encour-aging church and school attendance and daily prayers. The vicar of Hindolveston confided in Armstrong that he felt isolated because the surrounding clergy were 'aged and indolent'.

The Revd Denis Hill of neighbouring Gressenhall was also very much of the 'old school'. The Hills were the leading family in the village and had built the village school in 1842. Shortly after Armstrong's arrival in Dereham, he met Parson Hill on a train and Armstrong described him as 'a perfect specimen of a bygone class of clergy. With all their imperfections, however, it is impossible not to respect them, just as we do a dilapidated mansion because it is ancient and picturesque,

Elizabeth Hill
Gressenhall Rectory
Died Feby 20th 1863 · aged 71 yrs
Interned Sarlingham Church Yard

Revd Dennis Hill
Gressenhall Rectory
Died Feby 18th 1873 aged 90 yrs

11   The Revd Dennis Hill, rector of Gresenhall, and his wife. Armstrong described him as 'of the old school'.

though almost useless to anyone' (4/10/54). Armstrong visited Gressen-hall church for the first time in 1869 and described the parson as 'the greatest curiosity connected with the church'. Although over 80 years old he still shot regularly with large shooting parties, played bowls and 'drinks his daily bottle of port of which he has a famous cellar' (14/9/69).

Hill was certainly an exception. When Armstrong had had time to get to know the local clergy better, his view moderated somewhat:

During the evening I thought what a difference there is between the Rector fifty years back and our young incumbents. It runs through everything – their house, their 'views', their wives, their furniture, their dress. Now all is handsome and refined and in good taste. Everything is new and even in the remotest village we hear …. the latest new song of the season…. The same care is shown by these

young rectors for their church and school as for their houses... In
all respects they are vastly superior to the last generation. (8/11/54)

An example of the more hardworking new-style parson was
Armstrong's low church neighbour, Henry Tacey of Swanton Morley,
whom he first met in 1852 when he went to see how a new school there
was organised. Tacey had been given a home by an unrelated benefactor
who had found him as a child working on a stocking loom. He had
educated the boy and saw him through university. Tacey then became
a tutor to the family of the local squire, Mr Lombe, who later presented
him to the living of Swanton Morley with its income of £1,000 a year. By
the time Armstrong met him he had been in his parish for nearly thirty
years and been made a rural dean and honorary canon of Norwich. He
had himself helped pay for his curate to go to Cambridge (28/8/52).
Tacey's popularity as a preacher spread beyond his parish. In the 1820s
the farmer John Leeds from nearby Billingford frequently travelled to
hear him. He regarded him as 'A most excellent preacher ... certainly
one of the finest preachers I have ever had the opportunity of hearing,
being truly evangelical' and 'one who expands the scriptures in the most
exemplary manner.'[33] Perhaps not surprisingly, he was not popular with
the high church Armstrong, who frequently accused him of 'poaching'
his parishioners. He found that Tacey had been regularly visiting one of
his flock for spiritual purposes. 'He has not had the courtesy to apprise
me of this and is, in short, a fomenter of discord and schism in my
parish' (6/8/62). He believed that Tacey had always resented the fact
that he, a much younger man, had been appointed to the larger parish
of Dereham. There were however some topics which the two of them
could discuss on friendly terms. In a conversation Mr Tacey had given
his view that as the Test and Corporation Act (1828), allowing dissenters
to become MPs, and the Catholic Emancipation Act (1829) meant that
Parliament was not made up entirely of Anglican MPs, a new relationship between church and state was needed. 'He foresaw trouble ahead',
and this was a view with which Armstrong had sympathy.[34] When, in
1863, he was dying of cancer, Armstrong visited him and rather pomp-
ously recorded in his diary 'heard from the curate how gratified he was
and hoped I would call again. Divine charity and reality of his position
seemed to obliterate all previous opposition and divergence' (6/8/62

and 7/3/63). Tacey died a month later while Armstrong was in London. He was sorry to have missed his funeral, but 'How glad I am that we had made our peace' (18/4/63).

The Revd Henry Collinson was described by Armstrong as 'admirable in all matters not connected with his profession' (7/10/73). He occupied the family living of East Bilney and occupied a recently erected large, architect-designed gentleman's residence of a rectory. Elsewhere Collinson is described as owning a vineyard in South Africa and spending most of his time at his office in the City. 'He was more of a merchant than a priest' (18/8/81). Armstrong frequently dined at Bilney, where the welcome was always warm, the banquet splendid and the company usually from the gentry or younger branches of the local aristocracy. In May 1856 Collinson organised carriages to take his friends on a trip to Holkham. 'He is never so pleased as in getting his friends around him and affording them pleasure' (20/5/56). In September 1857 there was an archery party and in addition to this fashionable sport there was a band, lunch in a tent and dancing in the evening for the 200 people present. The church in Bilney, however, was 'in a wretched state'. The contrast between the church and the 'luxury of the rectory is most painful' (12/10/62). A similar thought struck Armstrong some years later when passing a brightly lit meeting house on his way to 'one of Collinson's great parties'. 'It conveyed a sort of reproach in my mind that we were going to fare sumptuously with one whose church is never lighted up for expectant guests' (7/10/73). Collinson's remoteness from his poorer parishioners is shown by his remark that there was no point in giving the inmates of Gressenhall workhouse handkerchiefs because they would not know what to do with them.[35] When he died at the age of 90 in 1881 the living passed to another member of the Collinson family.

The Revd Walter Marcon of Edgefield understood the problems of poverty rather better and took a far more sympathetic view than Collinson: 'We parsons have no right to expect our people to be moral, unless we see, as far as we can see, that their conditions conduce to that end in the same way as our own do.'[36] Armstrong was concerned that the 'monotony of toil' resulted in the poor being 'heavy and dull', leading in some cases to insanity in old age. 'There is much truth in what Dr Challice [Armstrong's brother-in-law] once said to me: "I find", said

12 The fine Tudoresque East Bilney rectory, built in 1837 and designed by Arthur Brown, was the home of Armstrong's affluent friend Henry Collinson, described by him in 1873 as 'admirable in all matters not connected with his profession'.

he, "that joking don't pay"' (9/12/53). Bearing in mind the social back-ground of most of the clergy, it is not surprising that by the middle of the nineteenth century they were increasingly identified with the landed interest which controlled village life and had so little understanding of the majority of their parishioners.

Although Oxford and Cambridge produced a large number of ordi-nands, until 1860 Trinity College Dublin came a close second. With its non-residential degree courses, it produced a 'back-door route' to grad-uation for impecunious Englishmen as well as the Irish.[37] The Irish vicar of West Bradenham, the Revd George Stone, features regularly in the diary. Armstrong was prejudiced against the Irish and later described his curate Mr Swann as having the Irish characteristics of being vain and quick to take offence (24/3/63): traits that he also ascribed to Stone. However, Stone and Armstrong seem to have been good colleagues, with Stone calling on Armstrong to talk over the problems he had with his squire, Armstrong's friend Captain Haggard: 'verily Squires love to have pre-eminence and I'm thankful there is not one in this parish' (24/10/57). The situation did not improve and two years later Stone preached at Dereham, staying for the evening and relating the quarrels between him and Haggard: 'I fear they will never get on together' (30/9/60). Armstrong's descriptions of Stone could have been lifted straight from Charlotte Brontë's *Shirley* – a book first published in 1849 and which he may well have read. Her Mr Malone was proud, arrogant and rude, with a towering passion, all of which Armstrong described in Stone. For this reason he was somewhat nervous when Captain Haggard asked him to give a lecture on his Irish trip at Bradenham school, knowing that Stone would be there. He removed from his lecture points that he thought might be controversial and indeed added some complimentary remarks. When Armstrong had finished, Stone stood up and lectured the audience, quoting at length from the Protestant Irish patriot, orator and lawyer, John Curran. When the audience began to be impatient with him he became furious, threw his book on the floor and left the room. This show of anger led Armstrong to write in his journal, 'Ireland is the best place for the Irish' (28/2/58). This short temper was again exhibited in 1860, when he went into the school in Bradenham and cut the children's hair, which he thought untidy and long. This was greeted by fury from their mothers, who then put up a notice near the vicarage which read, 'Hair cutting, gratis in the Irish fashion by G. Stone'. 'He might have known that nothing irritates mothers more than meddling with their children's hair' (15/2/60). Finally, in November, Stone left to return to Ireland 'to a living of 5,000 people, not above twenty of whom are Protestants, with a new house in the middle of a potato field … he will perhaps get on better among his own people than he did here' (21/11/60).

There were also some eccentric examples. The vicar of Cawston, a relative of the local land owner, Mr Bulwer, never attended church, but instead spent his time in 'the elevating task of mending pots and kettles' (5/7/52).

Of course there were a few bad apples. William Henslowe appears to have been a difficult character. He became rector of the fenland parish of Southery in 1838 and described the 'moral and spiritual condition of the people there most reprobate and abandoned'. There were ten beer houses, and 'poaching, gambling and cricketing' were amongst the lawless Sunday activities. He was immediately unpopular because of his efforts to close beer houses; his poultry was stolen and his horse let loose in revenge. Various efforts at founding a Sunday School and evening lectures failed and he was attacked outside one of the public houses one night. Feelings reached such a pitch that complaints were made to the bishop in 1840, who dismissed the case.[38] Later in the year Henslowe resigned Southery and moved to Tottenhill and Wormegay, where he was no more popular, and in 1876, the bishop asked for his removal. This followed an incident in which he had refused to baptise the dying child of a dissenter who lived in a remote fenland hamlet. His unpopularity meant that his churches were empty. 'He is so mentally deranged as to address his parishioners as heathens.' His answer to this was that it was their 'willful absence' that was emptying the churches. Such people who encouraged them not to attend 'cannot be Christian people'. 'Churches are not merely Houses for the idle entertainment of ill-natured critics and opponents, but God's especial house of prayer.'[39]

Arthur Loftus, possibly a relation of the Yarmouth MP William Loftus, was rector of Fincham and was accused in May 1845 at the Consistory Court of keeping two prostitutes as servants, claiming that this was on the advice of his doctor as he had been denied conjugal rights by his wife. Not surprisingly this defence failed and in 1846 he was deprived of his rectory, stipend and any further preferment.[40] There were accusations of 'soliciting the chastity' of two ladies against the Revd Thomas Berney of Bracon Ash, and whilst he was found guilty before the Episcopal Court of Arches in 1865, he won on appeal to the Privy Council and remained as rector until 1895.[41]

Armstrong described the parish of Attleborough as being at a 'low ebb' in 1872 because of the ill conduct of the previous incumbent (3/11/72), but no further details are recorded.

The life of a clergyman in an isolated rural village could be very lonely and disheartening. Armstrong's friend the Revd William Fothergill frequently came to stay and was the godfather to Armstrong's second son, Herbert, a fact that made Armstrong hope that they might see more of each other (13/8/52). When Armstrong arrived in Dereham, Fothergill was the curate of the neighbouring parish of North Tuddenham. From there he moved to the fenland parish of Wentworth, near Ely, where, in August 1857, Armstrong went to visit him. 'I was glad to find the countryside much prettier and less fen-like than I had expected.' However, the rectory was rambling, ill-furnished and dilapidated, with an abandoned garden. Armstrong was struck by the silence of the place. The little church had been restored and the parish consisted of two or three farms and a public house. The congregation at Evensong and Matins consisted only of the school teacher and Fothergill's servant (10/8/57). It was not surprising that he found the life lonely and depressing, feeling the need of companionship and conversation with his long-standing friend. Finally, after much heart-searching he followed other young high churchmen into the Roman Catholic Church (6/12/59).

The clergy's outside interests

The work of the church allowed time for a variety of other interests, and most clergymen followed a variety of outside pursuits. Armstrong visited the theatre and art exhibitions while in London, travelled both across the British Isles and abroad, as well as playing an active part in the affairs of the town, enjoying family activities and an evening's fishing. His garden and greenhouse also occupied him. A letter written by William Layng in 1843 described Lincolnshire clergy for whom gardening was also an important occupation. The clergy were 'the only resident gentlemen in the country [who] employ themselves entirely in their gardens and do their own carpentry'. The Louth Floral and Horticultural Show was dominated by clergy.[42] When the Dereham Horticultural Society was founded in 1862, Armstrong was vice-president.

However, for those with serious academic interests, the priesthood could provide time for quiet study and research, and there were many examples of such men to be found in rural Norfolk. Both the Norfolk and Norwich Archaeological Society and the Norfolk and Norwich Naturalists' Society began in the mid-nineteenth century and many clergymen were to be amongst their founding members. Antiquarianism was popular amongst the clergy, encouraged by their enthusiasm for church restoration and interest in the past practices of the church and of its buildings. In 1844 the Revd Richard Hart of Catton gave a lecture, later published, at the recently founded Norwich Museum on 'The Antiquities of Norfolk' which was illustrated by many of the objects that had found their way into the museum's collections. It was the first general description of the antiquities of the county.[43] The Norfolk and Norwich Archaeological Society (NNAS) was founded in 1846 at the instigation of the Revd George Munford of East Winch and the antiquarian George Minty of Norwich. In common with similar county bodies, about two-thirds of the committee members were clergy and the president was the Bishop of Norwich. In the 1860s, 70s and 80s, 69 per cent of the articles in the Society's journal, *Norfolk Archaeology*, were from clergymen,[44] covering subjects to do with church architecture, fabric, memorial brasses, plate, wall paintings and records. Others had a more general archaeological content such as finds of Roman coins and pedigrees of famous families. This pattern continued throughout the century. One of the aims of the founders was to keep the subscription as low as possible 'so as to bring it within the means of all, and especially with a view of creating a better taste among the class from which churchwardens are drawn'. [45] The Revd Charles Manning was secretary for much of the 1860s and wrote at least one article in every volume from 1864 to 1892, most of which were on church architecture and fittings, and he travelled widely across the county from his rectory in Diss, visiting churches and historic sites. In 1852 and 1866 he excavated the prehistoric flint mines at Grimes Graves, near Thetford, cutting trenches through pits which he believed were dwellings.[46] His friend the Revd John Bloom of Castle Acre made an in-depth study of the history of the priory and castle there, including details of the builders and founders, the De Warenne family.[47] In 1890 the Revd Edmund Farrer of Rickenhall published what must have been the result of many years work travelling around the county, producing a parish-by-parish list of Norfolk's monumental brasses.[48] Armstrong himself was never a member of the Society, although his clergyman son, John, had joined by the 1880s and was able to share his interest in monumental church brasses with other members.

The most prominent of the antiquarian clergy was Augustus Jessopp, who features in the later volumes of Armstrong's diary. He came to Norfolk as headmaster of Norwich Grammar School in 1859 but became rector of Scarning in 1879 and remained there until 1911. He wrote, 'I was burning my boats in taking a country living',[49] but in spite of that it was a decision he never regretted. 'I have found an abiding joy and pride in doing my best for my people and studying them and their ways in the present, while trying to learn something about their forefathers and *their* ways in the past.'[50] Jessopp preached at a service in aid of the school (27/6/80) and attended the opening of the new St Withburga's chapel in Dereham in 1880 (20/4/80), and in addition Armstrong asked him to lecture to a literary society he was helping set up. The subject was 'Monks and Monasteries in Norfolk' (2/12/80). He was soon a part of the local social scene and Armstrong found his company stimulating. After a 'friendly dinner' with the Jessopps, Armstrong wrote, 'conversation amusing and instructive which it always is with them' (20/7/82). It may well have been as a result of this friendship that John Armstrong, then a curate in Dereham, took up archaeology as a hobby and in 1881 gave a lecture to the Institute on church brasses, illustrated by rubbings that he had taken (7/2/81). Jessopp became a member of the council of the NNAS in 1872 and remained there until the early 1890s. He was a great supporter of the Society for the Preservation of Ancient Buildings (SPAB), founded in 1877 by William Morris in an effort to promote the authentic maintenance of medieval buildings, particularly churches, against the sort of 'restoration' that Morris, Jessopp and others thought 'destructive'. He died at the age of 90 in 1914, and was described in his obituary as 'a remarkable example of a lettered cleric with interests extending widely outside his own profession, a type less common now than it was when he took orders in 1848'.[51] He was a serious antiquarian researcher, publishing regularly in *Norfolk Archaeology* on a range of architectural, ecclesiastical and biographical subjects ranging from married clergy in thirteenth-century Norfolk,[52] and descriptions of Bowthorpe and Breccles Hall,[53] to studies of St William of Norwich and an obscure Catholic priest, Father Henry Walpole, in the time of Elizabeth I. Many of his essays were republished in book form, the best known of which were *Arcady, for Better or for Worse* (1887), *Studies of a Recluse in Cloister, Town and Country* (1892), *The Coming of the Friars and Other Essays* (1893) and *The Trials of a Country Parson* (1894). His most prolific period was the 1880s and 1890s, when he published at least eleven learned articles in each of the two decades. When he retired in 1911 his extensive library of over 600 items collected over a half-century of antiquarian studies was sold by Sotheby's for £3,000.[54]

However, Jessopp's interests were not only antiquarian. He wrote regularly for the *Nineteenth Century*, a periodical that circulated mainly among the London intelligentsia, as well as in the *Quarterly Review* and several American periodicals in which he described Norfolk rural life, condemning the condition of labourers' cottages. In an attempt to dispel the 'idyll' of country life fostered by town dwellers, he recorded the monotony and dullness of rural life, and bemoaned the decline of the small farm. He shared with his contemporaries a fascination with the supernatural and recorded his own ghostly experience while working in the library at Mannington Hall in 1879 on Henry Walpole. The article, published in the *Nineteenth Century*, described his seeing the ghost of the monk beside him. Other papers recounting ghostly experiences, such as 'The Phantom Coach' and 'A Night of Wakening', were published individually and in collected volumes.[55]

Much of this was stimulated by Jessopp's friendship with M.R. James, the medievalist and celebrated writer of ghost stories. James himself was the son of a clergyman and had a brother who followed their father into the church. He spent much of his childhood at the rectory in Great Livermere, Suffolk. James first met Jessopp when together they translated *The Life and Miracles of St William of Norwich*, published in 1896. The project was James's, but he wrote in his autobiography, *Eton and Kings*, published in 1926, 'I thought that Dr Jessopp would be the right person to handle a monument of Norwich history of this importance.... The resulting friendship with Dr Jessopp and the visit to Scarning were handsome rewards for any weariness entailed by the translation.'[56] Many of James's stories have an East Anglian provenance, as well as an antiquarian one. It is nice to speculate that some of the themes were discussed between the two men in front of the flickering firelight in the library at Scarning Rectory.

Of an earlier generation was the Revd Mr J.H. Dashwood, vicar of Stow Bardolph and rector of Wimbotsham. He was a Fellow of the Society of Antiquaries and his major work was the transcribing of the Visitation of Norfolk in 1563 from an original in the British Museum. This he annotated with extensive genealogical detail. The work was nearing completion on his death in 1869 and was finished by Augustus Jessopp and another clergyman, the Revd Grigson, with help from Armstrong's churchwarden, George Carthew, and Captain Bulwer of Quebec Hall. It was published by the NNAS in 1878.[57]

The Revd William Hart-Raven, vicar of the Suffolk village of Fressingfield-with-Withersdale within the Norwich diocese, wrote widely on archaeological subjects between 1893 and 1902. His works included a guide to the Roman fort at Burgh Castle. In the introduction he wrote that 'To render an excursion really enjoyable there ought always to be included in it a visit to some object of interest ... by looking at some old castle or church, or camp, the sight of which takes the mind back to distant times, and makes us think of the wonderful history of our country and the changes which have passed over its smiling surface.'[58]

Some clerical antiquarians were also archaeologists, opening burial mounds in their spare time. Following on from the work of Manning, between 1869 and 1871 Canon William Greenwell from Durham carried out excavations at Grimes Graves which indicated that the pits were in fact entrances to prehistoric flint mines.[59] Augustus Legge was rector of North Elmham from 1867 to 1894 and a friend of Armstrong's. The grounds of his fine Georgian rectory included the ruins of what was then called Tower Hills and which are now interpreted as a Norman bishop's chapel on the site of the cathedral of the Anglo-Saxon diocese. He believed that the great ditches which surrounded the manor house marked the site of a Roman fort, with the manor house in one corner, and in the1870s his antiquarian interests led to him to clear the site of undergrowth and excavate the area. Retaining walls were built and the site was left well tended.[60] He also transcribed and published privately the churchwardens' accounts for Elmham from 1537 to 1577 and, after his retirement, those for 1586–1714.[61]

Other related interests covered folklore and dialect. The Revd John Gunn contributed an article to volume 2 of *Norfolk Archaeology* (1849) on 'Proverbs and Popular Superstitions' and in volume 5 (1859) the Revd Grenville J. Chester wrote on 'Norfolk Words Not in Forby's Vocabulary'. Armstrong also noted usages, words and phrases that he saw as peculiar to Norfolk. For instance, he noticed that the word 'tempest' was frequently used in place of the word 'storm'.

Members of the Victorian clergy were also at the forefront of botanical and ornithological studies, building on the work of the Revd William Forby of Fincham, an eminent botanist of the 1790s. Indeed, the garden designer John Claude Loudon, writing in 1822, had recommended the study of 'Natural History' as a suitable pastime for the clergy. He regarded it as

> superior, in a social point of view, even to a taste in gardening. The sportsman often follows his amusements to the great annoyance of his parishioners ... and the classical or indoor student of any kind secludes himself in his closet or laboratory, but the naturalist is abroad in the fields ... not only invigorating his health, but affording ample opportunity for frequent intercourse with his parishioners. In this way their reciprocal acquaintance is cultivated, and the clergyman at last becomes an advisor and friend as well as a spiritual teacher.[62]

The first county flora was published by the Revd Kirby Trimmer in 1866. The Revd Richard Lubbock, rector of Eccles from 1837 to 1876, was a member of the committee of Norwich Museum from 1831 and published *Observations of the Fauna of Norfolk and More Particularly the District of the Broads* in 1845. In the tradition of the Revd Gilbert White and his *Natural History of Selbourne* completed a hundred years earlier was the Revd Francis William Galpin's *Flowering Plants and Birds of Harleston*, written over a five-year period and published in 1888.

The clergy provided many of the nineteenth century's leading ornithologists. In 1826 the Revd R. Sheppard and the Revd W. Whitear published an article in the Linnean Society's *Transactions*, 'A Catalogue of the Norfolk and Suffolk Birds with Remarks', which for the first time contained a complete list of birds for both counties. Whitear was also a keen sportsman and ironically was killed later the same year in his own woods at Starston by a member of his own anti-poaching party.[63] The Norfolk and Norwich Naturalists' Society was founded in 1869 with the Revd J. Crompton as its first chair and the clergy continued to be well represented in the membership lists.

It is not perhaps surprising, considering their classical and university education, that there were several authors amongst the clergy. The books and articles of Augustus Jessopp have already been mentioned, but he was not alone as a writer. The Revd Whitwell Elwin (1816–1900) came from a wealthy dynasty of clergymen and followed his kinsman Caleb Elwin to the family living of Booton in 1849. In 1852 he published a selection of letters and poems of Lord Byron and in 1853 he began writing for the *Quarterly Review*, in all contributing forty-two articles between 1853 and 1889. From 1853 to 1860, he was its editor, travelling to London four times a year to undertake the work. This literary publication took a moderate conservative political view and received articles from such figures as Lord Robert Cecil and William Gladstone. When he retired, Elwin concentrated on his parish work, but still found time to edit and publish five volumes of the works and letters of Alexander Pope, published in 1870–1871. He was described by Edward Bulwer-Lytton as 'one of the last true men of letters, scholarship, style, tenderness, discrimination with a vast knowledge of books and unlimited leisure'.[64] His work in rebuilding Booton church is described elsewhere.

Richard Cobbold, rector of Wortham, Suffolk, and a graduate of Gonville and Caius, was also a prolific writer, poet and illustrator. Between 1827 and 1847 he wrote and illustrated over twenty novels. His book *The Story of Margaret Catchpole, a Suffolk Girl*, published in 1845, telling the true story of a young convict who was transported to Australia and then became an admired nurse in the colony, brought him international acclaim, over 20,000 copies being sold in his own lifetime.[65]

Writing was also something that the Armstrong family enjoyed. Armstrong senior kept a detailed diary and his sister was a well-known

novelist. Benjamin's daughter Helen wrote short articles for local magazines, and in December 1880 a paper by her entitled 'Reminiscences of
a Tour on the Rhine', in which she had included poetry and historical
details, was read for her at the Dereham Athenaeum Club by her brother,
John (16/12/80). Not only did Armstrong keep a diary, but he had many
publications to his name. Sermons given in Crowle were published
in 1843 and in Dereham in 1853. His first book was a history of Little
Stanmore published in 1849. His *Manual of Devotion for Private and
Parochial Use*, reprinted in Dereham, was in its fifth edition by 1856. On
the publication of *Holy Catholic Church and the Communion of Saints*,
he wrote 'Every author of a book, however small, knows the satisfaction of seeing it fresh from the hands of the printer.' It was dedicated
to his father and ran to a hundred pages (1852 n.d). By 1853 his other
publications included *Lectures on the Morning Service, Questions and
Answers on the Catechism, Short Prayers for the House* and *A Sermon on
the Advantages of Daily Worship.* He also wrote articles for local magazines such as the *Norfolk Spectator.* In 1862 a piece criticising cathedral
services was published and in the same edition was one by 17-year-old
Helen on a two-day visit to Rouen (1/7/62). A copy of *The Advantages of
Daily Public Worship* survives in the Heritage Centre at the Millennium
Library in Norwich, while others are to be found at Cambridge University Library and the British Library.

Armstrong was not the only Norfolk parson to publish on religious
matters. Arthur Robert of Woodrising published seventeen volumes
of his sermons under titles such as *Plain Sermons on Gospel Miracles
Preached to a Village Congregation* in 1867 and six volumes of *Village
Sermons.*

Although Armstrong was well aware of the academic enthusiasms
of his fellow clergy he showed little in-depth interest in their activities.
The pastoral care of his parishioners was for him a full-time occupation.

It is clear that Professor Chadwick's statement, 'The list of interesting incumbents of villages could go on for many pages. The work
bred remarkable men',[66] was as true of Norfolk as elsewhere.

Notes

1   Mrs Cresswell, *Norfolk and the Squires, Clergy, Farmers and Labourers*, 1875, 22.
2   Charlotte Brontë, *Shirley*, 1994, 308.
3   PP 1835 XXII, table xv, 287.
4   A. Haig *The Victorian Clergy*, 1984, 4–5.
5   P. Virgin, *The Church in the Age of Negligence*, 1989, 161.
6   NRO, PD548/46.
7   Ibid.
8   O. Chadwick, *Victorian Miniature*, 1960, 35.
9   NRO, PD532/32.
10 O. Chadwick, *The Victorian Church*, vol. 2, 1971, 176.
11 A. Jessopp, *Trials of a Country Parson*, 1894, xviii.
12 PP 1835 xxii, table X, 281.
13 D. Dymond (ed.), *Parson and People in a Suffolk Village: Richard Cobbold's Wortham, 1824–77*, 2007, 2.
14 Haig 1984, 154.
15 F. Knight, *The Nineteenth-Century Church and English Society*, 1995, 115.
16 Virgin 1989, 279.
17 P.C. Hammond, *The Parson and the Victorian Parish*, 1977, 45.
18 W. White, *Norfolk Directory*, 1845, 577.
19 NRO, DN/CON 136.
20 Chadwick 1960, 37.
21 Jessopp 1894, 59.
22 NRO DN VIS 52/8.
23 Hammond 1977, 56, quoting A. Oxenden, *The Pastoral Office: Its Duties, Difficulties, Privileges and Prospects*, 1857.
24 R. Lee, *Rural Society and the Anglican Clergy 1815–1914: Encountering and Managing the Poor*, 2006, 40.
25 Ibid., 31.
26 Knight 1995, 145.
27 Virgin 1989, 279.
28 R. Jefferies, 'The Parson's Wife' (1880), in *Hodge and His Masters*, 1992, 111–19.
29 *Norfolk Chronicle*, 26 March 1851.
30 S. Wade-Martins, 'The County School Movement', *Rural History Today* **18**, January 2010, 4–5.
31 NRO, MC 150/52.
32 NRO MC 150/72.
33 NRO, MC681/1 802x7, Diary of John Leeds.
34 *Norfolk Chronicle*, 21 July 1857.
35 Quoted in Lee 2006, 95.
36 W.H. Marcon, *Reminiscences of a Norfolk Parson*, 1927, 20.
37 Haig 1984, 123.
38 NRO, D 314/51.
39 W.H. Henslowe, *The Accepted Rejection*, 1876, 9.
40 NRO, DN/CON 133 and 136.
41 J. Barney, 'Scandal at Bracon Ash', *The Annual* **24**, 2015, 3–8.

42 Quoted in J. Obelkevich, *Religion and Rural Society*, 1976, 126, from LAO, Misc. Dep. 165/4/1.

43 R. Hart, *The Antiquities of Norfolk*, Norwich, 1844.

44 Lee 2006, 42.

45 B. Cozens-Hardy, 'The Early Days of the Society', *Norfolk Archaeology* **29**, 1946, 1–7.

46 C.R. Manning, 'Grimes Graves, Weeting', *Norfolk Archaeology* **7**, 1872, 168–77.

47 J.H. Bloom, *Castle Acre Priory*, 1843.

48 E. Farrer, *List of Norfolk Monumental Brasses*, 1890.

49 Quoted in J.R.H. Weaver (rev. by M.C. Curthoys), 'Jessopp, Augustus, 1823–1914', *Oxford Dictionary of National Biography*, vol. 30, 2004, 95.

50 A. Jessopp, *Before the Great Pillage*, 1901, preface, vii.

51 *The Times*, 14 February 1914, 9.

52 A. Jessopp, 'On Married Clergy in the Thirteenth Century', *Norfolk Archaeology* **9**, 1884, 187 200.

53 A. Jessopp, 'Gilbert Haultoft's Will', 'Bowthore Hall' and 'Notes on the History of Breccles Hall', *Norfolk Archaeology* **8**, 1879, 171–82, 273–81, 303–18.

54 N. Hartley, *Augustus Jessopp, Norfolk's Antiquary*, 2017, 245.

55 Most recently republished in *The Phantom Coach and Other Ghost Stories of an Antiquarian*, ed. J.A. Salmonson, 1998.

56 M.R. James, *Eton and Kings*, 1926.

57 G.H. Dashwood, W.E.G.L. Bulwer, G.A. Carthew, W. Grigson and A. Jessopp, *The Visitation of Norfolk in the Year 1563* (2 vols), Norfolk and Norwich Archaeological Society, 1878.

58 William Hart-Raven, *Guide to the Roman Saxon Shore Fort of Burgh Castle*, n.d.

59 W. Greenwell, 'On the Opening of Grimes Graves', *Journal of the Ethnological Society* **n.s. 2**, 1870, 419–39.

60 G.A. Carthew, *The Hundred of Launditch and the Deanery of Brisley*, vol. 2, 1877, 517.

61 *East Anglian* **6, 7, 9**, 1895–1902.

62 J.C. Loudon, in *Magazine of Natural History*, 1822, quoted in D.E. Allen, *The Naturalist in Britain*, 1976, 22.

63 Lee 2006, 116.

64 N. Moore (rev. by H.C.G. Matthew), 'Elwin, Whitwell, 1816–1900', *Oxford Dictionary of National Biography*, vol. 18, 2004, 373–4.

65 Dymond ed. 2007, 2–3.

66 O. Chadwick, *The Victorian Church*, vol. 1, 1966, 127.

Four

Church Life

The holding of a rural parish presented many opportunities and challenges for the new recruit. In the early part of Victoria's reign most were young men straight from Dublin, Oxford or Cambridge universities with very little training for the post. Many would be the best-educated inhabitants of the parish, which may have left them feeling rather isolated, and this lack of intellectual stimulation must have been frustrating. The Revd Walter Marcon followed his father as vicar of Edgefield in 1880. 'I found life very slow and lonely.' He missed the give and take of ordinary conversation: no one initiated an idea, instead 'everyone waited for me to speak and then replied in monosyllables'. 'A country parson must be able to read silence.'[1] When Richard Cobbold moved from the urban life of Ipswich to the rural isolation of Wortham, a parish on the Norfolk–Suffolk border, he regretted the 'solitary confinement' of the rural clergy, who 'alone are compelled to spend three-quarters of the year in one parish'.[2] When the Revd Francis Massingberd, a graduate of Magdalen College, Oxford, moved to the Lincolnshire parish of South Ormsby shortly before 1838, he had hoped to continue an academic life, but found regular study difficult in the isolation of South Lindsey: 'great learning is now hopeless for me'.[3] John Rashdall moved to a neighbouring parish from Trinity College, Cambridge, followed by Cheltenham, where he had a wide circle of Evangelical friends, to 'the lonely usefulness of a country curate's life'.[4] Armstrong sometimes records the 'monotony of the work', and looked forward to his six weeks' holiday a year when he visited friends, family in London, the seaside with his family and made longer trips, often abroad, with his father. Nor was there much sense of corporate identity among the rural clergy as a whole, although this was to change over the period, especially as the railway made it easier to travel to meetings in their cathedral city and Bishop Pelham instituted regular gatherings of his clergy at his palace in Norwich.

A report to the Church Congress of 1893 stated that 'The great disease which afflicts the country clergy is want of work.'[5] Books of advice aimed at young clergymen stressed the dangers of 'becoming enamoured of a peaceable and retired life and of literary tastes'. These could include 'the library, the drawing room, the garden even the ballroom, card table and hunting field'.[6] This was certainly not true of Armstrong, who, on his arrival in Dereham, wasted no time in putting together his plans for the parish. 'Tomorrow we open our campaign' (undated, 1850, vol. 1). The three main duties of a clergyman were towards the church, the school and the poor, and along with his curate, Mr Gilbert, he set about revising the church services. He was determined to introduce a second, and later a third, Sunday service in Dereham, with one every Sunday in the much smaller sister-parish of Hoe. There should be a monthly Communion. As well as this there should be a mid-week service and saints' days were to be recognised. Singing was to be introduced and worship should be conducted by a surpliced clergyman. In his attempts to introduce these high church reforms, Armstrong was very much following a trend being established by the many new, young, high church parsons. While one service on a Sunday and a Communion only four times a year at the church festivals was regarded as adequate by most Georgian clergy, by the 1860s two to three services on a Sunday, including a monthly Communion, with weekday services as well, were usual and often required by the reforming bishops such as Wilberforce in Oxford.[7] Holy Week was particularly important, with the Good Friday service being well attended in Dereham: 'some masters pay their men all the same on condition that they go to church – hence a lot of rough fellows come tramping in late looking scared and bewildered' (18/4/62). Armstrong noted in 1853 that 639 churches in England had a daily service, while only 11 in Norfolk did (3/4/53).

It was through the church service that parishioners were likely to become acquainted with their parish priest for the first time. Although limited by the words of the Prayer Book, the style of service could vary considerably from parish to parish and also over the years. The *Book of Common Prayer* was regarded as the cornerstone of worship, but resulted in very long services, two hours in the morning and ninety minutes in the afternoon. Not surprisingly, it was the shorter afternoon service that was more popular. At the flourishing small north Norfolk

port of Blakeney there would be 200 at the morning service, but typically 500 in the afternoon in the 1830s.[8] Changes made by the Act of
Uniformity Amendment Act of 1872 allowed clergy to select the parts
of the service to be used. This meant the length of the morning service
could be limited to under an hour.

An almost universal change of the Victorian period was the replacing of
the singing gallery with an organ, often enclosed in an ornate gothic case,
to accompany a choir singing from stalls in the chancel. This elite project
was usually almost entirely financed by the parson and his patron, and the
organ itself would often be played by the parson's wife, or sometimes by
the schoolteacher. The end of the singing gallery meant that 'The Anglican
church rid itself of the embarrassment of being patron of a lower-class
form of musical expression.'[9] At Briston there is a remarkable survival
from this earlier era where an iron cello made by the local blacksmith is
displayed at the back of the church. A question in the 1838 archdeacon's
visitation asked whether there was singing in the church. Many replied
that there was. At Bale the Sunday School children sang two hymns, and
similarly at Bacton, 'the school children sing', while at Brinton, 'there was
no singing'.[10] George Crabbe, rector of Merton, recorded in 1870 that
congregational singing began there in August of that year. 'Lady Walsingham played the harmonium in her pew the first two Sundays, after
which Miss Woods played in the chancel.'[11] The widespread adoption of
Hymns Ancient and Modern after its publication in 1861 increased the
importance of congregational singing, even if it led to the standardisa-
tion of hymns rather than the perpetuation of local versions. In Dereham
it was introduced by Armstrong in 1863 and replaced a selection of
hymns published by Armstrong himself and printed locally as recently
as 1856. Previously it had been Wollaston's collection of metrical psalms
printed by H. Barker of Dereham in 1825 that had been used. Services in
Hoe were said to be 'thronged' after singing was introduced and people
came from neighbouring Swanton Morley and Gressenhall to hear the
choir and take part (8/9/57). In June 1876 a new organ was installed in
Dereham and choir stalls introduced. Armstrong regarded this as the
'culminating improvement of his vicarate'. 'What makes the satisfaction
almost a triumph is to see these people <u>enjoying</u> the service' (17/9/76). An
important change took place in Dereham at Christmas 1880, when carols
were sung in the church for the first time (25/12/80).

Answers for the archdeacon's visitation in 1845 show change in progress. While two services on a Sunday were normal across Norfolk, Communion was still only celebrated four times a year and attended only by the elite. Gradually the singing of hymns as part of the service increased. At Brisley the singing was said to be 'of a rustic kind, though not offensive'. At Scarning, 'we had singers about two years since, but they quarrelled and separated themselves'. At Carlton Rode, 'the children sing accompanied by a barrel organ'.[12]

As more high church ideas filtered down to rural parishes, more formal ritual came into use. Surpliced choirs became more usual, and in 1865 Armstrong introduced the wearing of them at all services in Dereham. On his arrival, Armstrong introduced a monthly Communion and numbers of communicants changed little over the years, averaging about 150, with Easter Communion attracting 200. Finally, in 1865 Armstrong felt in a strong enough position to introduce a weekly Communion.

In 1857 Armstrong tried to introduce a third (evening) service, but there were objections as 'servants should not be out at night' and the idea was dropped for the time being (23/8/57). Notwithstanding the complaints, the experiment was tried during the summer of 1858, but was only possible during the summer months because of the lack of lighting. An offer of candles was refused, because Armstrong thought it would distract attention from the need for gas. At the end of the year Mr Harvey, a retired Dereham builder who had originally left money in his will for the paving of the town, offered, now that the town was paved, to change his will to provide gas lighting for the church. Armstrong queried why it was necessary to wait for his death to receive the bequest and in January 1859 took him to Swaffham to see the lights there, after which Mr Harvey agreed to pay for the lighting immediately. On the second of March the lighting was finished and on the following Sunday the evening service was resumed (6/3/59). Unlike other services, all the seats at the evening service were to be free, rather than some being allocated through pew rents to particular individuals, a system which was usual in churches at the time but to which Armstrong firmly objected. In 1854 Armstrong's father had paid 'to engage the best sittings we can obtain' at Trinity Church (London). 'Finding we were unlikely to improve our position, engaged and paid £2.10. od for two sittings in Pew 63 for the present year.'[13]

The new sung services and hymns were led not by a group of rustics but by a disciplined choir of men and boys. All the Dereham choir received Christmas boxes for their efforts and the boys were taken for an annual treat by the vicar. In 1855, this consisted of a day's outing by train to Lowestoft. Only three of the boys had ever seen the sea and so the day offered a whole range of new experiences and excitements, vividly described by Armstrong in his diary. In later years the outing was usually to Norwich, including a visit to the cathedral and a river trip to Whitlingham. Some of the boys had never been on a boat. In July 1858 a different trip was planned. For several months a 'Monster Fete' to be held on the cricket ground in Norwich had been advertised, where there would be performers, bands, a tournament, hawking, archery, a roasted ox, fireworks and much more. The excitement in Norwich was such that all the shops were closed and the streets full of those going to the ground where the advertised festivities were to take place. In fact it was a 'monster humbug and a great disappointment. The knight had no-one to fight with, and the hawks flew away.' Only the fireworks were worth seeing and the disgruntled crowds, many of whom had come from London and Cambridge, made their way to the station. 'Our train, the longest I had ever seen, arrived at Dereham at one o'clock, with the junior members of the choir fast asleep and all thoroughly tired out' (6/7/58).

Occasionally some discipline was required, as in the case of the choirboy who was suspended for a month for lying and fraud. To this punishment, the boy's father had added his own: 'to stand in the middle of the room with a Bible in each hand raised above his head for half an hour!'. The father was persuaded to change this ordeal to reading the Bible instead (28/1/56). In November 1856 Armstrong found it necessary to reprove the choir master for taking some of the boys into a public house (22/11/56).

Armstrong's curates

Armstrong's first curate was Mr Gilbert, and with his help two Sunday services and a monthly Communion were soon established after his arrival in Dereham, a pattern maintained under later curates, many of whom did not stay long. Mr Clarke, who replaced Gilbert in 1853, did not last and left under a cloud because of his alleged drunkenness. 'What a trouble curates are!' (7/2/55). He was followed by Frederick William Kingsford, who was far more satisfactory and stayed until 1857. However, even he caused some unease. In April 1856 he announced his engagement to Miss Long of Dillington Hall. Although the family was very 'respectable', Armstrong felt he could have done better 'as regards wealth and position', but 'a curate engaged is better than a flirting curate'. Sadly, the next day 'the fair Emily retracted her acceptance', which left Kingsford forlorn for several days (5/4/56). However, Emily changed her mind again, which meant that Kingsford was looking for a post which would allow him to support a wife. The offer of a position in India allowed the pair to marry and the wedding took place in Dereham church.

> The affair went off as such things do: smiles, flowers, speeches, eatables, tears and an old shoe thrown after the coach as the 'happy pair' whisk away on the road of life. (7/10/56)

Armstrong was responsible for both Hoe and Dereham churches and he and his curate shared duties at Hoe. From the end of 1855 Armstrong's father agreed to pay £40 a year towards the cost of a curate responsible for Hoe alone to ease the burden on his son, and Mr Valpy took on the role. Curates generally stayed about three years. Kingsford and Armstrong seem to have worked well together and Armstrong thought a replacement would be difficult to find. Kingsford was followed in 1857 by George Dove, with whom Armstrong formed a good team, but who left with his new wife for Adelaide in 1860. He was followed by Walter William Skeat. He was well-off and clever and planned to marry and settle locally, but 'he lacked zeal'; so was 'not perfect, but curates very scarce' (22/10/60). When he left at the end of 1862 he was described as 'too tame a preacher' (2/11/62). His problems preaching may have been the result of a throat illness which curtailed his clerical career. After a short period in Godalming, he returned to Cambridge in 1864 and there became an eminent scholar of medieval English literature, his publications including definitive editions of *Piers Ploughman* and the works of Geoffrey Chaucer.[14] There followed several months without a curate, when Armstrong found the work of visiting sometimes as many as six sick people a day as well as the daily services and three with a sermon on Sunday very wearying. He frequently found neighbouring clergy to take one of the Sunday services. Finally, he found a new curate in Mr Swann. Armstrong's main observation was that he was Irish and thus likely to be vain and easily take offence (24/3/63). The next curate recorded by Armstrong was George William Minns, who 'promises well' (4/11/66). His interest in medieval wall paintings and rood screens would have found favour with Armstrong. Then Mr Winslow arrived in September 1868 but left 'much regretted' in August the following year (5/8/69), to be replaced in October by Mr Sandon. In October 1872, Revd William Wollaston died, thus ending an outdated system of sine-cures. Although Wollaston was not to be buried in Dereham, where he had not lived for thirty years, Armstrong felt it necessary to preach a sermon in his honour. This was difficult, as he had not been popular in the town. However, he had been a generous benefactor, paying for all the work in the chancel as well as investing money for the benefit of the school, providing annually for the purchase of coals and giving £100 towards the hospital. The rectorial tithes which he had received now reverted to the Ecclesiastical Commission and Armstrong was anxious that some, if not all of it, should be returned to the parish. Eventually it was agreed that the tithes could be used to appoint a second curate, something for which Armstrong was grateful, as the town's population continued to grow, creating more work for him. The stipend offered for the second curate (£126 a year) was not enough to attract a candidate, so Armstrong asked the Ecclesiastical Commission for more. Finally the post was filled in October 1873 and Armstrong hoped that with more support he would be able to do less preaching.

Later in the year a new curate, Mr Norwood, arrived, only to resign in April the following year because he did not want to work with a second curate. 'He had no zeal and was unpopular' (15/4/73). He was followed by Mr Watts, who had been trained at Samuel Wilberforce's Cuddesdon Theological College, one of the first of its kind. 'He will be a valuable curate' (15/6/73). The theological colleges were becoming an important source of non-graduate clergy, and although these men usually preferred urban parishes, Armstrong noted at a service for the re-opening of neighbouring Mileham church, 'some young curates unknown to me who wore novel hoods of yellow, plum colour and so forth', who would have come from the colleges rather than the universities (21/2/82).

In the summer of 1873 several of his previous curates came to stay at the vicarage, and he took the opportunity of commenting on their qualities in his diary, 'Very few seem to have realised what the work of ministry is.' Gibson and Dove had been the best and 'Watts bids fair' (12/8/73). He always complained that curates were difficult to find, but the problem could sometimes be the other way around. Bennett, in compiling his biographies of Lincolnshire clergy, found several examples of men who remained curates for over twenty years before finding a parish.[15] However, some of these men may not have been particularly able. Armstrong had dismissed Johnson after his twenty-seven years at Crowle because of his inability to take a service or preach (p.) Perhaps Armstrong's difficulties were as much to do with his uncompromising high church views as with the lack of candidates.

The sermon

An important part of the church service was the sermon. It was often on the quality of his sermon that the reputation of the parson rested and a good preacher might well attract worshippers from outside the parish. Sir John Boileau resented the fact that outsiders came to hear the Revd William Andrew preach at Ketteringham, while John Leeds travelled the few miles from Billingford to Swanton Morley to hear Mr Tacey.[16]

Handbooks for young clergymen devoted large sections to preaching and included lengthy programmes of reading. Public speaking of the type required when addressing a congregation including illiterate labourers as well as professional men was something entirely new to them. Their only experience would have been the learned disputations prepared at university. The role and type of sermon was changing during Victoria's reign. The highly academic and lengthy sermon, often lasting over an hour, was being replaced by a more colloquial, plain style, which was more accessible to a mixed audience, though the language remained dignified. While the earlier handbooks had condemned extempore sermons, they became more acceptable later in the century. In his handbook *Parochial Work* (1850), Munro described the 'unreality of the written sermon'. [17]

Preparing a sermon could take much of the parson's time, and preaching could be the single most important event in the parson's week. John Gott, dean of Worcester, suggested that five or six hours were needed to compose a sermon, although after a little experience, four or five might be sufficient.[18] Its delivery could range from forty-five minutes to over an hour. By the 1860s Armstrong was frequently preaching two sermons on a Sunday and rarely preached the same one twice. Holding a congregation's attention could be a challenge. His elevated position in the pulpit meant that the parson could see if there were sleepers in the pews below and knowing that they were being watched might have helped keep the congregation looking attentive. In a period before modern media, it was most likely in church or chapel that people first encountered public speaking. Sermons could help explain the stories in the Bible, as well as give a particular message. Politics was to be avoided. The clergy would encourage paternalism in the rich and acceptance and resignation in the poor. It was the duty of the rich to be charitable to the poor, and to give generously towards the restoration of the church and the building of schools.

The Preachers' Books for Dereham list the names of visiting clergy and the subjects of their sermons.[19] They show a great variety of titles for sermons, some of which were based on the Bible readings for the day, others on matters of doctrine and Christian behaviour. During 1860 fourteen neighbouring clergy came to preach, some more than once. Not surprisingly, considering Armstrong's own leanings, they were mostly high church (1/12/60). Mr Bloom of Castle Acre (the author of the first guide book to the ruins of Castle Acre Priory) was considered 'certainly the best preacher here abouts' (12/7/60). When Armstrong's friend William Duncombe came to stay he would take his turn in the pulpit. Visiting clergy from further afield also came to preach, often on behalf of foreign missions, or on their work in the slums of London. On 20 May 1858, the Bishop of Cape Town preached on behalf of the African mission. All these men, entertained at the vicarage, provided variety in the style and types of sermons preached.

A big event was when the Bishop of Oxford, Samuel Wilberforce, preached in Norwich on behalf of the SPG. He was known as one of the best public speakers of his day. A contingent went from Dereham, and the bishop 'electrified the whole audience' (14/6/58). Armstrong, a strong supporter of the SPG who frequently preached in other churches on its behalf, gave the toast after the following lunch.

Armstrong took great pains in the preparation of sermons. Rather than writing them week by week, he often composed them well in advance. When he was away he would spend time at his desk writing in the morning. At the end of December 1854 he was busy writing a sermon, 'my stock being preached out', and the following February was hoping to find time to write some fresh ones (21/2/55). Sometimes he would reuse sermons, but 'how much easier to preach new sermons than old' (19/8/55). In Lent 1852, he preached his first extempore sermon. It lasted fifty-five minutes and 'I experienced no hesitation'. This was not an unusual length. At a Lent service in 1854 he preached for an hour and he recorded in his diary the praise of an 'aged man' who claimed he was 'the plainest spoken church parson that he had ever heard' (28/3/55). Armstrong emphasised in his diary the importance for sermons to be 'plain' (15/7/56). It was not just the words used, but the method of presentation that made for a good sermon. Armstrong advocated 'a flexibility of voice, judicious emphasis, the use of the eye and sometimes the hand – how very rare it is though to find a preacher of this stamp' (6/5/55). The last months of 1855 found him editing his sermons. He hoped they might be of use to his son, who at the age of only five was showing an inclination towards entering the church! Two of Armstrong's sermons were published, one on the value of daily public worship in 1853 and one to the Rifle Volunteers in 1861 and he was happy to lend his sermons to others. In March 1855 he had a request from 'his first love', now married to a Devon parson, the Revd Robert James, for the loan of two dozen. In April 1861 he 'sent off a large packet of sermons to William Duncombe and Dean Bull (in Ireland); 'they do more good being preached than lying idle in my box' (26/4/61). With the arrival of the second curate Armstrong felt that after thirty years of preaching he might be able to leave some sermons to his curates. He was tired of his sermons, although his congregation assured him they were not (9/10/73).

The sermon was particularly prominent where the parson was of a low church persuasion. Andrew at Ketteringham could preach for an hour and was quite happy to personalize his criticisms of members of the congregation from the pulpit, including even his patron sitting immediately below him. He did not restrict his preaching activities to within the walls of the church, but on one occasion spoke to a wagon-load of thirteen people and on another preached at the roadside on his way home.[20]

As well as the two or three Sunday services at Dereham and one at Hoe, sometimes there was a 'mission service' at Etling Green in the school. Here the congregation was more 'rustic' and Armstrong noted that the old-fashioned practice of men sitting on one side and women on the other was usual (11/2/64). In Lent 1852 there were 'Lectures' at Etling Green on Tuesdays and in the church on Thursdays. In 1856 a daily service was held during Holy Week. The experiment was repeated in 1857, and then became a permanent arrangement. As the population of Dereham grew (it had risen by 800 in ten years to 5,120 by 1871) and was spreading out along the road to Toftwood, a second 'mission' was set up there with regular services from 1872.

National controversies

Arguments between the high and low factions within the church reached a fever pitch in the 1850s and reached the generally low church county of Norfolk. The Revd John Spurgin, vicar of Hockham, wrote thirty-one 'anti-tractarian tracts', the titles of three of which were 'Confession', 'Priestly Absolution' and 'Intoning', while in December of 1851 the Norwich Operatives Protestant Association held a lecture at the Assembly Rooms with the title 'The Corruption of Romanism'.[21] In the same year George Denison, Archdeacon of Taunton and the model for Archdeacon Grantly in Trollope's *Barchester Chronicles*, insisted that ordinands accepted his views on the sacrament of Holy Communion, which, it was claimed, were contrary to those put forward in the Thirty-Nine Articles of the Church of England. He then preached in Wells to support his views and years of acrimony followed, the case going from one ecclesiastical court to the next until it reached the Queen's Bench, by which time too long had elapsed since the original sermon (1853) and the appeal to the court (1856) for the case to be heard. Armstrong followed all this in his diary.

However, it was arguments over ritual rather than theology which were likely to affect the average churchgoer and which were more immediate to him or her than academic disputes. The balance between preaching and the sacraments (the altar and the pulpit) was more relevant at the local level. The Reformation had pushed the focus to the pulpit, and this trend had continued through the eighteenth century. The Tractarians, however, redirected attention to the altar and placed it in a restored chancel with a cross and lighted candles upon it. As the chancel became more ornate, they believed the altar itself should also be decorated, rather than simply being covered by the 'fair linen cloth' laid down in the 1662 *Book of Common Prayer*. Churches such as St Paul's in Knightsbridge and St Barnabas's in Pimlico, both places regularly visited and admired by Armstrong when he was in London, had installed chancel screens, sanctuary rails, lighted candles and priestly vestments, while the service itself was mostly sung. This, its detractors argued, went beyond what was laid down by Parliament in 1662 and several lawsuits ensued. At the same time the Roman Catholic Church was establishing its own Archbishopric of Westminster and a national pattern of dioceses. Anti-Catholic feeling reached a level which only served to emphasise the divisions between high and low within the Anglican church. In December 1850, only a couple of months after Armstrong had been installed at Dereham, Lord Townshend proposed at a crowded meeting in the Shire Hall in Norwich a motion disapproving of those who swerved from 'the simple modes of worship in general use amongst us'. It was carried unanimously.[22] Armstrong always noticed with distaste those of his fellow clergymen, such as Mr Tacey, 'the ultra-Evangelical Rector of Swanton Morley', who did not follow the more formal services or treat the altar with due reverence. On a visit to Swanton Morley church, he was horrified to find a baited rat trap on the altar into which a sparrow had fallen. 'Took the liberty of displacing so painful an object from the altar, if so wretched a thing can be so described' (25/10/61).

Not all his parishioners approved of the changes he was making; there was always 'a little clique of dissatisfied ones who are always for stirring up the waters of strife' (7/10/55). Later he commentated that country towns were 'proverbial for narrow-mindedness, jealousy, pride and gossip (7/5/56). In January 1853 Henry Cooper resigned as churchwarden, being one of the small group of malcontents' (29/1/53). Armstrong noted in detail the results of the case of *Liddell* v. *West-*

erton, settled in December 1855.The legal arguments concerned what the rubric in the *Book of Common Prayer* meant exactly. The judgment took three hours to deliver. Altars were to be simple, jewelled crosses of metal or wood should not stand on it and embroidered altar frontals were not permitted. However, candles and rood screens, so long as they did not have a large cross at the centre, were lawful. 'The Infidel, the Dissenter and the Papist will no doubt make fine fun of all this' (7/12/55). Further cases rumbled on through the 1850s with the question being finally settled in 1857 in a judgment in the *Brodrick* v. *Freemantle* case in favour of the high church practice and more concessions were made to vary the requirements of the 1662 Prayer Book.[23] Opposition to the increasing use of ritual continued, with further cases going through the courts. This led in 1859 to the founding of the English Church Union (ECU) to oppose civil courts deciding what forms of worship were acceptable, as well as to defend the church's influence on education. The Norfolk branch was formed in 1862, with Armstrong as its vice-chairman. In 1865 Armstrong was voted chairman and the Union petitioned the cathedral, asking for a weekly Communion service. Armstrong records that the cathedral chapter was not happy but 'notice was taken' (17/6/65). In June 1866 a west Norfolk Branch of the ECU was established with Armstrong as vice-president, and in 1868 a further branch 'for this neighbourhood' (8/2/68). However, because of the far-flung nature of the small, isolated parishes in the local branch and the difficulty of attending meetings, Armstrong reluctantly closed it in July 1872. Similar was the Church Defence Association, whose main aim was to ensure its views were heard by Parliament when addressing legislation affecting the church, and by 1876 Armstrong was on its committee.

Increasingly, when commenting in his diary on services in other churches, it was always the use of candles, surplices and chanting that Armstrong noted. Whether or not there were candles and whether or not they were lit during services were all-important to the different factions. The Prime Minister, Lord Palmerston, was accused of choosing low church bishops and Bishop Hinds of Norwich (1849–57) was of a low church persuasion. Armstrong felt that the cathedral services lacked ritual and his diary entries give details of the style of service in neighbouring churches, condemning those where the service was not sung and the parson did not wear a surplice. The revived ritual and sense of mystery lifted the role of parson to a higher level. His priestly duties were emphasised. He now faced east during the Communion service, away from the people and towards God as represented in the altar, rather than west towards the people, and this in itself was cause for legal intervention. Armstrong admired churches such as St Alban's in Holborn and St Mary's, Munster Square in London and the parish church in Brighton where the Communion service was called 'Mass', with their chanting, wearing of vestments, lighted candles on the altar and highly decorated chancels. In some churches incense was burnt, although this was considered by many a step too far. 'How things have changed: twenty years ago surplices were thought too Roman Catholic' (22/1/65).

Feelings continued to run so high that more legal cases were brought against the high church party. Armstrong records the judgment of Sir Robert Phillimore over ritual at St Alban's. Vestments, lighted candles during Holy Communion and 'excessive kneeling' were all lawful, but incense, except before and after the service, was not (3/4/68). Cases continued to be brought, with previous judgments being overturned. Armstrong's support was always for the 'ritualists', whose only object was 'to make our services as glorious and beautiful as any in the world – but public feeling is too strong for the attempt to succeed' (5/1/69). However, he did confide to his diary that some of the 'high ritualists' had gone beyond Rome (23/5/70). Matters came to a head after the Purchas ruling of 1871, when, amongst other things, vestments at the Eucharist were ruled illegal. Armstrong decided to abide by the law but signed a petition, along with 4,500 other clergy, against the Purchas judgment and was relieved when it was clear that the law could not be enforced and the case was to be reheard. Suggestions that there should be a Royal Commission on Ritual were not pursued. A further case against the Revd Mr Bennett of Frome in 1872 was reported by Armstrong 'as coming down in favour of the Catholic Party' (7/6/72).

Finally, as a member of the House of Lords, Archbishop Tait of Canterbury introduced a Private Member's Bill to limit what he perceived as the growing ritualism in the church that became law in 1874.[24] It allowed members of a parish to complain to their bishop if they felt that church law was being infringed by the introduction of

extra decoration, rites or ceremonies not specifically directed in the
Book of Common Prayer of 1662. If there could be no agreement, then
the matter could be sent for trial, and Armstrong watched with horror
as several clergymen were sent to prison. He agreed reluctantly to take
the Communion service standing to the north of the altar, rather than
facing east, as was the more high church practice.

Whilst Armstrong was following these debates and recording them
in detail in his diary, a far more fundamental argument was being played
out on the national stage that seems to have been of no interest to him.
Geologists had already begun to challenge the teachings at the beginning of the book of Genesis that the world was created in six days, and
replacing it with an evolutionary theory that proposed a process over
millions of years. The debate intensified with the publication in 1859 of
Charles Darwin's *The Origin of Species* with its theory of evolution based
on natural selection. Science and Christianity were now at loggerheads.
The idea that chance rather than divine providence was responsible for
the natural order resulted in many churchmen feeling that the very foundations of their beliefs were being undermined. Bishop Wilberforce's
review in *The Times* expressed this view in colourful language, calling
it 'the most pestilential book ever vomited from the jaws of hell'.[25] The
review of *The Origin* in the weekly Anglican newspaper the *Guardian*,
founded in 1846, was more measured, saying that Anglican assump-
tions had to be 'closed with and tested face to face in the light of fact
and history'.[26] The philosopher Thomas Huxley was a friend of Darwin's
with whom had had shared his ideas before the publication of his book,
and Huxley reviewed it favourably in the *Quarterly Review*. Huxley
and Wilberforce finally met to debate at the British Association for the
Advancement of Science annual meeting in the library of the Natural
History Museum in Oxford in the summer of 1860. Sadly, no transcript
of the debate survives and it only received short notices in the press,
but Wilberforce as the more eloquent speaker may well have swayed
the audience of 700 in his favour. It is strange that nothing of this is
mentioned by Armstrong in his diary and that it does not appear to have
excited interest among his clerical friends. He almost certainly read the
Quarterly Review, the *Guardian* and *The Times*, but his concerns and
interests were elsewhere. The greater controversy which followed the
publication of *Essays and Reviews* a year after Darwin's book marks the

beginning of questioning about the literal interpretation of Genesis's description of the creation of the world within six days, and is only mentioned in passing in the diary (see below).

A parson's daily work

There was more to a conscientious parson's work than taking church services and arguments about ritual. Armstrong described in his diary for 5 July 1853 a clergyman's typical working day.

> Examined the Dereham schools as usual ... afterwards drove to Etling Green school for the same purpose. Attended the monthly meeting of the District Visiting Society. Visited a few sick. Said the Even-song and took the chair at a meeting of the Institute. A good day.

He admitted that he was not an early riser, but then would work all day, at least until nine in the evening, but sometimes nearer midnight. 'I do not allow myself amusing books, newspapers or to light a pipe' (6/12/55).

Armstrong always stressed the threefold role of the clergyman – the church, the school and the cottage. House-to-house visiting was seen as second only in importance to preaching. The more diligent incumbents made regular visits to their parishioners and took particular note of the literacy of families and whether children were being sent to school. Pocket books were even produced for the parson to note down relevant details. *The Clergyman's Private Register* was printed from 1838 and allowed four pages for each family. The general character of the family, what books they read and what clubs they belonged to could all be noted. The *Speculum Parochiale*, printed from 1859, allowed for details of the sanitation around the cottage to be included as well.[27] In the nearby parish of Bawdeswell, this duty was left to the curate, who visited the 144 households within the parish in 1842. He noted whether the parents and children could read and write, whether the children were likely to be confirmed, as well as including a description of each person. Widow Adcock was described as 'A proud charwoman, husband killed, eldest son in prison for stealing ducks, girl well-behaved, son giddy and ignorant', while a labouring couple were 'a comfortable pair, wife attended Lent prayer'. The husband, however, was 'rather blunt and opposed to church'. Very importantly the curate recorded the complex interrelationships between many families.[28] On the other hand, in some of the very small Norfolk parishes there would be little visiting to be done. The rector of Fishley, near Acle, held his living from the 1880s until 1904, during which time the population dropped to eighteen people, which included the rectory household.[29]

There was plenty of advice in the textbooks as to how clergy visiting should be conducted. The visitor should 'take no liberties'. He should not sit down until offered a chair and should always take his hat off when visiting a house. There should be no over-familiarity and he certainly should give no money. Conversation should not be 'vapid or gossipy, conventional or pointless'. On the other hand, he 'should not be for ever pressing religious expressions or passages from the Bible'. Instead he should show sympathy for earthly concerns and interest in the family and children, which would 'pave the way to deeper conversations'.[30]

Armstrong 'conducted a visitation' throughout the parish annually and because of the scattered nature of the hamlets around the town found a horse necessary to his work. In one day he visited Dillington, 2 miles from the vicarage, to baptise a child, Badley Moor, 2 miles in the other direction, to 'give Holy Communion to eight poor people' and then to Toftwood Common, a mile further on to visit a sick person (14/5/69). He was particularly concerned to visit the sick and, contrary to the advice given above, he often gave little doles to them. An old man of 91 in Hoe, 'one of the humblest and most pious of men', was given porter daily and supplied with tobacco (8/5/57). These personal observations and enquiries were an essential part of parish work and 'the most gratifying'. It meant that the vicar was known as a person and not someone remote, known only 'as living in extensive and well-wooded grounds and preaching on a Sunday' (22/11/57). He was probably more aware than many of the better-off townspeople of the conditions in which the poor lived. When it came to the distributing of bread, coal and meat tickets, he knew which were the families who needed them. The motives for these visits were not simply humanitarian. He hoped to persuade parents to have their children baptised and to send them to the church school, and for young people to be confirmed.

If the incumbent was a 'committee man' there were plenty of opportunities by the second half of the nineteenth century for him to meet up
with his fellow clergymen. Societies in which Armstrong was involved
included the Church Building Society, the National Society for Additional Curates, the Society for the Promotion of Christian Knowledge
(SPCK) and the Church of England Temperance Society, which had its
first local meeting in 1878 (22/3/78). The SPG, mainly concerned with
foreign mission, had been founded as early as 1701 but was increasingly active in the nineteenth century, meeting frequently in Norwich,
with a local branch in Dereham, with Armstrong and his wife regular
attenders. Bishops like Samuel Wilberforce in Oxford encouraged
meetings of their clergy and the idea was taken up by most reforming
bishops. The arrival of the railways made it much easier for rural clergy
to attend meetings, and from the 1850s diocesan synods were being rein-
troduced, firstly in Exeter in 1851 (undated, 1851). In 1852 Armstrong,
along with 100 other clergy, went to a 'convocation' in Norwich Cathedral (16/8/52) organised by Bishop Hinds.

The retirement of Bishop Hinds in 1857 left the way open for a more
outgoing man in Bishop Pelham. Descended from an eminent and aristocratic Whig family, he was a breath of fresh air after Hinds. He was
described by Armstrong as 'very tall and huge, no great scholar, but hard
working' (5/9/59). Armstrong attended his enthronement in June 1857
before joining his family in Yarmouth. Still of a low church persuasion,
he was more conciliatory than his predecessors and so more supportive
of men like Armstrong. In December 1860 Armstrong visited him to
discuss the appointment of his new curate. He was invited to lunch, at
which the bishop was 'gracious' and talked of visiting Dereham. He was
pleased with the visit and felt welcome, 'in spite of a difference of views'
(14/12/60). Following the example of Wilberforce, an innovation was
the calling of regular meetings of his clergy at the Bishop's Palace where
items of wider concern would be discussed. Even if 'nothing new was
elicited, it brought us together', thus helping to relieve the isolation felt
by rural clergy in small parishes (5/9/59).

In 1861 Armstrong went to Norwich for the inaugural meeting of
the Pastoral Work Association, whose was to give the clergy mutual
support, and Armstrong joined the committee (19/12/61). It provided
a forum for the clergy to discuss practical issues of their ministry and

Armstrong was always a regular attender. At its meeting in November 1864 there were two papers, one by the Revd Mr Govett on the 'Visitation of the Sick', while Armstrong spoke on the 'Visitation of the Whole'.[31]

As well as meetings in Norwich there were also opportunities for more local discussions. Following a visitation in Swaffham, the bishop initiated a debate on how to 'improve the devotional manner in church'. Armstrong's remedy was that all sittings should be free and pews should be of a bench rather than box design, there should be a daily service and churches should always be open. The universality of the church ('the Communion of Saints') should be preached from all pulpits (26/6/58). At a rural deanery chapter in Yaxham the subjects for consideration suggested by the bishop included a proposal that the clergyman's wife should 'speak to the females about unchastity, so prevalent in East Anglia'. Armstrong felt that this should not be left to others, 'difficult as this part of his [the priest's] work was'. Following a long discussion, Armstrong's views were defeated by one vote (15/3/59). There is no record of his wife, Nellie, having any such conversations with the young women of Dereham.

Sometimes it was matters of concern to the Anglican church nationally that were discussed. At a chapter meeting in 1861, time was spent considering the volume *Essays and Reviews*, published in March the previous year. The book had caused a furore within the church. It contained seven essays, each written by a different churchman. The book was significant in that it was written shortly after the publication of Darwin's *Origin of Species* (of which Armstrong makes no mention in his diaries). Benjamin Jowett, Regius Professor of Greek at Oxford, never referred to the theory of evolution directly in his essay, but support for it is implied when he wrote that the 'two witnesses to the Being of God were the order of nature in the world and the progress of the mind of man'. A rearguard action could not be fought against geologists, biologists and philosophers.[32] The two most controversial essays were those by Rowland Williams of St David's College, Lampeter, who denied the predictive character of the Old Testament prophesies, and Henry Wilson of St John's College, Oxford, who appeared to deny some of the assertions of the Thirty-Nine Articles, accepted by all clergymen at ordination. Other essays were condemned for describing the early part of the Book of Genesis as allegory rather than fact, as well as claiming that there were no texts in the New Testament that proved the divinity of Christ. Armstrong was shocked that men in high positions and also serving clergy like Dr Williams should promote such heretical views (19/2/61). There were demands nationally for the resignation of Williams and Wilson, and both were found guilty of heresy by the ecclesiastical courts, but finally in 1864 acquitted by the Judicial Committee of the Privy Council. A few days before the meeting attended by Armstrong, the Archbishop of Canterbury, Charles Longley, had made a general declaration on behalf of all his bishops implying that views in the book were contrary to the beliefs of the Church of England.

Although Armstrong disagreed with Bishop Pelham on many points, he appreciated his attempt to get to know his clergy. In February 1862 thirty-five of the diocesan clergy were invited by the bishop to dine and stay the night at the palace. The dinner was elegant and Armstrong thought it was a long time since such a group had sat down to hobnob together. 'The Bishop may be below par in doctrine and scholarship, but not in hospitality' (13/2/62). By 1862 there were also deanery synods and Armstrong went with his churchwardens to one in Barnham Broom to petition against Sir Samuel Morton Peto's bill seeking to allow dissenters to officiate at funerals in churchyards (13/6/62).

Not only did the bishop extend annual hospitality to his clergy, allowing them to get together socially, and support local and full diocesan meetings, but he also encouraged greater involvement of the laity. The idea of a diocesan synod was aired by the bishop in January 1869. Such synods were already being held in many other dioceses and the archbishop was known to be in favour, but, in Armstrong's rather biased view, were 'held up by the Puritan party who are antagonistic to any move to bring life into the church' (20/1/69). Finally, however, a diocesan conference was held at St Andrew's Hall in October 1870, attended by 900 laity and clergy. Subjects for discussion in the morning included the relationship of the laity to the church and in the afternoon, education. Laity as well as clergy were at the local deanery meeting at Yaxham in March 1871, where the burial and education bills were discussed.

In spite of the controversies within the church and the voices raised against Armstrong's changes, the congregations remained large at both morning and afternoon services. In a church with space for nearly 2,000 worshippers (including galleries to the west, north and south), there were usually a thousand at the afternoon service, with fewer in the morning. The afternoon service was more popular with the lower classes in the town, while the 'more intelligent parishioners' such as the squire, the lawyers, doctors and principal tradesmen, described by Armstrong as 'The old bald heads which give weight to every congregation', came in the morning (13/4/79). Numbers for Confirmation were usually about 300, but these services were not held every year. Even with such large numbers, newcomers were noticed and a subject of interest. The Revd Mr Mason, a 'low slow' clergyman, had moved to Dereham and in 1856 his married daughters came to stay. Unlike their father, they 'are the opposite of low slow' and attended church where they caused quite a stir. 'Their dress so stylish and their manner so devotional, as to create quite a sensation amongst our cold, plain undemonstrative people.' They were well travelled and 'even acknowledged that they sometimes smoked a cigar' (13/3/56).

He was annoyed that Mr Tacey of Swanton Morley had started a Bible Society meeting in the Corn Hall on Sunday evenings to coincide with his newly established third Sunday service and wrote to him to complain. However, he was able to report in his diary that it was 'chiefly attended by poor from distant parishes attracted by a brilliantly lighted room with a good fire' (10/2/58). By April the services were closed, ending on Good Friday with a tea (10/4/59). In a similar vein there was a protracted correspondence in the *Norfolk News* between Armstrong and the Revd William Haslam of Buckenham Ferry about the irregularity of preaching in another man's parish.[33] The *Norfolk News* reported on Haslam's special Lent meetings on Wednesday afternoons in 1867, held in St Nicholas Hall. His address 'was marked by the same simplicity and correctness as previous discourses'. 'Tea was plenteously supplied.'[34]

One group who would be unlikely to be accepted in church by the congregation were unmarried mothers. In November 1856 Armstrong persuaded two single mothers with five children between them to have them baptized. 'To avoid the embarrassment' for the mothers of coming to church, he baptised them in the rainwater tub outside their cottage (22/11/56).

Armstrong not only aimed to bring the church services into line with a more elaborate pattern of worship, but he was also anxious to make the church part of the lives of a wider range of worshippers. A meeting of the Diocesan Pastoral Work Association in November 1862 had debated how to attract young men between leaving school and marriage to the church but 'nothing new was elicited' (13/11/62). Armstrong acknowledged that young men were the most difficult to engage, and in 1866 he decided to found the Guild of St Nicholas for young men, aimed at religious instruction and church work. In February 1867 he sent invitations to the young shop assistants inviting them to join, 'This class being very hard to get at and a constant prey to dissenting proselyters' (23/2/67). His aim was to attract those working in shops, offices and banks. The first meeting was held in July, with twenty attending. Further meetings and services for the Guild are mentioned occasionally in the diary. The annual service just before Christmas in 1872 was a grand affair, with a procession headed by a splendid embroidered banner. The chancel was crowded with members and their friends (19/12/72). The Guild continued to 'show zeal, conducting mission services and raising money for the work of the church' (12/8/73) Its annual services became ever-more popular through the 1870s.

A second initiative was the creation of a 'Union of Church Helpers', the proposal for which was circulated in August 1871. Armstrong's annual report of 1872 listed nineteen different charitable institutions run by the church and active in the parish (27/2/72), and a dissenter who read the report commented that Armstrong 'did more good in the town than the dissenting ministers put together' (7/3/72). The aim of the Union would be to 'create a spirit of unity' amongst the sixty-seven people who currently helped as parish visitors and charity workers, encouraging them 'to think and act together for the common good' (28/8/71). It would meet four times a year, the first being in August, with fifty members. Associate members were also invited, and at the second meeting thirty 'Associates' from amongst the principal tradesmen were added to the membership (20/12/71). By September 1872 there were 100 members. At a meeting in September 1873 fifty members discussed the vexed question of free sittings. The compromise was that once the bell had tolled announcing the services, any unoccupied reserved seats would be regarded as free (17/9/73).

A later innovation was a Bible class for young men under the guidance of Armstrong's son, John, who became a curate in Dereham in 1880. He was a great help to his father during his later years and developed the Bible class into the Churchman's Society. In 1884 it had forty members. John also organised social evenings for them with music, short addresses and cricket in the summer. Although Armstrong accepted that such events were 'a necessary expedient to bring all classes together', he did not enjoy them and was happy to leave the arrangements to John (23/4/84).

Beyond the confines of the Anglican church with its arguments over ritual were the dissenters, or non-conformists, with their own chapels, and Dereham catered for a wide range of denominations. The Independents and Baptists were the oldest groups, dating back to the seventeenth century, with chapels built in Dereham in the early nineteenth century, while three branches of Methodists (Wesleyan, Primitive and Wesleyan Reform) all had a presence in the town. Armstrong's attitude to them all was one of condescending tolerance. He felt that a clergyman 'compromises his principles' by working with dissenters for religious purposes, 'but [there is[no reason why not on secular matters' (18/3/61). He wrote disparagingly of a 'clown in a troupe of players in Dereham who preached in one of the meeting houses' (28/2/58). He did recognise, however, that they knew how to attract people to their services. 'There are tea drinkings, speeches and revivals while we go on without any change' (11/3/60). In May 1861, the

> congregation was thinned by a camp meeting and love feast got up by the dissenters. At the conclusion of my service about thirty of them came into the church and seemed astonished at the beauty of the decorations ... they were a rough lot, full of argument and private judgement.... I loved their enthusiasm – some had travelled 25 miles. About ten came to the afternoon service, but two walked out when I ascended the pulpit. (5/5/61)

The Wesleyan chapel in Theatre Street was a small building and the Primitive chapel was not built until 1864, so for large 'revival' meetings the newly converted theatre, known as St Nicholas Hall, was hired. In 1861 a Methodist preached there on Sunday evenings 'but church attendance not reduced' (21/10/61), although the numbers of dissenters was increasing 'owing to the late revival and lectures in St Nicholas Hall' (8/12/61). In 1866 Armstrong objected to the bishop about an 'Irish Revival priest' who was lecturing in the Corn Hall on Wednesday evenings, but the bishop saw no need to take any action. There were always those who switched happily between the churches. One of Armstrong's congregation had ceased coming to church and joined the dissenters after a 'revival'. Two years later he returned and Armstrong questioned him before accepting him for Communion to see whether he was going to come regularly. In 1862 the Baptist minister went so far as to publish a pamphlet entitled 'Why I am a Dissenter', to which Armstrong's curate, Mr Skeat, wrote a reply, 'Why Should Anyone be a Dissenter' (8/10/62).

In June 1865, the Pastoral Work Association discussed what the attitude of the parish priest should be towards dissenters and Armstrong spoke, saying that it was right that they should work together on secular matters, such as running the savings bank or the Institute but that they 'should never fraternize on any religious subject'. 'The meeting seemed to agree, except for a very small number' (15/6/65). His own view was very clear – 'the Church of England was of divine origin while all the sects were of human origin' (3/4/68) – and he took some delight in the confusion into which the Baptists and Independents in Dereham were thrown in 1878. 'The Baptist minister, the Revd Mr Freeman, has married a wealthy woman, built himself a grand house and retired into private life.' Mr Tyas, the Independent pastor, had displeased his congregation by introducing Anglican prayers into his services. Later in the year, he joined the Church of England, with some encouragement from Armstrong, who suspected that the Baptist would soon follow suit (19/8/78). The next we hear of Mr Freeman, described as 'a clever man', is in 1885, when he was 'seized with paralysis' and Armstrong went to see him in his fine house with 'a smoking divan at the top of a campanile'(7/1/85). There is no indication that he had in fact defected to the Church of England.

In 1851, for the only time in the history of the decennial census, a record of the numbers attending churches of the various denominations on a chosen Sunday in March was included. The parish church in Dereham attracted much larger congregations than those in the neighbouring market towns, with 906 at the morning and 1,510 at the afternoon service. The dissenting denominations were all well represented, with Primitive and Wesleyan Methodists, Baptists and Independents all with congregations of over 100.[35] Numbers at the parish church in Swaffham, where the Revd Salisbury Everard was unpopular, were 583 in the morning and 779 in the afternoon. Unlike in Dereham, the Primitive and Wesleyan Methodists, Baptists and Bible Christians between them attracted as many worshippers as the Anglican church.[36] The same was true in the smaller towns of Fakenham and North Walsham.[37] Only in Dereham were there small groups of Latter Day Saints (Mormons), while no Roman Catholics are recorded. By 1853 Armstrong was visiting 'a poor papist family who have recently moved into the parish' (8/9/53).

In the winter of 1865/6 the *Norfolk News,* a newspaper described by Armstrong as 'very radical and dissenting' (12/2/66), sent reporters across the county to report on 'Sundays in the Country'. In fact they confined their visits to the market towns easily accessed by train. In North Walsham they found a rector more interested in the restoration of his church than the well-being of his parishioners. In Swaffham, Mr Everard was 'high church in principal and would be high in practice if his people would let him'. His service was 'proper' and 'becoming', having 'a cold beauty like the glitter of moonlight on a stagnant lake'. His sermon was limited to eighteen minutes but seemed to consist mainly of praising the church.[38] A third visit was to Dereham, where 'the high practice of the vicar was well known'. The service began with a procession headed by the choir and followed by Armstrong. In spite of his reputation, Armstrong was not robed and there was 'no incense or intoning'. However, the prayers were read very fast and the chants and hymns sung too fast as well. The sermon was addressed to the 'poorer class of parishioners of whom the congregation principally consisted'. It was on the subject of prayer, and his hearers were encouraged to think of death, judgment, heaven and hell before they said their prayers.[39] The paper reported that Armstrong was the moving force behind many of the local charities and that their success was due to his 'unfailing energy and perseverance'. He was also even-handed towards his own congregation and the dissenters when distributing help.[40] Clothing clubs specially providing for new-born babies were typical of many parishes. In Blakeney, a 'Clothing Society' in the 1830s was said to be very useful for the poor.[41] They were often, as in Dereham, the responsibility of the parson's wife.

A growing dissenting revivalist movement in the nineteenth century was that of the Primitive Methodists, often described as 'ranters' by their detractors. Beginning in the midland counties, by 1825 they had spread to Norfolk, with 'circuits' based in Fakenham and Norwich, and the following fifteen years saw a rapid expansion across the county.[42] By 1851 they had nearly as many chapels at all the other Wesleyan groups put together.[43] In 1851 they had a meeting house on Etling Green which attracted fifty-five people to its morning service and forty in the afternoon.[44] Their chapel in Dereham was described by the *Norfolk News* reporters of 1866 as 'well attended'. In 1851 there were three services on a Sunday, with 104 at the morning, 187 at the afternoon and 107 at the evening service.[45] Although there were congregations in many villages by this date, it was not until later in the century that many of these groups could afford to build permanent chapels. In 1881 Armstrong commented on the number of 'tiny meeting houses springing up in the smaller hamlets. The peasantry <u>do</u> love earnest preaching which indeed is their sole means of satisfaction' (17/6/81).

Armstrong commented that generally it was the morning services that were attended by the gentry and 'better class of people', while the poor came in the afternoon. He noticed when preaching in neighbouring North Elmham that although the congregation was large, it mainly consisted of the cottagers and aristocrats, with few of the middle class (19/1/68). This may well have been true in Dereham, too, with the more independent-minded tradesmen supporting the chapels.

The third role which was generally seen as within the duties of the parson was the promotion of the church school and, as we will see (Chapter 6), it was one that Armstrong took very seriously.

Notes

1 W.H. Marcon, *Reminiscences of a Norfolk Parson*, 1927, 16.
2 D. Dymond (ed.), *Parson and People in a Suffolk Village: Richard Cobbold's Wortham, 1824–77*, 2007, 4.
3 F. Knight, *The Nineteenth-Century Church and English Society*, 1995, 142.
4 Ibid.
5 *Church Congress Reports*, 1893, 219.

6   Quoted in J. Obelkevich, *Religion and Rural Society*, 1976, 125.

7   D. McClatchey, *Oxfordshire Clergy, 1777–1869*, 1960, 84.

8   NRO, DN VIS 64/4.

9   R. Lee, 'Paternalism, Distance and Dignity', *Norfolk Archaeology* **44**, 2002, 1–14, 10.

10 NRO, DN VIS 64/4.

11 NRO, PD 532/32.

12 NRO, DN VIS 73/13.

13 C. Armstrong (ed.), *Under the Parson's Nose*, 2012, 322, n. 3

14 K. Sisam and C. Brewer, 'Walter William Skeat', in *Oxford Dictionary of National Biography*, vol. 50, 2004, 817–18.

15 N. Bennett *Lincolnshire Parish Clergy c.1214–1968*, 2013, vol. 1, xxxvi.

16 NRO, MC681/1 802x7, Diary of John Leeds.

17 A. Russell, *The Clerical Profession*, 1980, 85–99.

18 P.C. Hammond, *The Parson and the Victorian Parish*, 1977, 116.

19 NRO, PD86/45

20 O. Chadwick, *Victorian Miniature*, 1960, 52–3.

21 *Norfolk News*, 22 November 1851.

22 Chadwick 1960, 12.

23 O. Chadwick, *The Victorian Church*, vol. 1, 1971, 495–7.

24 PP 37 and 38 Vict. C.85.

25 D. Bowen *The Idea of the Victorian Church*, 1968, 164, n. 17.

26 Ibid., 164.

27 Russell 1980, 117.

28 NRO, MF/RO 207/5.

29 Hammond 1977, 138, quoting F.R. Barry, *Period of My Life*, 1970, 159.

30 *Manual of Clerical Work by Various Authors*, 1888, 131–2.

31 *Norfolk Chronicle*, 12 November 1864.

32 Bowen 1968, 166, 169.

33 *Norfolk News*, 6 October 1866.

34 Ibid., 16 March 1867.

35 J. Ede and N. Virgo, *Religious Worship in Norfolk: The 1851 Census of Accommodation and Attendance at Worship*, Norfolk Record Society 62, 1998, 243–5.

36 Ibid., 339–41.

37 Ibid., 262–3, 69–70.

38 *Norfolk News*, 13 January 1866.

39 Ibid., 10 February 1866.

40 Ibid.

41 NRO, DN VIS 64/4.

42 N. Scotland, *Methodism and the Revolt of the Field: A Study of the Methodist Contribution to Agricultural Trade Unionism in East Anglia, 1872–96*, 1981, 24.

43 Ede and Virgo 1998, introduction.

44 Ibid., 243.

45 Ibid.

Five

The Building Legacy

Many Victorian clergy left a lasting built legacy in their parishes, changing the appearance and layout of their churches and building new rectories and schools. In this Armstrong was no exception. In his first couple of years in Dereham he visited the restored neighbouring churches in Yaxham, Billingford, Necton, Reymerstone and Cranworth. He was able to write, 'How wonderful is the move towards restoration. Not long hence the <u>un</u>restored church will be an exception', and to comment, 'Those not renovated just make me feel sad' (31/7/52).

The maintenance of their churches was a duty taken seriously by the majority of clergymen, but their perception of what this should involve changed over the period in question. As antiquarians acquired an increasing understanding of the development of medieval architecture, so a more sympathetic 'restoration' rather than 'alteration' dominated. To encourage true 'restoration', the Cambridge Camden Society (later the Ecclesiological Society) and the Oxford Society for Promoting the Study of Gothic Architecture were both founded in 1839. The mentor of the movement was Augustus Pugin, actively involved in ecclesiastical work in the 1840s. It was not so much the size of the church which was significant, rather its form, so that it suited the rituals to be performed within it. Importance was placed on the chancel, with an ornamental reredos behind the altar, a bell tower and, most significantly, stained glass. The promotion of restoration was articulated in Ruskin's *The Seven Lamps of Architecture,* written in 1849, in which he deplored the practice of gutting churches and renewing what could in fact have been repaired. It was the high church rectors in particular who were responsible for the Gothic revival and who wanted to restore church buildings, and also much of the ceremonial, to their pre-Reformation glory. Galleries, box pews and with them pew rents were seen as eighteenth-century additions to be removed. Emphasis on the pulpit, often a three-decker, with its clerk's reading desk, highlighting the role of the priest as preacher and teacher, was to be replaced by a focus on the altar and the priest as mediator between God and man.[1] Pulpits were moved to the side to allow a clear view of the altar. It could also be difficult to see the altar from galleries down the north and south side aisles (as at Dereham) – another reason to remove them. Edward Stanley, Bishop of Norwich from 1837 to 1849 and president of the Archaeological Institute until 1848, wrote that Protestants should no longer fear symbols of ritual such as statues and crucifixes as 'objects of superstitious worship' as in former times, because 'the present era is an enlightened one'.[2] Later bishops were not so sympathetic towards the changes of the ritualists. Bishop Pelham objected to the stained-glass windows proposed by William Maxey Allen, the high church rector of Shouldham, because they did not include texts, such as the beatitudes, as part of the design.[3]

Armstrong's restoration work in Dereham

On his arrival in Dereham, Armstrong was determined to give the church a high church appearance. Like many country churches of the time, the building itself was in poor repair. A drawing now hanging in the church shows the interior shortly before Armstrong's arrival. There were galleries around three sides, which along with box pews below (some of which had been removed by Armstrong's predecessor), provided 1,800 sittings, 500 of which were free (8/5/60). There was a rounded plaster ceiling which Armstrong was to take down and replace. Ritual played a minor role in church services in the Georgian period and so the chancel in many churches was often under-used or derelict. At Dereham Armstrong described it as little more than a lumber room with broken paving for storing discarded furniture. The picture hanging in the church shows the classical reredos under the east window which Armstrong so disliked, clear glass in the east window and no sign of an altar. One of Armstrong's first projects was to 'restore and beautify' the chancel, which involved inserting a Gothic stone reredos, installing stained glass in the east window, putting the altar at the east end and placing a cross behind it. His reredos is still in place, although the saints

13   The interior of St Nicholas's as it was when Armstrong arrived, with box pews and galleries around the west end and north and south sides and the 'Grecian cornice' on the east wall of the chancel to which Armstrong objected so strongly.

14   The restored piscina and reredos installed by Armstrong in 1851

on it were repainted in 1927. It was the rich stained glass that had impressed Armstrong so much on his continental tour, and installing it at Dereham was a top priority. His east window was replaced in 1901 but some of the glass from it is in the west window in the north aisle.[4] The upkeep of chancels was the responsibility of rectors and Mr Wollaston paid for the work. The first phase was completed in less than a year, and 'On Whitsun Eve I was permitted to complete the restoration of the Chancel at Dereham up to a point; a painted east window and handsome reredos of stone are being made at the expense of the sinecure rector' (undated, 1851, vol. 1). In 1853 he showed two eminent visitors around the church 'and they were pleased with the restoration' (12/4/53). By August 1854, he was able to write, 'How complete is the difference between the former and present appearance of the chancel of Dereham Church.... Now it is beautifully painted and restored and daily filled with a devout and attentive congregation. With candles lighted and the instrument playing, and the departing daylight still coming through the painted glass, the effect is really fine' (28/8/54). There was obviously still more to do, as in 1857 Armstrong recorded in his diary, 'Our chancel being under repair the Passion week services were held in the nave' (6/4/57). What Armstrong does not tell us is what he had removed. He may well have been right that the area was little used, but there was a fine reredos and Grecian cornice shown in the pre-restoration picture. It was probably the work of James Verdun, rector between 1677 and 1740,[5] but the cornice was removed by Armstrong in the final phase of 'restoration' in 1857. In January, 'After service I saw a builder relative to removing the ugly Grecian cornice which is the last disfigurement of our noble chancel' (7/1/57). Two of the heads on the piscina were restored, something to which the Dereham-based antiquarian George Carthew objected. Work was completed in April and the chancel reopened for services. To celebrate this, the choir wore surplices for the first time and the service was sung, having been rehearsed by Armstrong's wife. The plaster ceiling had been removed and a lofty barrel roof restored at Mr Wollaston's expense (9/1/57). The Early English style was adopted to replace the original fifteenth-century Perpendicular north and south chancel windows. They were then filled with stained glass by the popular craftsman William Wailes of Newcastle. 'The effect of the whole was admirable' (25/4/57). Later,

15 St Nicholas's from the east as it is now and much as it would have been in Armstrong's time.

in 1862, a new south door, again paid for by the sinecure rector, was cut into the chancel to replace a very plain one and soon became the main entrance to the church from the town. Armstrong gave a floriated cross, which was placed on the roof ridge (9/8/55). Much of the chancel remained unpainted until June 1862, when the sedilia and piscina were decorated. In 1864 much of the stonework in the chancel was painted in chequered blue, red and gold. 'Perhaps ours is now the most beautiful chancel I have ever seen' (11/9/64). In 1871 the final painting and gilding was completed and Armstrong was relieved that all his changes had been greeted by very little opposition. Although Armstrong often described his improvements as 'final', unspecified work continued until the end of the 1870s. Fashions have changed again and the wall painting has now disappeared, but the scale of Armstrong's work is still obvious: the high barrel ceiling, the steps up to the altar and the reredos under the large east window all made a fitting setting for his elaborate services.

Once the chancel was restored, a use needed to be found for it. In line with Catholic tradition the priest assisted by a lay choir sang much of the service, while those in the nave would be spiritually uplifted and led to God by events taking place in the chancel. To begin with, the daily service which Armstrong introduced was said in the chancel; later, when the third Sunday service was added in 1858, a choir of men and surpliced boys sang there. Subsequently Armstrong achieved his ambition of a fully surpliced choir in the chancel for all services.

To the north of the church is St Withburga's Well, so called because of the association of St Withburga with Dereham. When Armstrong arrived it was covered by what he described as a 'bath house' and a 'vile modern structure' which he was determined to take down and replace with 'a fountain and parterre'. He first proposed this in 1855, but was defeated. Two years later he was more successful. He immediately ordered its demolition and hoped to create a cascade and flower border. In May 1857 Armstrong was planning a garden with roses and creepers and later in the year railings were installed to allow a garden to be planted within (8/7/57). Armstrong and his gardener planted the area up in the spring of 1858 and in July it was 'doing well' (29/7/58). In 1860 its maintenance was taken over by Miss Steele, 'one of those delightful old maids you read about in novels' (5/6/60). The garden around the well survives very much as Armstrong intended.

16 St Withburga's Well, just west of the church, very much as restored by Armstrong in 1867.

The ownership and therefore the responsibility for the repair of the body of the church as distinct from the chancel was unclear and remained unresolved after the abolition of church rates in 1868. These rates for the upkeep of the building were levied on all rate payers whether Anglican or not. They could be imposed by churchwardens through a vestry meeting, but overturned by a parish meeting open to all parishioners, and so remained a source of local disputes until their abolition. In default of any clear guidance, however, it was generally accepted that the church was part of 'the parson's freehold' which he was granted on being inducted into his church. As part of the ceremony he was presented by the archdeacon with the keys of the church and directed to lock himself in and ring the bell. Surely, the argument went, this showed that the church was part of his freehold and he was responsible for it. 'If he does not take the whole burden of collecting the money [for repairs or restoration] and seeing the work through and making himself personally responsible for the cost, in nine cases out of ten it will not be done at all.'[6] After 1868, therefore, repairs were usually left to the parson or his patron: 'A local Philistine with a long purse and no more conscience or sentiment than a gorilla may do almost as he pleases.'[7]

Church restoration would therefore be financed in various ways. In some cases it was the local patron, while more often it was the result of voluntary subscription. The installation of gas lighting at Dereham was paid for by a local builder, as we saw in an earlier chapter, and brass standards were installed. On 1 March 1 1859, there was 'an experimental illumination of the church' and the following Sunday 1,200 people attended the evening service to see the 'grand effect', which resembled more 'a cathedral abroad than the ordinary appearance of an Anglican church'. Work in the chancel having been completed, the final phase of Victorian work at Dereham involved the nave. At a vestry meeting in April 1884 it was agreed to take down the plaster ceiling and remove the galleries (15/4/84). The nave roof was in a poor state and those accommodated in the galleries, which had been erected on the south side in 1775 and on the north in 1814, could easily find seats below now that the large box pews had been replaced by bench pews. The south gallery had always been known as the tradesmen's gallery because of the group of townspeople who had sat there.[8] Later in the month a Restoration Committee was set up to raise the £3,000 needed for the work. A subscription list was opened, headed by the churchwardens, who gave £200, followed by Colonel Bulwer, who gave £100. Armstrong himself gave £25.[9] In January the following year a faculty for the work was granted to include the replacement of the clerestory windows, new doors to the south porch and, most importantly, a heating system under a newly tiled floor. The galleries were removed and a new barrel roof inserted. The work was completed by the end of the year and formally revealed in December. The opening service was followed by a lunch at the King's Arms with speeches (9/12/85). The various fundraising activities undertaken included the Dereham Dramatic Society performing an evening of short plays in aid of the restoration fund and a grand two-day bazaar at Quebec Hall that was arranged later in the month. A 'living waxworks' was put on in the Corn Hall in December in which Armstrong's daughter-in-law Mary appeared as a milkmaid.[10] While being grateful for all these efforts to pay off the loan, Armstrong was uncomfortable about them: 'I cannot say I like these ways of "raising the wind"' (8/7/86).

The restoration movement across Norfolk

Elsewhere, the Revd Bartholomew Edward of Ashill, a man with 'ample private means', 'restored and reseated his church at his own expense',[11] and the Revd Whitwell Elwin paid for the rebuilding of Booton. The Revd Barnham Johnson paid for the rebuilding of the chancel at the tiny church in Welborne in 1875, including the screen by John Purley.[12] However, the major works at North Elmham in 1863, which involved refacing the whole of the church, except the tower, with best Brandon flint, as well as restoring the south aisle roof and rebuilding buttresses, was partly paid for from parish income and the rest advanced in the form of a loan from one of the churchwardens.[13] The Revd George Winter, rector of Bradenham, chose a different route. He 'produced and sold sketches of hunting scenes to an Oxford print seller and uses the money for church restoration' (30/4/53). In 1858 he told Armstrong that he had made £300 from his drawings (19/10/58).[14] Individuals too could make personal donations. Armstrong recorded how Mr Hales, a surgeon and businessman of Holt, set apart the money he made on Sundays to pay for a window in the parish church.

When Augustus Jessopp arrived in Scarning in 1870 the roof was in imminent danger of falling in. A new roof was put on and other essential repairs undertaken. 'The cost of this was partly defrayed by subscriptions and partly, I am sorry to say, by the sale of the lead from the old roof.'[15] A second round of repairs was needed in 1892 and to help pay for this he inserted a leaflet in the front of his latest volume of essays encouraging his readers – 'if they derived any pleasure, instruction or suggestions from my writings' – to contribute towards the restoration of the flint tower, walls and buttresses. Scarning was a parish with no resident squire to help finance the work and Jessopp's own income was not sufficient. 'I am not in a position to sacrifice three years' income of my benefice, and am sorry that I am not.' He sought donations of not less than half a crown (2s 6d/12½p) and expected the work to cost about £1,000, of which £500 was raised as a result of this appeal.[16] Some larger landowners not only paid for work on the church in their local parish, but for others across their estates. Lord Leicester of Holkham did not take the initiative, but acted in support of his tenants, contributing to the cost of work in villages such as Longham and Castle Acre. Between 1850 and 1880 he donated £15,000 to church building in his parishes. In 1851 the vicar of the Holkham-owned village of West Lexham described his church as 'in a wretched condition' and received £551 from the estate towards the cost of gates to the churchyard. The rest of the work he paid for himself. Work at Holkham church itself cost nearly £8,000.[17]

At a visitation in Hingham in 1854 the archdeacon commented that as many as a third of churches within the diocese were 'restored' (16/5/54), but the major period of restoration reached a peak in Norfolk in the 1860s and 70s, with as many as sixty-four churches undergoing major works between 1861 and 1865.[18] This was a period when, conversely, the population of most Norfolk villages was declining, but this enthusiasm can be accounted for in several ways.

First, as is obvious from the etchings by Robert Ladbrooke made in the 1820s, many churches were in a very poor state of repair as a result of centuries of neglect. Ladbrooke was a founding member of the Norwich School of painters, although few of his paintings survive. A major project of later life was to make drawings of all 700 of Norfolk's churches, which were then etched for printing by his son, bound and sold in five volumes. They provided a remarkable and important record of what churches looked like before the period of intensive building activity. They show both the medieval masterpieces which were to survive, externally at least, little altered, but also the many smaller, simpler buildings, often single-celled and thatched, with low towers and few windows, which were typical of many remote rural villages. Some, such as the church at Glandford, were ruinous, to be rebuilt by the landowner Sir Alfred Joderell at the end of the century. The collapsed tower at Ryston was rebuilt by the local Pratt family in 1858. Shernbourne was rebuilt at the expense of the Prince of Wales, while North Wootton, Shouldham Thorpe and East Bilney were also completely remodelled by local land-owners. A feature common to all of Ladbrooke's illustrations is the lack of stained glass. The installation of new, often memorial, windows is something few churches escaped in the later Victorian period.

Second, the parson and his patron were often making a statement and asserting their social control. At Ketteringham, the patron's control was emphasised by the building of galleries at the west end, with the inscription 'Erected September 26th 1841 by Sir John Boileau, Bart.' emblazoned in capital letters across the front.

Third, the reason could be liturgical. During Queen Victoria's reign the high and low church movements were both to have a lasting material effect on church buildings within Norfolk as elsewhere. The high church's encouragement of ritual within the service went along-side an increasing interest in antiquarianism and particularly in English medieval architecture. The Evangelical wing of the church was also concerned that a revival of Anglican Christianity should be demon-strated in well-maintained churches. The Ecclesiological Society provided guidance on what the ideal new or restored church should look like. Gothic was the preferred style, and for liturgical reasons the chancel and nave should be separated.

Of the 700 rural parish churches in Norfolk, over 500 went through a period of major restoration or were completely newly built between 1830 and 1900. Over half of the new churches were in the towns, with others on newly drained land. Walpole Highway church was built in 1844 and Welney in 1848. At Walpole Highway, the rector instigated the building of a new church as a chapel of ease to Walpole St Peter. J.C. Butler was the architect and unusually chose to build in a Norman style. The involvement of the rector, the Revd Arthur Moore, was such that he carved and painted the screen and poppy heads on the pews as well as designing the stained glass.[19] After 1880, as agricultural depression began to bite and population decline in the countryside increased, no new churches were built in rural areas.

Those churches that were completely rebuilt were frequently funded with help from the Incorporated Church Building Society, the various diocesan building societies and donations from the local landlord. A variety of local and sometimes famous national architects were employed, such as Anthony Salvin at North Wootton and Shouldham Thorpe. The most Anglo-Catholic of church buildings in Norfolk is St Mary's, West Tofts, and it was greatly admired by Armstrong when he visited in 1871. It was extended and decorated by the Pugins, father and son, between 1845 and 1850. This included an elaborate and highly ornate memorial chapel to Jane Mary Sutton of nearby Lynford Hall, a north aisle, south porch and chancel. All was elaborately painted and the windows filled with stained glass.[20] Armstrong described it as 'in the most perfect taste imaginable' (23/10/71). S.S. Teulon was working on nearby Shadwell Park and was commissioned by Lady Buxton to rebuild the almost ruinous Brettenham church in 1852. Although mostly in a restrained Decorated style, the octagonal vestry is more typical of Teulon's flamboyant approach. A new church to replace the ruinous one at Hainford was designed by the diocesan surveyor, John Brown, in 1838–40. It is a plain cruciform building, but externally the flintwork is decorated with brick dressings. Brown was also responsible for the churches at Thorpe Hamlet, Lakenham and New Catton within the rapidly expanding suburbs of Norwich. At Hunstanton it was the landowner, Henry Le Strange, who designed much of the interior decoration as well as repainting part of the ceilings in Ely Cathedral. Perhaps the most striking work in the region is the elaborately decorated ceiling at Huntingfield, near Halesworth, Suffolk, painted by Mildred Holland, the wife of the rector, which took eight months in 1859/60.

Nationally well-known architects could be involved in restoration as well as new builds. Sir Gilbert Scott was responsible for thirteen projects in Norfolk.[21] Teulon worked at Sandringham church in 1857–8 for the then owner, Mrs Harriet Cowper. The estate was bought by the Prince of Wales in 1862 and in 1890 he commisioned Arthur Blomfield, the architect son of the Bishop of London, to build a south transept and north aisle.[22]

Booton church is unique in that it was not only funded by the local landowner/incumbent, the Revd Whitwell Elwin, but also designed by him. He was rector for fifty years, dying at the age of 83 in 1900. A man of culture, he began work on the church in 1875 and completed it in 1891. The Victorian antiquarians, supported by the publications of the Ecclesiological Society, believed that Early English was the purest form of medieval architecture (it was also the simplest and therefore cheapest form of gothic) and encouraged the use of this style in church building. This was the form adopted at Booton. Having rebuilt the chancel, Elwin went on a tour of English cathedrals, measuring details that he wished to include at Booton. The result is a 'lavish building designed with a knowledge of Early English detail but a happy disregard for principles of Early English composition.... The architecture and fittings are the result of one man's personal and idiosyncratic vision.'[23] The two strange, slender west towers are a landmark visible for many miles around.

After about 1850 styles other than Early English became popular. At Martham the chancel was rebuilt in a general church restoration as a memorial to the Revd Jonathan Dawson between 1855 and 1861 at the expense of Mrs Alice Lagley, and designed by the architect Phillip Boyce, otherwise unknown in Norfolk. The result is a building with ornate windows and an elaborate chancel arch. A Norman style was used at Roydon and Gillingham, where both churches were ruinous, but with Norman features. At Gillingham, 'one of the glories of Victorian architecture', the architect T. Prentice, 'convinced that he knew Norman better than the Normans', added an aisled nave and chancel to the decaying Norman church in 1859–60.[24] James Colling was responsible for the 'severe' restoration of Holkham church at the expense of the Countess of Leicester between1868 and 1871.[25] Gradually high Victorian styles took over, including the use of decorative brickwork, as at Fulmodeston, where the old church was abandoned and a new one built in 1882. The interior of the new one is lined in polychromatic brick and the exterior is flint-faced.

A problem which was particularly obvious in rural Norfolk was the fact that over the centuries since churches were first built, the population had moved away and left the church isolated. In 1884 the vicar of

Edgefield, the Revd Walter Marcon, solved the problem with the help of a grant from the Incorporated Church Building Society, by taking down the medieval isolated church, leaving only the octagonal tower and graveyard in its original place. The original stonework, windows and pillars were used by the architect J.D. Sedding, much influenced by the Arts and Crafts movement, to rebuild it on the glebe, nearer the modern settlement.[26]

A development of the Victorian period was the reintroduction of stained-glass windows, often inserted as memorials to landowners and incumbents, something Armstrong always commented on favourably on his visits to France as well as to other Norfolk churches. So many Norfolk churches had large, plain glass windows, while stained glass gave 'a dim religious light'. This was all part of the wish to return the churches to their medieval glory. The work of Wailes of Newcastle was popular but much high-quality glass was made locally. One of the most prolific Norfolk glass firms was that of Samuel Carter Yarrington, and between 1860 and 1870 the firm installed over 300 new windows. The firm of J. and J. King was also important, producing high-quality glass with strong, clear colours throughout the period.[27]

The faculty system

Before major works were carried out in a church, the incumbent was supposed to submit his scheme to the diocesan authorities and obtain a faculty. It is clear that this was not always done, and indeed the antiquarian vicar Augustus Jessopp of Scarning describes a church to which

> a very hurricane of a man had been recently appointed, and which he had already set himself to restore.... He had an army of brick-layers picking and slopping about the sacred edifice tearing down and digging up that and smalming over the other.... 'Of course you have a Faculty for this?' I suggested. 'Not I! Faculty indeed! I have made up my mind to have nothing whatever to do with any officials or professionals of any sort or kind.'[28]

There is no evidence that clergy were held to account for this sort of omission. With this proviso however, the record of faculties granted through the Victorian period does give some indication of the sort of work taking place.[29]

Faculties of the 1830s and 40s are mainly concerned with the replacement of lead roofs with slates, the excavation of burial vaults, erection of railings around graves and the building of schools in churchyards. Internally, old pews were replaced and sometimes galleries for schoolchildren inserted. From the 1850s more faculties deal with rebuilding. In 1856 for instance a faculty for Croxton was granted, allowing for the 'taking down of the north and east wall of the nave and rebuilding the south aisle', while a more general faculty grant for Gresham simply stated, 'To restore the church', work that was undertaken in 1856.[30] Faculties for the 1870s continue to cover general restoration, as well as the first applications for stained-glass windows, organs and organ lofts.

The fervour for 'restoration' could come from both ends of the Anglican spectrum, and according to Jessopp both were equally damaging. The high church ritualist, seeking to emphasise the importance of the sacraments in church services, rather than the role of preaching, 'gets rid of the Jacobean pulpit, or the royal arms, or the ten commandments and sets up a construction which he calls a reredos, all tinsel and putty and *papier mâché* … and intones the service, keeping well within the chancel'.[31] Jessopp regarded the low church 'Evangelical' as just as destructive. 'Then the axes and hammers come out with a vengeance. None of your pagan inscriptions for him … none of your crosses and remains of frescoes on the walls…. As for the rood screen – away with it…. If you must have a division between the nave and chancel, set up a pulpit there, tall, prominent and significant.'[32] Jessopp's concern was that, particularly since the abolition of church rates, a clergyman could do almost what he wanted with his church, and, judging from the number of examples of Victorian restoration in Norfolk, many of them did.

Changes within the church

A major change of the Victorian period was in the internal layout of the church. In the early nineteenth century much of the seating was 'appropriated', that is, reserved for the use of particular families. Sometimes this involved a pew rent, but also it could simply be the result of custom. Much of this seating would have been in enclosed box pews, with open benches for the poorer members of the congregation. By the 1840s box pews were seen as interfering with ritual as well as symbolising private property and exclusiveness rather than the open character of the church and its interior. There was a move away from this socially divisive arrangement to make all seating free and in open benches. Armstrong was firmly against pew rents. A feature of his third (evening) Sunday service was that all pews were free.

A faculty application for Redenhall, for instance, explains the need for change:

> The parish church of Redenhall ... is badly and insufficiently pewed, the pews being high and for the most part double seated so that kneeling is almost impossible and many are compelled to sit with their backs to the minister ... [and] from constant changes of inhabitants and from increased attendance in the said church confusion and uncertainty prevail to a great and prejudicial extent. [33]

In some parishes old habits died slowly and certain pews were recognised as 'belonging' to certain families into the twentieth century. At Thurning church, which still retains its box pews in the north aisle allocated to individual farms, with open benches in the nave for the farm labourers, the old reservations were still acknowledged in the 1920s.

There was one other person within the parish who could well be concerned with church restoration and he was the patron/squire. His social control was as obvious in church as elsewhere. The Revd Mr Nelson of Lexham was not allowed to begin the service until the squire, Mr Keppel, and his family arrived (31/3/54). Armstrong sometimes took a service at North Elmham for his friend Augustus Legge, where Lord Sondes was the major landowner. He was treated deferentially. 'No one left the church until Lord Sondes had gone.... I prefer a town church where there is more general intelligence and less overpowering influence' (19/1/68). We have already seen that several landowners were responsible for large-scale restoration and rebuilding of churches, but smaller-scale additions and alterations could also be very significant. The rector of Merton had been presented to the living by the local patron, Lord Walsingham, in 1851 and noted in his *Annals* the various additions to the church made during his long incumbency. Lord Walsingham paid for a new north door in the 'decorated style' in 1854 and an east window in 1855. In 1856 there was a new south porch. In 1859 the nave was cleaned and plaster removed.[34]

The many faculties for vaults would have been landowner-inspired, as Victorian fashion dictated that local families of standing should be buried in them and due respect had to be shown by the incumbent to the landowner, who might well be his patron. Even in death there were inescapable social barriers.

The most famous of the inevitable disagreements between squire and incumbent – famous because the diaries of both the squire and the incumbent survived – is that between Sir John Boileau and his priest at Ketteringham, William Andrew, the subject of a book by Owen Chadwick.[35] Unlike Armstrong, Andrew was on the Evangelical wing of the church. His sermons were long (sometimes over an hour) and direct, often identifying personalities and never moderating his denunciation of sin. Sir John bought the estate from Mrs Atkyns, and on taking up permanent residence at Ketteringham in 1841, immediately embarked on a scheme for improving the layout of the church. He installed a gallery for the schoolchildren, altered his own and the servants' pews and whitened the walls of the church.[36] Andrew did not object to any of these changes, but the real disagreements came over the question of a family vault. The list of faculties granted by the diocese for the digging of family vaults during Victoria's reign is an indication of the importance that was attached to them. Like many others, Sir John felt it appropriate 'that a squire and his family should be buried in the chancel vault of the squire's church'.[37] He knew that there was already a vault in the chancel, to which he had the key. On investigation it appeared that it was full of coffins, but only one had an inscription and was dated 1702. As the vault could not be enlarged because that would undermine the foundations of the church, and as the only identifiable coffin had been placed there over 150 years previously, Sir John came to the radical conclusion that he should rebury the coffins outside and use the vault for his family, not realising that there were in fact more recent coffins in the vault of people with relatives still living locally. The idea of moving the coffins horrified Andrew, but Sir

John had managed to gain the tacit permission of the bishop, although privately the bishop also believed it was illegal. As Sir John understood that there were probably no living descendants of the dead, and the removals could be carried out surreptitiously, Andrew had little choice but to acquiesce, if reluctantly. Although the removal of the coffins took place after dark it soon became known in the village and also to a Mr Pemberton of Bourn Hall, Claxton, in Cambridgeshire, whose sister-in-law had been buried there. Local feelings ran high and the coffins had to be returned to the vault and the entrance paved over. The whole sorry escapade was reported in lurid detail in the *Norfolk Chronicle*[38] and Andrew inevitably was implicated in the whole incident. The relationship between squire and parson reached a new low. Finally, Sir John got permission to build his own mausoleum in the churchyard and commissioned Thomas Jeckyll to design a classical building which survives today. Andrew determined no longer to submit to his squire and demonstrated this new-found independence. When Sir John requested that there should only be one prayer at the harvest festival of 1854, Andrew wrote in his diary 'I however commenced my future mode of conduct.... I have found my past yielding everything has not brought peace. Henceforth I shall act with distinctiveness and decision.' He read two prayers.[39] While this is an extreme example of the disagreements that might arise between the clergyman and his patron, the situation could undoubtedly be problematic and is one that was often identified in Victorian fiction.[40]

Expanding urban populations resulted in the building of new churches. Not content with all he had achieved, within both the church and the community, in 1879 Armstrong embarked on a project to build a small mission church on the Norwich Road out of Dereham to serve the rapidly expanding town in this direction. In March he set up a committee to take forward the project and spent much time out and about 'begging' for money to build it. He then looked into the difference in price between a prefabricated iron construction of the type manufactured by Norwich-based Boulton and Paul and a flint and brick building, and settled on a flint building. By the end of March, a tender to build the church had been accepted. A concert was held to raise funds for the building and by May the foundations had been dug. Building went ahead at a pace and on 3 March 1880 the new church, dedicated to St Withburga, was licensed by the bishop, with an opening service on 4 April. Gradually the congregation increased and the first baptisms were performed. The altar was 'furnished with candlesticks and flower vases' (31/5/80) and in September a fund to provide gas lighting was opened. It was with great satisfaction that Armstrong noted in his diary in November 1880 that the final payment for building the church had been made (20/11/80).

Restoration and rebuilding in the Victorian period ensured that the diocese was served by structurally sound churches adapted for the new and reformed ideas of worship and liturgy. Medieval features had been brought back into use and the post-Reformation inheritance swept away and replaced by a distinctly Victorian version of the original.[41]

It was not only Anglican churches which were restored to what the Victorians saw as their gothic glory; those of the dissenters were often rebuilt in the same style. In Dereham, Armstrong was horrified when the house of the poet and hymn writer William Cowper on the Market Place was bought by the Independents, to be pulled down and a new church built in its place. In September 1874 Armstrong visited the new church. He praised it as a 'fine gothic structure, surmounted by a very bold cross'. A steeple was to be added. Inside it seemed to have borrowed much from the Anglican restoration movement, with stained-glass windows. 'But alas notwithstanding the fabric it is no more a CHURCH than its humble predecessor in Swan Lane' (25/9/72). The Wesleyan chapel, too, in Theatre Street was rebuilt in high gothic style in 1881.

Rectories

One of the first things a new reforming parson would turn his attention to was the provision of a parsonage that matched his station. Robert Kerr, in his book *The Gentleman's House, or How to Plan English Residences from the Parsonage to the Palace* (second edition, 1865), advocated a modest house appropriate to 'the domestic habits of a refined person'.[42] Plenty of advice on what sort of house the parsonage should be was available:

> The parsonage should be a kind of pattern house. There should be
> an air of neatness, sobriety and cheerfulness about it, but nothing

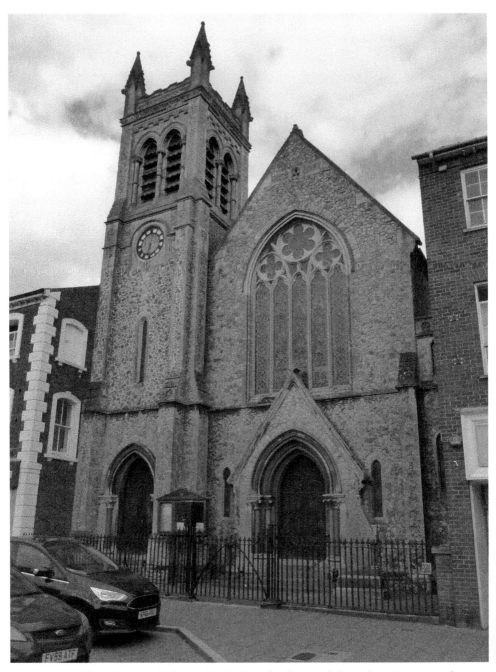

17   The Cowper 'Independent' chapel, designed by John Brown and opened in 1874. Armstrong continued to call it a 'meeting house' and wrote, 'Alas, notwithstanding the fabric, it is no more a CHURCH than its humble predecessor in Swan Lane.'

like extravagance or needless display ... a lordly parsonage is incon-
sistent with our character who come not to be ministered unto but
to minister.[43]

The parsonage often displayed the increasing social standing of the
clergy. That at Charlton in Oxfordshire was described in 1855 as being
built 'in a substantial manner, at once to convey to posterity a proof of
[the incumbent's] superior state and public spirit'.[44]

The provision and maintenance of a parsonage were the responsibility of the incumbent, and to enforce residence it was necessary for
the clergy to have houses within their parishes. The Parsonages Act of
1838 allowed bishops to require the incumbent to build or repair the
parsonage in livings worth more than £100 per year. Mostly this was
done willingly, even if it involved the incumbent mortgaging his living
and thus reducing his income, but sometimes coercion was needed
by the bishop and the archdeacons. An Act of 1777 had empowered
the trustees of a fund known as Queen Anne's Bounty to make loans
for the building and repair of parsonages. From the 1810s the trustees
of Queen Anne's Bounty established the Church of England Fund to
help poor clergymen and to issue mortgages for new parsonages. From
an enhanced income the clergyman would be expected to repay the
mortgage over a long period of years. To qualify for the mortgage, plans
had to be submitted to the trustees and many of these plans survive.
Applicants also had to declare that 'there was no parsonage on the
Glebe and whether there was any standing timber that could be used
to build it'.[45]

Nationally, this building programme was one of the success stories of
the Victorian church. In Oxfordshire, returns for 1855 show that since
1800, of the 178 parishes who sent in returns, the parsonage had been
rebuilt or newly built in 112. Between 1840 and 1869 a further £200,000
was spent on improving or rebuilding houses.[46] It was during Edward
Stanley's time as Bishop of Norwich that there was a great upsurge in
the building of parsonages in Norfolk. According to the diocesan plans
in the Norfolk Record Office, eighty-four new rectories were built or
substantially altered between 1840 and 1849, fifty-eight between 1850
and 1859, eighty-five between 1860 and 1869 and eighty between 1870
and 1879.[47]

When Armstrong visited Dereham with a view to moving there, he wrote that the vicarage built by his predecessor in 1806 was suitable for a gentleman, but would be too small for his family, so after Easter in 1852 work began to add two bays containing five rooms to the existing three-bay building. To enable the work to progress, he took his family for a month's visit to London and Northchurch. The enlarged house contained five bedrooms, three with dressing-rooms, a day and night nursery, a study, dining- and drawing-rooms, as well as a WC. There was a servants' stair passage, a 'necessary' and tradesman's entrance. 'What passes on either side of the boundary [between servants and family] shall be both invisible and inaudible to the other.'[48] The kitchen quarters consisted of scullery, butler's room and pantry, larder, dairy and knife house, with a cellar below. Outside was the garden 'necessary', stoke house and manure bin. As well as stabling, there was a coach house, gig house and harness room.[49]

How Armstrong funded the new building is not clear. Certainly his father gave financial help towards decorating and improvements, and he may well have paid for the work. Family wealth would probably have meant Armstrong did not need a loan; it is possible that the sinecure rector as patron also provided some of the funding.

Some parsonages were paid for entirely by the patron or a wealthy incumbent with no outside help at all. Many of these buildings, as in Dereham, were of a plain Georgian style typical of the period and would not have been out of place as the residences of the minor gentry, from which class, of course, many of their occupants came. Gradually the typical style changed from classical Georgian to the Tudor-gothic which was fashionable during the middle decades of the century, to high Victorian towards its end.[50] When the new rector arrived in Blakeney shortly before 1838 a new room was added to the house because 'it was not large enough for my family'.[51] William Donthorn of Swaffham worked on many gentry houses as well as public buildings and workhouses. He also designed at least five Norfolk parsonages.[52] Parsonages at Horning (1820) and at East Bilney (1837) were the work of the Norwich architect Arthur Browne. That at Bilney, built for Armstrong's friend and member of the local landowning family the Revd Henry Collinson, was in a Tudor style and on a grand scale, with a footman's room beside the entrance. That at Horning, standing in a prestigious position overlooking the river, was classical.[53] Arthur Browne's son John built several parsonages, including Foxley (1841) and West Lexham (1850), both in a plain, rather austere classical style. They included a drawing- and dining-room, as well as a study and extensive kitchens. Four bedrooms, one with a dressing-room, and a nursery were typical. A maids' and menservants' room was usually approached by a separate staircase.[54] Teulon built ornate Tudor-style rectories at Bressingham (1842) and North Creake (1845), while at Booton in 1860 Thomas Allom favoured Jacobean.[55] For those who did not want to employ their own architect there were books of designs, such as T.F. Hunt's *Designs for Parsonage Houses* published in the 1830s, which included a plan for 'a clergyman's house on a moderate scale' in which 'frugality may be exercised without the appearance of poverty'.[56]

These buildings, with the air of a gentleman's residence, emphasised the improved social standing of the clergy during the Victorian period. To obtain a grant through Queen Anne's Bounty a parsonage had to have two sitting-rooms, a study, kitchen, pantry and scullery and wine cellar, dustbins and coal house together with five bedrooms, linen closet and WC. By the 1870s most clergy were resident and there were more parsonages for them to live in, partly because there were more men available, more money to pay them and the conviction that they should reside in their parishes was strong.

The rector of Yaxham built his own rectory, 'a curious little cottage with odd contrivances such as speaking tubes instead of bells' (25/9/79). Presumably this was because he found the huge classical vicarage, built in 1822 and designed by the well-known architect Robert Lugar who illustrated it in his book *Villa Architecture*, published in 1828,[57] too large for his bachelor requirements.

By the 1860s features fashionable at the time, such as bay windows to drawing-rooms, made an appearance and the designs were more typically Victorian. Even buildings on this scale did not always satisfy the incumbent. When Armstrong visited his son at his first curacy in Thatcham in Berkshire he found that the parson had let the vicarage, 'which was not considered sufficiently grand for the squire's daughter he took for his third wife'. Armstrong regarded the new house as 'somewhat pretentious', but 'in the very best style and replete with every comfort and luxury, conservatory, baths etc.'. The only drawback was that it was too far from the church (10/1/74). Parsonages remained large, with up to eight family bedrooms as well as provision for servants' rooms, providing space not only for large families, but also for live-in pupils. In 1861 the Revd Mr Valpy of Garvestone took in boarders and ran a school. By the 1870s and 80s few new parsonages were being built, but extensions and improvements were carried out at existing ones. In 1875 at Woodbastwick, a new servants' hall and kitchen were added, with further rooms upstairs.[58] At Attleborough, the rectory was said to be 'a fine mansion' (3/11/72).

A third building which was also very much the parson's responsibility was the school, and this will be discussed in the following chapter.

Notes

1 N. Yates, *Buildings, Faith and Worship*, 1991, 170–4.
2 E. Stanley, 'Church Decoration', *The Builder* **3**, no. 121, May 1845, 263, quoted in S. Muthesius, 'Provinciality and the Victorians: Church Design in Nineteenth-Century East Anglia', in T.A. Heslop, E. Mellings and M. Thofnor (eds), *Art, Faith and Place in East Anglia*, 2012, 214.
3 E. Baty, 'Victorian Church Building and Restoration', PhD thesis, University of East Anglia, 1987, 25.
4 N. Boston and E. Puddy, *Dereham: The Biography of a Country Town*, 1962, 170.
5 Ibid., 132.
6 A. Jessopp, *The Trials of a Country Parson*, 1894, 155.
7 Ibid., xxiv.
8 *Norwich Mercury* 12 July 1884.
9 *Norwich Mercury*, 11 October 1884.
10 *Norwich Mercury*, 18 December 1886.
11 NRO, PD 548/46.
12 N. Pevsner and B. Wilson, *Buildings of England: Norwich and North East Norfolk*, 1997, 757.
13 NRO, PD209/42.
14 Leaflet in A. Jessopp, *Studies by a Recluse in Cloister, Town and Country*, 1892.
15 Ibid.
16 N. Hartley, *Augustus Jessopp, Norfolk's Antiquary*, 2017, 212.
17 S. Wade Martins, *A Great Estate at Work: Holkham and Its Inhabitants in the Nineteenth Century*, 1980, 202–3.
18 Pevsner and Wilson 1997; N. Pevsner and B. Wilson, *Buildings of England: North-West and South Norfolk*, 1999, passim.
19 Pevsner and Wilson 1999, 744.
20 Ibid., 770.
21 Muthesius 2012, 210.

22 Pevsner and Wilson 1999, 626.
23 Pevsner and Wilson 1997, 409.
24 Pevsner and Wilson 1999, 140.
25 Ibid., 411.
26 Pevsner and Wilson 1997, 454, Baty 1987, 34.
27 Pevsner and Wilson 1999, 144.
28 Jessopp 1894, 69.
29 NRO, DN/FCB/6-9.
30 NRO, DN/FCB/7217 and 230; Pevsner and Wilson 1999, 529.
31 Jessopp 1894, 70.
32 Ibid., 71.
33 NRO, DN/FCB7, quoted in R. Lee, *Rural Society and the Anglican Clergy*, 2006, 46.
34 NRO, PD532/32.
35 O. Chadwick, *A Victorian Miniature*, 1960.
36 Ibid., 75.
37 Ibid., 133.
38 *Norfolk Chronicle*, 17 December 1853
39 Chadwick 1960, 146.
40 For example, Anthony Trollope's *Framley Parsonage.*
41 Baty 1987, 121.
42 Quoted in K. Tiller, *Parsonages*, 2016, 64.
43 A. Oxenden, *The Pastoral Office: Its Duties, Difficulties, Privileges and Prospects*, 1857, 270.
44 McClatchey *Oxfordshire Clergy, 1777–1869*, 1960, 23.
45 F. Knight, *The Nineteenth-Century Church and English Society*, 1995, 136.
46 McCluskey 1960, 22–3.
47 NRO, DN/DPL.
48 Quoted in Tiller 2016, 64.
49 NRO, PD86/83.
50 T. Brittain-Catlin, *The English Parsonage in the Early Nineteenth Century*, 2008, 21.
51 NRO, DN VIS 64/4.
52 H. Colvin, *Dictionary of British Architects 1600–1840*, 3rd edn, 1995, 318.
53 Pevsner and Wilson 1997 and 1999.
54 NRO, DN/DPL 2/1/3, 2/3/119, 1/1/9, 2/5/172.
55 Pevsner and Wilson 1997, 146; NRO, DN/DPL 2/1/41 and 1/1/12.
56 Quoted in P.C. Hammond, *The Parson and the Victorian Parish*, 1977, 55.
57 Colvin 1995, 625.
58 NRO, DN/DPL 2/9/327.

Six

Schools

The Anglican church had long been involved with the provision of education, mainly through individual trusts associated with churches, where schools established as a result of bequests were often housed in an upper room above the church porch. By the early nineteenth century it was clear that these charity schools were no longer sufficient and so the Church of England National Society for Promoting the Education of the Poor was founded (1811), with the aim of providing a school in every parish. In 1812 the Norfolk branch was set up and was responsible for either supporting or founding most of the rural schools in Norfolk established before 1870. At its inaugural meeting, called by the Lord Lieutenant and attended by some of the county's leading landowners and churchmen, the Bishop of Norwich was appointed patron. In his letter of acceptance, the Whig-supporting Bishop Bathurst made it clear that he did not want there to be any antagonism between non-conformists and the Anglican schools, but all should work together.[1] This is what we would expect from this liberal-minded man, who had many Unitarian friends and who later voted in the House of Lords for Catholic emancipation. Following this, a questionnaire was sent by the archdeacon to all incumbents asking them what educational provision there was within their parishes and what opportunities existed for setting up schools. Answers were received from 175 clergy and survive amongst the diocesan records.[2] Forty-nine parishes had Sunday Schools, twenty-one had day schools and in forty-three education was provided part-time or on Sundays. There were plans for schools in seventeen parishes, but in forty-two none were proposed. Sub-committees were then formed in each deanery and these contributed towards the purchase of or providing schoolrooms, the salary of the teacher and provision of teaching materials.[3] The first school to be founded outside Norwich with support from the National Society was at Hingham in 1812. It was to serve Hingham and its surrounding parishes and was open every afternoon. An annual grant of £16 was allocated and books and slates for 100 children donated.[4] Schools that had already been founded by clergy and other individuals were accepted into the National Society, offered an annual grant and provided with books.

Not all schools operated daily. Some were open only in the afternoons, while many were Sunday or evening schools. Thornham school was an afternoon school when it became a National School in 1812.[5] The Sunday School at Harleston and Redenhall joined the National Society in May 1813 but 'as soon as a fit room can be procured ... instruction will be extended to four afternoons, two for boys and two for girls'.[6] In March 1813 £20 was granted for the extension of the schoolroom at Blofield and later that year £15 was granted towards the building of a school in Litcham and £12 for fitting out a schoolroom in Postwick. Sixty pounds was granted for the building of a school at North Creake for 200 children.[7] A board inside Baconsthorpe school lists the original donors in 1816. As well as the £70 from the National Society in London and £60 from the local branch, local gentry and churchmen gave £314.

In November 1814 a meeting was held in Dereham, attended by the leading local landowners and all the clergy in the deanery of Brisley and those parishes of the deanery of Hingham which were in the Mitford and Launditch Union, of which Dereham was a part. William Lee-Warner of Quebec Hall was made chairman, and Charles Hyde Wollaston of Dereham, secretary. Each incumbent was then urged to open subscriptions for the opening of a school within his parish. The landowners present were appointed as general visitors to the schools and it was agreed that the committee should meet twice a year in Dereham.[8] A small National School was duly founded, whether on the site of the later school building in Theatre Street is unclear.

Supporting the local school was, along with the church and the cottage, one of the three main duties of the clergyman as listed by Armstrong. By 1846 nearly 200 Norfolk schools were under the National Society's umbrella.[9] However, the Society was always short of money. Teachers were trained at two central schools in Norwich, suitable books were provided and directions on educational ideology came from the centre, but otherwise schools relied heavily on voluntary contributions

18 Dereham British School. The inscription over the original door states that it was built by voluntary subscription 'liberally supported' by W. Lee-Warner in 1841. The windows on either side were part of the new build when it was taken over by the School Board after 1870.

EAST DEREHAM,

NATIONAL CHURCH SCHOOL. 1841.

19 Dereham Church School, rebuilt in 1841 and little changed during Armstrong's lifetime.

to survive. Armstrong spent many weary days walking around Dereham collecting subscriptions.

Where there was a resident squire, the responsibility might be shared with the landowner, but this was not to be the case in Dereham. In 1841 Mr Lee-Warner of Quebec Hall, 'who wavered between church and dissent' (16/6/52), provided the funds for the competing non-conformist British Society to build a school in Norwich Street. With this lack of support for a National School from the leading family, it was up to the priest to secure funding through subscriptions. By 1840 the Dereham school building was inadequate for the number of children attending and efforts to raise money for a new building began. A 'Fancy Bazaar' supported by Lord and Lady Sondes and all the local aristocracy, as well as leading members of the town community, was held. A second bazaar was run in the following year.[10] A building for 300 children and a schoolmaster's house was finally opened to compete with the British School in December 1841.[11] Unlike many church schools, it was not built on the glebe near the church but on a site away from the centre of the town at the far end of Theatre Street. A small branch school was set up by Armstrong in 1852 in the hamlet at Etling Green which he visited regularly.

Alongside the formal National and British schools were the smaller and unregulated 'dame schools'. These were generally frowned upon by the recognised schools and very little is known about them. A few such schools existed in the town and the log-book for the church school records on the first of December 1873 that 'twelve children were admitted, some from the Board [previously British] school and from various dame schools'.[12]

The role of the parson

The promoting of elementary education within their parishes was taken very seriously by Victorian clergy, and Armstrong certainly spent many hours encouraging attendance, testing children on their understanding of the Christian faith as laid down in the Catechism (beliefs of the Church of England in the form of questions and answers which were regularly learnt and recited in church schools), collecting subscriptions, writing the annual report and accounts and obtaining government grants for improvements. The school log-books show that he came into the school at least once a week, working with different classes in turn. When in London he made a point of buying books for the school, and in 1862 'Miss Armstrong' (presumably his daughter, Helen) was in charge of issuing books from the school library.[13] He also accompanied the diocesan inspectors on their visits. In July 1856 he spent 'all day with the Diocesan Inspectors at school' (29/7/56). In October 1860 the diocesan inspector dined at the vicarage, 'a superior and intellectual man'. In 1861 the inspectors reported that the school 'was very much improved on last year' (17/10/61). One of Armstrong's aims on his regular visits to the poor was to encourage them to send children to school, and the report for 1862 stated that the school 'maintains its high character of efficiency – for which I can take credit as I took it on in a deplorable state' (4/12/62).

In 1855 he persuaded Mrs North of Hoe to bring fourteen children from that parish to the school in Dereham. She became a subscriber and paid for them all for a month. This was unusual support from a farmer's wife, as the farmers generally did not want to lose children from their labour force. Armstrong was encouraged by such support in the face of 'the sneers of farmers' (19/5/55). Collecting subscriptions around the town could be a time-consuming task. However, in 1857 he was pleased because it was not only the old subscribers who supported him, but new subscribers as well (31/3/57).

Armstrong's involvement was not limited to the curriculum. In addition, various treats might be arranged. In January 1857 he took the schoolchildren to see a panorama of Sebastopol at the Corn Hall (27/1/57), something that would have been relevant to those who had fathers in the army. In the summer he played cricket with the first class, 'which I allow to come to the vicarage to play every Wednesday evening'. A select group was often invited to the vicarage on Christmas Day to share any entertainment which Armstrong had laid on for his children and to receive a small present from the Christmas tree. In March 1859 Armstrong took 160 children to see an 'exhibition of dogs and monkeys' in the Assembly Rooms', and in April 1861 the senior children were taken to a concert given by 'Dr Martin's Band of children.... The children were probably orphans taken in by Dr Martin in order that he could train them for his band' (18/4/61).

The school fête was another red-letter day. It was held either in the vicarage garden or Quebec Hall and was the one event in the year which could be ruined by the weather. It usually took place in August, and in 1851, under blue skies and after a good tea, the children enjoyed games in the 'tastefully decorated grounds' until about nine o'clock, when they 'were dismissed to their respective homes, no doubt highly gratified and thankful to their kind benefactor for the treats they had that day so richly enjoyed'.[14] In 1854 it rained for the procession to the church, but then cleared up in time for tea for 300 children as well as subscribers. This was followed by games and finally a fire balloon was sent up over the town (21/8/54).[15] The following year, however, Armstrong did not give a school feast, as the parents had 'come to regard it as a right rather than a favour' (2/10/55), and in 1857 it was held at Quebec Hall, to which 325 children marched with banners and music (29/9/57). The next year Armstrong tried to persuade Mrs Lee-Warner to have the fête at the Hall again but she refused, 'as it might become an annual thing – but what if it did? Neither squire nor farmers are very liberal' (23/6/58). Instead it once again took place in the vicarage garden: the day was fine, the music good and there were 320 children in the procession with banners. Church was followed by tea, dancing, sports, games and fireworks (15/9/58). In 1861, perhaps because of a fear of wet weather, the tea was held in St Nicholas Hall, newly converted from the old Theatre; 350 children sat down to tea, 25 to a table, each of which had been provided by 'ladies at their own expense'. Afterwards there were games in the vicarage grounds. One thousand people enjoyed the garden. The Rifle band played for dancing and the evening ended with a fire balloon being sent up (29/7/61).

The motives of the clergy in promoting education were undoubtedly mixed. While there was a general concern over the lack of literacy amongst the poor, there was also a wish to ensure that they received a sound religious education and developed a suitably deferential attitude. Armstrong visited the schools in Dereham and Etling Green twice a week on Tuesdays and Thursdays for an hour, teaching the children the Catechism and hearing them recite it. He was afraid that this emphasis on the teachings of the Church of England might result in dissenters leaving. There is no evidence that this happened and certainly numbers kept up. He was, however, unpopular when he tried to distribute 'tracts' for children at two dame schools in Toftwood because the teachers were afraid that the parents might withdraw their children (20/3/54).

Bishop Wilberforce, writing in 1848, was clear about how far the clergy should be involved in school life. 'Your teaching in the school must be that of a pastor, not a school master', and 'You did not promise God through your bishop at your ordination that you would be a teacher of useful knowledge, but that out of Scripture you would instruct the people committed to your charge.'[16] In an emergency, however, Armstrong or his curate would teach in the school, and on one occasion Armstrong had to take a boy who had fallen off a form and cut his ear open to the doctor to be bandaged up. He then took him home to a very concerned mother (31/3/57). Rather surprisingly perhaps, Armstrong did not feel he could sack a schoolmaster, but instead had to persuade him to resign if he thought he was inadequate (27/11/56). By July 1857 a new permanent master had been recruited and a letter was sent to parents encouraging them to send children to school. This was followed up by visits, and by September the numbers in the school had increased greatly. However, within a few months he was without a master again. 'The school master and wife found the work too hard and left for Gressenhall with no warning' (16/1/58). Within a month a new master was found and was formerly elected at the annual school meeting. 'Mr Trollope was elected new master as he is certificated (to which we have not hitherto aspired), he will go in for capitation grants and pupil teachers and so raise the school to a higher grade than hitherto contemplated' (17/2/58). Under his leadership the school staff grew to two pupil-teachers, two sewing mistresses (one of whom was his wife) and an infant assistant.[17] Standards began to rise and discipline improved. The inspection of March reported that there had been 'a marked and decided improvement': the number of pupils had increased and the management improved.[18] New parallel forms and desks were ordered, and by 1859 the 'school was reduced to perfect order' and the school inspectors were 'pleased' (10/4 and 6/6/59). In 1861 Armstrong negotiated a government grant of £21 to replace the stone floor in the school with a wooden one (24/2/61).

Pupil-teachers

The system of pupil-teachers was introduced into National Schools in 1846. Pupils who were first appointed as monitors could progress to become pupil-teachers, which involved studying in the evenings and taking examinations. Once there was a certificated teacher in Dereham, the appointment of such pupils was possible, and in January 1859 three pupil-teachers were apprenticed. Armstrong addressed 'their parents, the master and mistress and gave them a bottle of wine' (31/1/59). Three years later Armstrong noted that they had done very well in their examinations (19/10/61) and in the autumn he 'signed indentures for a new pupil teacher' (11/11/61). An apprenticeship as a pupil-teacher could lead to better life prospects. In 1864 Armstrong noted with satisfaction that he had managed to obtain a post for a young girl as a pupil-teacher, 'otherwise she would have been a maid of all work' (29/6/64). In October 1863 William Gee and Charles Sharpe finished their apprenticeship and monitors were selected to take their place. (This may be the same 'Mr Gee' who later became the master at neighbouring North Elmham school.) However, the system was not always easy to operate. In 1872 Alice Barnes was apprenticed as a pupil-teacher but was said to be 'making little progress'. In March 1873 she 'continued to neglect her home lessons'. Sometimes she was late and in October was reported because 'she knew nothing of the lessons set her last night'. Mr Trollope complained of her lethargy and her carelessness in making up the register. She missed the teachers' lessons. Finally, at the end of October 1873 she was given notice that she was no longer a pupil-teacher 'owing to the neglect of her studies'.[19] Studying of an evening in an overcrowded cottage with no proper light to read by would have been no easy task. In the neighbouring parish of North Elmham, the school log-books make it clear that pupil-teachers were difficult to recruit. In April 1870 Lydia Hammond 'thinks her health will not allow her to continue as a pupil teacher but is willing to go on as monitress'. In 1876 the schoolmaster wrote, 'Like all the boys in this neighbourhood, George Willimot declines to become a candidate for pupil teachership because of the lessons he will have to learn.'[20]

The story of Maria Utting of North Elmham is a typical of many. In April 1865 she commenced 'teaching a class (on trial)'. Presumably the trial was deemed successful, as she was later appointed a monitress and was teaching Mrs Gee's (the wife of the schoolmaster) class as she was unwell. By 1866 she was a pupil-teacher and was absent without leave on the first day of term. This was followed by further absences and in 1868 Mr Gee cautioned her 'to mind what I say to her more'. She was absent again the next day. The school inspector also commented on Miss Utting, saying her work must improve. In November 1868 Mr Gee wrote, 'Maria did not know her lessons today – I do not think she tries to get them up.' There were further complaints. She could not keep her class quiet, and 'It is very little use setting Maria Utting work to do in the evening as it is very seldom done.' She was obviously not suited to the work and was frequently absent. Finally her father came to the school and 'cancelled her indentures as her health would not stand it'. 'A very good thing', wrote Mr Gee, 'as she was quite valueless as a pupil teacher.'[21]

Generally, teaching seems to have been done by pupil-teachers and the class was then examined by the master, who would take over the class if it was particularly backward. There are many examples in school log-books of pupil-teachers and monitors finding it difficult to control children. At Elmham in April, 1872 a monitoress was suspended for beating a child in the infant school.

Religious instruction

The list of books supplied by the National Society gives some indication of the influence of the church on the curriculum. Requests for psalters, prayer books, catechisms, extracts from the Bible and 'other books which will improve' arrived regularly at the Society's headquarters from Norfolk schools.[22] Books used at Fritton National School in 1844 included Bishop Gastrell's *Faith and Duty of a Christian*, the *Church Catechism Broken into Short Questions and Answers*, Wilkinson's *Short Catechism* and Parry's *Infant Catechism and Hymns for the Young*.[23] It is clear from this emphasis on religious education that the local clergyman was likely to be directly involved in the running of the school. In July 1852 Armstrong undertook 'a diligent visitation all over the parish with a view of getting parents to send their children to school' (31/7/52). He noted the ignorance of many of his parishioners, and what really concerned him was that 'in religion they are excessively vague' (31/7/52). In October 1855 he recorded in his diary that he visited 'fifty chubby little children' at Etling Green and found to his satisfaction that their knowledge of the Catechism was improving (5/10/55). If the teacher was absent for any reason, then Armstrong would fill his place (16/12/56). Only in the school holidays was there any respite. In August, 'As the parochial schools are dismissed, the poor are in the harvest fields and the rich are at the seaside, there is not much to be done' (25/8/53).

Other local clergyman also saw the importance of church-controlled education. William Andrew at Ketteringham not only kept a close eye on the school, but also on the activities of the schoolteacher. She found herself caught between Sir John Boileau, the landowner, and Mr Andrew. When an invitation to the New Year ball arrived from Sir John, the vicar urged her not to accept, as dancing should not be condoned by a schoolteacher; however, she was anxious not to offend Sir John. Andrew was pleased to find that in the end she did not attend, complaining of a headache.[24]

Stephen Allen of Shouldham fought long and hard to build a school in his parish. When the school was finally opened in 1866 he claimed it had taken him sixteen years of 'steady perseverance' to obtain the land and enlist enough subscribers. It is clear from the opening ceremony that he saw the school very much as a religious institution. In his opening address, which followed an elaborate church service and procession with banners, he pronounced the occasion as the 'most important day after [his] ordination in [his] life'.[25]

The Dereham schools, in common with all National Schools, would have had strict rules about tidiness and neat dress. In some cases, this would have prevented children attending. In 1859 Mary Hales, a close friend of Armstrong's, set up a 'boot and shoe club' which would have encouraged parents to save a little a week to buy boots for the winter (10/4/59). By 1862 this was being run by Helen Armstrong. She closed the club on 11 November and on the 24th, 'Many returned to school having received their boots from the club'.[26] The new club began taking subscriptions on 2 December.

Keeping children in education was a problem for all schools. Parents could see little point in sending them, there was no home support and so any excuse kept children away. Attendance on Dereham market day (a Friday) was always thin, and poor weather kept children at home. In February 1862 there was an exhibition of wild beasts which drew children away.[27] Average attendance was usually between 200 and 300, which only represented a small proportion of the school-age children in the town (800 in the 1871 census). No records survive of either the British (non-conformist) School or of the Board School that replaced it for this period, but an admissions book covering the period 1890–4 shows between fifty and seventy children being admitted every year, which, if children remained at school for seven years, suggests a total of 350 pupils.[28]

One solution to the difficulty of getting children to school during the day was to set up a night school, and in 1859 the rector of nearby Billingford built, at his own expense, a small schoolroom, which still stands at the old rectory gate, to which both adults and children were encouraged to come. The school ran for six years, and at its most successful it was attended by between fifty and sixty adults and children. It 'was discontinued owing to the attendance falling off'. The existence of the night school was used as an excuse for employing children during the day. Over the six years of its existence, the average age of those attending gradually reduced and when he finally closed the school the rector wrote, 'I considered my night school not suitable for weary little boys who had all day been exposed to the cold and wet in the fields.'[29] The Dereham school log-book mentioned twenty-three children being at the evening school in 1864, but there are no other references to it.[30]

Increasing government involvement

The problem of finding enough elementary school places for all children was very much one of finance, and gradually state funding became available. Initially, after 1833 grants were provided for building from national government, with the state taking no control over what was taught. Armstrong noted with approval in his diary in March 1856 a law recently passed, which would compel Boards of Guardians to require those to whom they were giving regular outdoor relief to send their children to school. This would be paid for out of the rates. 'This is clearly the first step towards a compulsory State Education, without something of which kind, our peasantry will always be behind other nations in intelligence' (19/3/56).

In 1862, as a result of the findings of the Newcastle Commission, a new system of funding schools came into force. Progress through the school was divided into six standards, six being the highest, and a strictly controlled syllabus, or 'Revised Code', was introduced on which children would be tested annually. In November 1862 the syllabus in Dereham was 'regulated to fit the new Code'.[31] The level of success in this oral test decided the level of state grant. This 'payment by results' system was condemned in a series of articles in the *Norfolk Chronicle* which claimed that the new system would result in the 'cramming into little heads of little capacity the knowledge which a long course of adult study could alone master'.[32] In July 1866, 'only a portion of the scholars; those who are considered competent for the ordeal' were examined and only three did not come up to the required standard. 'The Inspector expressed a very favourable opinion of the school.'[33] In 1867 the bishop visited Dereham and went to the school, where 'he examined the children who performed admirably' (4/4/67). In the same year improvements in the school building were proposed and Armstrong preached a sermon to help pay for 'new warming apparatus'.[34] A warm school might well have attracted children from cold, damp cottages to attend. A conscience clause in the new system was introduced by which parents could remove their children from religious education. This was firmly opposed by men such as Stephen Allen of Shouldham, who resented the idea that the clergy 'would not be able to teach in their own schools'.[35] In 1864 Armstrong organised a petition against the conscience clause, but it remained in force. He pointed out that dissenters were happy to send their children to the best (National) school and did not object to the Catechism during the week, but took their children to their own Sunday Schools and 'make dissenters of them' (51/3/65). To induce them back he organised a Sunday School feast in the vicarage garden (3/6/65) and in August 1867 the *Norfolk News* described the event in glowing terms:

The weather was fine and the repast was spread amidst the flowers and beauties of nature. The young folk amused themselves in innocent games until night threw her sable mantle on the scene, compelling them to return to their homes after hearty expressions of gratitude for the treats so kindly provided for them.[36]

Again, in 1868 the Sunday School feast for 178 children was held in the Armstrongs' garden but attendance was strictly limited to Sunday School rather than day-school children to prevent dissenters going to two feasts (2/9/68). The Sunday School tea soon became an annual event, and by 1872 it 'was more a festival for the whole parish' (20/8/72). In 1871 Armstrong decided that the Sunday School should meet in the afternoon as well as the morning, as children who came in the morning were often sent to the dissenting one in the afternoon, 'parents sending them there to get them out of their way' (9/7/71).

Sunday Schools, too, were for general as well as religious education, and in Dereham the girls were taught in the vestry and boys in the church. In April 1861 the needlework teacher resigned and by end of the year it was thought necessary to reorganise the Sunday School, and Armstrong held various meetings with the teachers about this (3/9 and 1/10/61). Armstrong's friend Salisbury Everard, the high church vicar of Swaffham, insisted that children who attended the church school should also go to the church Sunday School. In Dereham many of the poor went to the dissenting Sunday School. 'However, I hope that the re-organising of the Sunday Schools may in some measure remedy this' (25/10/61).

The beginning of secular education

By 1870 it was becoming clear that the voluntary sector would be unable to provide enough schools for all children and if education was to be made compulsory, the state was going to have to fill the gap. At meetings of the Norwich Diocesan Church Association and Pastoral Schools Society in January 1868, fears that an education rate might be imposed and schools become secular were expressed. The current system whereby the state gave grants to all schools, whatever denomination, was preferable to a 'generalised and godless system' (25/1/68). This argument did not find favour with those who felt that education should be secular and the result was the Forster Education Act of 1870, which stated that where there was not adequate provision for all children a local School Board could be set up funded by a school rate and run by elected school managers who could build and run a school. Existing schools which did not come up to the required standard could be enlarged and new ones built. The threat of this secular system spurred the clergy into action. 'The loss of a church school would be an irreparable injury to the discharge of pastoral office.'[37] In Fulmodeston the school consisted of a small room and the children were taught by the vicar as the only teacher. There was no school in neighbouring Barney and as the vicar failed to raise any interest in improving and enlarging the school, a joint Board for the two parishes 'will be forced upon us'.[38] Perhaps because of the fear of state control unless there were improvements, Armstrong preached in Dereham in July 1870 to raise money for the school. With the help of a legacy of £100 it was possible to build a new classroom and enlarge the master's house, which was completed by August 1870. In 1874 an enlargement of South Creake school was ordered by the Education Department. 'If we fail to do this, a School Board will be ordered.' In Foxley the vicar wrote to the neighbouring landlord, Lord Leicester, 'I hope we will be able to avoid Boards by inducing the occupiers and owners to contribute their rateable portions voluntarily.'[39] Armstrong recorded a meeting of Dereham rate-payers held because the Education Department was requiring the building of schools in outlying hamlets. 'I fear the School Board is inevitable, but I shall, if possible, maintain the independent position of the church schools' (19/2/73). The first election for a School Board was held on 5 May 1873 and its first meeting was held in the Assembly Rooms on the 22nd, with the Dereham solicitor Halcott Cooper as chair. Unlike the National School under the leadership of Armstrong, the non-conformists' British School in London Road was struggling and was handed over to the School Board in 1873. It was not for another two years that Board Schools at Etling Green for seventy children and in the expanding hamlet of Toftwood for eighty were opened.[40] Armstrong continued to take a close interest in the church school, hosting the annual school feast in the vicarage grounds. However, during the 1880s he handed over much of the responsibility to his curate son, who in 1886 had to cope with a crisis when the schoolmaster was 'unable to do anything' through illness for much of the year (29/7/86). In 1885 the annual sermon in support of the school was given by a visiting clergyman: 'His help a bonus. I am somewhat tired of this subject' (11/7/85).

While there was generally a decline in the involvement of the church in education after 1870, there were many School Boards where the incumbent was a member and sometimes the chairman. At Flitcham the rector, Mr Jones, was chairman of the managers, his wife also a manager and the three Jones children taught in the school. 'It appears to be the case of Jones unlimited.'[41] Rarely, however, were the clergy this involved and gradually their role became more of an advisory one.

Armstrong occasionally visited the school at the Union workhouse at Gressenhall. He was impressed with what he found and commented that 'the education was very exact and creditable to the master' (29/7/71).

The church's involvement with education was much resented by non-conformists. The Agricultural Union leader, Joseph Arch, speaking in the Corn Hall in East Dereham in December 1870, claimed that the labourer who took his child out of school while the Catechism was being taught, as was his right, 'was a marked man' and would suffer when parish doles were being handed out. The local leader of the union, George Rix, took up the theme: children should be educated, 'not in creeds and Catechisms for those never did any good and never would'. Instead, they wanted 'a good sound education administered for their children and not schools where the parson reigned supreme'.[42]

By the time Armstrong retired in 1888 there were Board Schools at Toftwood and Etling Green as well as the old British School, which was also now run by the Board. However, the National School was thriving and through his efforts it was well funded and staffed and always received good reports from the inspectors. Only rarely did he receive any credit for his efforts. However, in January 1880 a father came to see him to thank him for the education his son had received. 'This is recorded as being almost the only instance of any expression of gratitude ever met with' (26/1/80).

Notes

1   *Norfolk Chronicle*, 25 July 1812.
2   NRO, DN/NDS/275/1–4.
3   R. Iremonger, *Suggestions to the Promoters of Dr Bell's System of Tuition*, 1813, 51.
4   NRO, DN/NDS 137, 8–9.
5   NRO, DN/NDS 137, 10.

6   NRO, DN/NDS 137, 19.
7   NRO, DN/NDS 137, 16, 23, 24, 33.
8   *Norfolk Chronicle*, 12 November 1814.
9   A. Longcroft and S. Wade-Martins (eds), *Building an Education: An Historical and Architectural Study of Rural Schools and Schooling in Norfolk, c.1800–1944*, 2013, 25.
10 *Norfolk Chronicle*, 5 December 1840 and 27 February 1841.
11 *Norfolk Chronicle*, 4 December 1841.
12 NRO, C/ED 151/1.
13 NRO, C/ED/ 151/1.
14 *Norfolk Chronicle*, 16 August 1851.
15 *Norfolk Chronicle*, 2 September 1854.
16 Quoted in D. McClatchey, *Oxfordshire Clergy, 1777–1869*, 1960, 141.
17 NRO, C/ED 151/1
18 *Norfolk Chronicle*, 6 March 1858.
19 NRO, C/ED 151/1.
20 Elmham School Log-Books, 1. NRO CED/145/1 Acc 2009/72.
21 Ibid.
22 NRO, DN/NDS 239.
23 NRO, MC/534/56/1–18.
24 O. Chadwick, *Victorian Miniature*, 1960.
25 *Lynn News*, 4 August 1866.
26 NRO, C/ED/151/1151/1.
27 Ibid.
28 NRO, MC 762/4 825x1.
29 NRO, PD 210/45.
30 NRO, C/ED/151/1.
31 Ibid.
32 *Norfolk News*, 4 October 1861.
33 *Norfolk Chronicle*, 28 July 1866.
34 *Norfolk News*, 4 May 1867.
35 *Lynn News*, 4 August 1866.
36 *Norfolk News*, 24 August 1867.
37 *Manual of Clerical Work by Various Authors*, 1888, 251.
38 Holkham MS ES/10.
39 Holkham MS ES/1.
40 NRO, C/ED 3/61.
41 Holkham MS ES/9.
42 *Norfolk News*, 2 December 1870.

Seven

Town Life

No branch of the responsibilities of an English clergyman is more important than the duty of regularly, and at their houses, visiting his flock ... he should mingle with them on the most intimate and social terms.[1]

The Revd Benjamin Armstrong would have been a familiar figure in the town. In his dark frock coat, wide-brimmed hat and clerical collar he was to be seen visiting friends such as Mrs Gooch at Hill House and George Carthew in Quebec Street behind the Corn Hall, as well as the many houses of the 'middling sort' near the Market Place and the poor dwelling in the overcrowded yards. Further afield were the small terrace houses of the railway and industrial workers and beyond were the often squalid cottages of Toftwood, Badley Moor and Etling and Dumpling Green, all of which were regularly visited, particularly when their inhabitants were sick. These parishioners would also be encouraged to get infants baptised, children to school and older ones confirmed. There was also business to conduct and shops to be visited in the town. A typical morning was that of 29 April 1857:

> To the Police Station about disorderly conduct of certain people on Sunday – to stone mason about legend to be inserted in St Withburga's crypt, to plumber about some stained glass.

After this he returned home to write a piece for the local paper about the chancel restoration, prepare a testimonial for a young man from the school, which he then delivered, and in addition he gave instructions to the gardener. The next day he was in the town again to see his lawyer, Mr Cooper, about tithe arrangements.

Parish visiting

As well as the church and school, Armstrong listed amongst the duties of a clergyman 'the poor', and this was something he took very seriously. This diligent visiting was something that marked the Victorian clergy off from their perfunctory predecessors, and the involvement of lay (usually female) help was something growing in popularity. The General Society for Promoting of District Visiting was had begun in London in 1828 and by the 1830s lay visiting was recommended in the clergy handbooks. Samuel Best in 1839 encouraged the establishment of properly organised district visiting groups. In this way a 'surveillance could be effected' and 'perfect order established'. The parson need only be called upon in special circumstances.[2] Charles Kemble was so impressed by the value of female visitors in his London parish that he wrote, in his book *Suggestive Hints on Parochial Machinery*, published in 1859, that these visitors diffused 'Christian influence through all classes; presented Christianity under its practical aspect ... effecting a moral improvement in society to edify God's church'. Ideally the visitor would be a married woman 'who knows the world and its trials'.[3]

On his arrival in Dereham, Armstrong therefore divided the parish into twenty-five districts, each with a lay visitor. They met together regularly once a month to provide a list of visits made and report on the sick and any others they thought should be followed up by the vicar. Although their role had charitable rather than religious ends, they were provided with bibles, prayer books and other religious material to distribute. They also had £150 a year between them with which to provide emergency relief. In December 1853 Armstrong set up linen and clothing clubs to be managed by the visitors. Their chairman in the 1850s was Mrs Lee-Warner, whose earlier family links with the non-conformists may well have made her acceptable to the rival religious groups within the town. However, on her death in 1858 a new president was to be elected and Armstrong was chosen by thirteen votes to four. The four were low church people who would have preferred a woman (19/10/58) and within a few weeks a rival Benevolent Society had been set up. The District Society then passed a resolution that only members of the Church of England could be eligible to be a visitor (2/11/58), which resulted in a division in the charitable work within the town. The two societies continued to work separately, with the Benevolent Society supported by the low church and dissenters. In spite of the rivalry, both clubs were thriving into the 1860s (11/11/61).

Armstrong himself was responsible for distributing the money from the weekly offertory. At Christmas there were 400 loaves, provided by the Barnwell and Taylor charities, to be given at church. In 1853 this resulted in the church being crowded the Sunday before Christmas by those seeking bread. In 1854 this caused such confusion that rather than giving them out then and there, Armstrong drove around the whole parish giving loaves where he felt they were most deserved. In the particularly cold winter of 1853/4 he was responsible for organising coal tickets for the poor. In 1859 coal tickets were given to all the cottages in Hoe, 'it being such a small place it seemed the only way to avoid jealousy' (2/2/59). The vicar and churchwardens administered several other minor charities providing clothes and small doles. The Gooch charity, for instance, provided for thirty-six of 'the honest and most demeaned poor'.[4] Over the winter of 1857/8 the churchwardens distributed a total of £153 2s (£153.10) to 365 people in doles varying from 2s 6d (12½p) to 10s (50p).[5] Many of these doles had traditionally been distributed just before Christmas, and this 'as usual brought a large number to church and many who came mainly for the sake of them were much disgusted when told they had previously been given to the poorest and most needy' (20/12/54). By 1858 he felt he had lived in the parish long enough to know which of the 500 applicants for the endowed charities were in greatest need (16/2/58). In July 1864 both the clothing club and school suffered with the failure of the East of England bank. Again in 1870 with the collapse of Harvey's bank the clothing club lost £80. This was soon recouped and an account opened at Gurney's.

Self-help was something to be promoted, and in 1852, with the help of Lord Sondes of North Elmham, Armstrong set up a savings bank in Dereham for those with small sums to invest. In 1859 he chaired a public meeting at the Assembly Rooms concerning the setting up of a penny savings bank. It was well attended, mostly by the 'working classes'. Deposits could be anything between 1d and £1.[6] Mr Hyde, a relation of the sinecure rector and now living in Mrs Wollaston's old house at Moorgate, was also involved (13/10/59). Whether this replaced the earlier bank is not clear.

A vibrant town

Not only did Armstrong visit all his parishioners once a year, but he was involved in many projects for their well-being. Although he initially had qualms over sitting on a committee with dissenters to further the building of a secular Institute and Library, he agreed to chair the meetings and was active in collecting subscriptions to pay for the books. Finally, in July 1853, the Institute was opened with a suitable selection of reading material and 'a good number enrolled'. 'I hope by this means to get some little hold on apprentices, mechanics and those sort of people who are for the most part out of a clergyman's reach.' In November the first lecture was held in the Institute and was attended by 297 people. The somewhat obscure title was 'Physical Science in Relation to the Arts and Conveniences of Life'. Armstrong felt that most of it was 'rather too deep' for the audience, although demonstrations of a hydraulic press and electric telegraph went down well. He flattered himself that his twenty-minute vote of thanks was appreciated more than the lecture (9/11/53). In 1854 he was in London buying books for the Institute library. These included ten volumes of biography, Shakespeare, 'Brand's Popular Antiquities', a history of British India and 'Lectures to a Mechanics' Institute' (26/6/54). In 1855 the 'amiable and respectful' Independent minister, Mr Jefferies, of whom he recorded that he 'regretted from the heart that his departure from the church prevented further intimacy', asked him to give a lecture on his visit to France. The lecture which was illustrated with 'pictures of my own drawing', lasted two hours and was well received by the local paper (31/1/55). Takings from the lecture meant that the Institute's debts were fully paid off. Later he gave a private reading of the lecture at the vicarage to which he invited 'our better sort of parishioners' (9/5/55). Lectures were fortnightly and included a well-attended one by the antiquarian George Carthew on 'The Town We Live In, Its Origins and History' (18/4/55). In 1857 Armstrong spoke again after his Irish trip, and then again after his Scottish tour about his experiences there (21/3/59). The *Norfolk Chronicle*, after its announcement of the lecture commented, 'from the popularity of the vicar as a lecturer a large attendance is to be expected'.[7] In March 1858 a lecture on the missions in India was 'listened to with great attention, and the repeated plaudits of the audience testified to the pleasure they derived from such an eloquent discourse'.[8] One on astronomy by the dissenting minister was described by Armstrong as 'too learned' (21/11/58). A much more popular talk given in the Assembly Rooms was on 'The Dark Side of London' and attracted a large crowd of working men (28/3/59). In 1857 Armstrong took the chair at the Annual Meeting and spoke 'on the need of self-control, the advantages of literature and the necessity of having resource to pleasure within ourselves'. The speech was 'much appreciated, although many of the company dissenters' (30/9/57). A similar lecture was given at the opening of Watton Young Men's Society in 1858 under the title 'What Young Men Owe to Themselves' (20/11/58). It was printed in full in the *Norfolk Herald*. In March 1861 Mr Skeat, the curate, read some of Hood's poems. A clash of dates meant that on 23 February 1861 a lecture on Greece at the Assembly Rooms for the Institute was to be given at the same time as one 'under the presidency of the dissenting minister' at the Corn Hall. As a result the one at the Assembly Rooms was badly attended. The following year support for the Institute was waning and there was only one lecture in 1863, on the parks of London. Disagreements with the dissenters had become so strong that they left and set up their own Mutual Improvement Society with its own lecturers. This did not upset Armstrong. Rather he hoped that the Institute would become 'distinctly Church of England' (28/1/62). The Institute had recovered by 1864 and had a library of over 1,000 volumes 'and a well-supplied newsroom'.[9] By 1867 'Penny Readings' were given fortnightly and the last of the season was well attended, although there were some noisy youths who stamped their feet.[10] At the end of that year Armstrong gave up the presidency.

A slightly different project involved the setting up of a 'parochial and school lending library', many of which were being founded in the county at the time, and for which he was seeking subscriptions in 1856.

Armstrong was also president of the Book Society, a socially elite group which had been founded in 1805 by a previous vicar; as a result the incumbent was always the president and attended the annual dinner.

Concerts of variable quality were given in the town, to which Armstrong occasionally took his children. He was amused by the titles the performers gave themselves, such as 'Professor Martin'. 'Herr Rust' claimed to be of 'Her Majesty's private band', but was in fact 'plain

Bill Rust whose father shoes horses and mother sells cakes and fruit' (8/2/55). In November 1860 the Dereham band gave its first concert and played 'admirably'. However, the choral society was not so popular, and in March 1861 gave its last concert as support for it was 'waning' (23/4/61).

In May 1862 the Dereham Horticultural Society was founded, with Armstrong as vice-president. In June its first exhibition was held in the Corn Hall, which was crowded all day. Lord Sondes sent flowers, peaches and melons. 'Dereham is celebrated for the number of glasshouses, fine gardens and interest taken in gardens' (28/6/62). The following year the exhibition was 'very fine', and Armstrong commented on the flowers and 'prodigious size of the potatoes' (30/9/63). Confusingly, Armstrong described the show of May 1864 as 'the first Dereham Flower Show'. The following year there was a poor display on account of the drought (21/6/65). In 1867 the horticultural show was held in Elmham Park.

Travelling entertainers also visited the town. In June 1861 Bell's circus arrived with acrobats, clowns, performing elephants and lions and Armstrong took his children (15/6/61). In April 1879 Armstrong was upset to hear that the 'mesmeric enchantress' 'Madame Card' was intending to give an entertainment at the Corn Hall on the evening of Good Friday. He wrote a protest to the managers of the hall. Two days later Madame Card and the manager called on Armstrong. Madame Card, 'a fine and masterful woman', was concerned that changing the date to the Monday would reduce the size of the audience but was finally persuaded to do so. Armstrong had no objection to the entertainment in itself and promised to attend (7/4/79). There is no record in his diary of what he thought of the performance.

Whit Sunday was the day of the procession of the Oddfellows Friendly Society. It was quite a sight as they marched with their banners through the town to the church for their annual service. Afterwards Armstrong joined the 300 members for dinner in the Assembly House, 'where everyone sat naturally in their place. The finest grades of superiority being acknowledged in the position of the guests' (29/5/55). After dinner out came the clay pipes.

In 1859, there were fears over the intentions of Napoleon III of France. Plans to build the Suez Canal were seen by Palmerston, now prime minister for the second time, as a threat to British interests in

India, while the building by the French navy of iron-clad ships was seen as a direct threat and a royal commission on national defence was set up. The alarm this raised led to the establishment of a volunteer movement, strongly supported by Queen Victoria and Prince Albert.[11] In June Armstrong attended a meeting at the Corn Hall proposing the formation of a Rifle Volunteer Corps in Dereham. The following year the Dereham Rifle Volunteers were established, with about seventy men and Armstrong as their chaplain. In June 1861 he preached on why military life was not incompatible with religion, an address which was later published. In September 2,000 volunteers from across the county gathered at Holkham. The excitement in Dereham was such that all the shops were closed as almost the entire population of the town filled the trains and flocked to see the event (12/9/61). The Volunteer band of pipes and drums performed regularly and they attended camps, which Armstrong much enjoyed. In September 1863 the annual camp was at Letton Hall, where bands played and local gentry and clergy were present. The 1868 camp was at Hunstanton and lasted six days. There were 500 men and 40 officers, all men from the north of the county, who were entertained to dinner in the Hall. Each corps produced private theatricals in the evening and on the final day there was a 'Grand Review' in the park watched by thousands of spectators (27/6 and 1/7/68). In October the band gave a concert at the Corn Hall. Although much time was spent practising at the rifle butts, the opening of which in May 1867 was an occasion for Armstrong to wear his uniform, there were plenty of other recreational activities for the Volunteers. On 10 January 1867 they presented two theatrical performances in the Corn Hall at which prizes were distributed and 'the bachelors gave a ball'. When the Penny Readings ended for the season in March, there was a musical evening with the Volunteer band, the church choir and amateur singing. However, not all those who attended were of the 'reading class'. There were catcalls from some 'roughs' who had to be 'controlled' (26/3/67). By 1872, however, the band had ceased performing. Armstrong's support for the Volunteers never wavered. He went regularly to their camps, although in later years he did not stay long. There was always an annual church parade. Almost the last entry in his diary is about the officers' dinner in Dereham, to which he did not go because he 'did not feel up to it' (12/5/87).

The wedding of the Prince of Wales in March 1862 provided further excitement. The Dereham Volunteers fired a volley and over 2,000 were fed with roast beef and plum pudding in the Corn Hall and Market Place. Captain Bulwer of Quebec Hall gave two loyal toasts. The sports had to be cancelled because of snow, so 'the pubs filled and respectable families went home' (10/3/62). The deferred sports took place a month later, with 'donkey racing, greasy pole climbing etc. –old English sports' (7/4/62).

One of the biggest events for Dereham in the 1860s was the choice of the town, in July 1862, for the annual county agricultural show. Six triumphal arches were erected about the town and several thousand flags were flying. One banner, put up by a pork butcher, quoted the words of Seneca: 'Land, however fertile, needs farming to be profitable.' The show was held on two fields near the station, one for implements and one for stock. A steam plough demonstrated ploughing four furrows at a time at 4 miles an hour. Three silver cups were presented by the town to be given as prizes. The day was regarded as a holiday in the town and there were more admissions to the show than had been expected. There was a grand dinner attended by 180 leading farmers at which Armstrong sat at high table and gave a speech replying to the toast to the bishop and clergy. In it he recognised that farming had become an 'organised science'. He had been impressed by the steam ploughing demonstration and foresaw that such machines would result in a reduction of labour. Intelligent and skilled men would be needed, not idle and ignorant ones such as those caricatured in *Punch*. 'Let them [the farmers] look well to it that while they filled their barns and increased their stores they did not forget the welfare of their labourers.'[12] Labourers' children should go to school 'to cultivate the mind as well as the soil'. Although his speech was applauded by his farmer audience, they would have taken issue with him as many did not want to see children attending school, thus depriving them of child labour on their farms. The show ended with fireworks in the Market Place. The county show again visited Dereham in 1879, running from 10–11 June, but hardly features in Armstrong's diary. The Duncombes came to stay in order to visit the show on the first day, and on the 11th Armstrong went to the show again with another group of friends and sat in the stand to see the hunters jump, but the event had to be postponed because of the heavy rain.

Dereham society

Society in Dereham, as in most other communities in Victorian England, was strictly divided by class. At the top were the landowners. The Lee-Warners at Quebec Hall on the edge of town were the leading local family. The old squire, who died in London in June 1852, had for many years 'wavered between church and dissent' and had provided much of the finance for building the British (non-conformist) school in the town, but latterly had become a regular church-goer. His widow and family were on friendly visiting terms with the Armstrongs, but may not have been seen frequently at church. Armstrong noted a Sunday in November 1854 when they came to church, thus setting a good example to the townsfolk (30/11/54). Elsewhere he wrote of 'how completely external to the church the mass of the higher classes are'. However, by 1856 Mrs Lee-Warner was a leading light amongst the District Visitors (10/12/56). Miss Lee-Warner, described by Armstrong as 'the young Squireen', was a favourite of his, and made a point of coming into the vestry to tell him of her engagement to Captain Bulwer, a member of the Bulwer family at nearby Heydon. The wedding in July 1855 was a memorable occasion for the town. The church was decorated with wreaths and crammed with people. The schoolchildren lined the path into the church and, headed by Armstrong's two daughters, scattered petals along the way. Shortly after the marriage, the Bulwers took up residence at Quebec Hall.

Armstrong's position in the social hierarchy was certainly improved by the fact of his wife's aristocratic links. This gave him entrée to the landed gentry and the Armstrongs were frequent dinner guests at Quebec Hall, where 'one is sure to meet first-class people' (8/2/54). In December 1853 the guests included the brother of Lord Suffield, the sister of Lord Hastings, Mr Marsham, the squire of Stratton Strawless and the Walsingham branch of the Lee-Warner family. At the beginning of the month the Armstrongs had attended the Assembly in Dereham: 'a very brilliant affair … nothing could exceed the taste in dresses' and 'as we know all the families for miles around, the meeting was pleasant enough' (1/12/53). His description of the Assembly of 10 December 1855 was, however, more caustic: 'It began as it annually does, at an hour when people ought to be going to bed – a perfect haze of gauze, lights, music, colour and artificial flowers.' In spite of this view, he listed the aristocracy present as Lord Sondes and Lord Leicester, and noted with satisfaction that he now knew most of the 'county people'. But the following year he and his wife were 'pleased that a combination of circumstances means that we cannot go to the Assembly this evening' (3/12/56). The Assembly in 1862 was 'not well attended or as brilliant as usual'. However, Helen found plenty of partners and his wife was with her friends, so Armstrong was able to slip away and read quietly by his study fire until they returned at 2 a.m. (4/12/62). The following year numbers at the Assembly were thinned by 'a violent storm bringing down trees' (3/12/63). The year after that, Helen announced that she did not want to go to the Assembly, 'partly because of my disapproval of the aristocratic and worldly set'. He felt they were 'mentally inferior to his intelligent daughters' (8/12/64). Although he frequently complained of the vacuous nature of much of the conversation on society occasions, Armstrong always listed with some pride the titled people he met and with whom he was on friendly and visiting terms. There was admiration of their superior social status. The local gentry, and the junior branches of the aristocracy, were included among the guests invited to the vicarage. The Haggards of Bradenham and the Brampton Gurdons of Letton were frequent guests.

A little further down the social scale were those who 'could not be well asked to dinner' but were in fact 'people of good conversation and intelligence'. Instead they were asked to a 'parochial evening party': 'tea in the garden with music, very pleasant' (17/7/57). 'A children's evening party' in the Christmas season was part of the annual social calendar. It appears that parents as well as children were invited. 'This annual re-union enables us to invite many whom we could not have to dinner and is useful in a parochial as well as social way' (22/1/61).

The most influential groups in Dereham were the tradesmen, both active and retired, described by Armstrong as 'the middle class of parishioners', 'respectable and well off', amongst whom he found 'a liberality of sentiment and purse'. Not all were equally honest. In his wanderings through the shops he spoke to a chemist, probably one of the four mentioned in the 1864 *Directory* with shops in the High Street and Market Place, who showed him a huge box that 'he filled weekly with pills for a travelling quack, who always disposed of his stock in that time. They were made, he said, of soap and other things which could do no harm' (10/5/54). In August 1853 he visited 'some of the middle classes who tend to be overlooked and not so readily coming into our sphere as the peasantry or the rich' (17/8/53). Amongst these were numbered the lawyers and doctors 'who formed the component part of every parson's parties' (14/12/53). Occasionally he enjoyed a cigar with the local doctor, Mr Hastings. There was Mr Barwell, a wine merchant on the Market Place, who was also an artist with a studio in the High Street. Armstrong visited him to see the painting he was completing for the Royal Academy exhibition (12/3/61). In April 1878 Armstrong married Barwell to his partner of twenty years and with whom he had two grown-up children (17/4/78). He was a man of many talents, being a musician and linguist and 'a man of taste' (22/2/79). Sadly, he was also an alcoholic and died as a result. He had been popular in the town and his funeral was well attended by the local tradesmen and professional people (22/2/79). No doubt this group constituted the 'respectable parishioners' who were allowed to walk around the vicarage grounds on a Sunday and attended church in the morning rather than the afternoon (13/4/79). However, even among this group there were divisions. The dispute over the building of the Corn Hall and the following court case divided the town. 'The professionals and traders are fully occupied in squabbling about the Corn Exchange or making money by their business' (24/11/57). Some of the worldly members of the professions saw the poor as 'a race too low for their consideration' (8/1/55). In 1852 Armstrong held an evening party at the end of the year for forty parishioners 'with the aim of promoting peace and good will and unity amongst them … they remained until 3a.m. and were highly pleased'. In January 1854 he and his wife went to a party at Mr Weston's, 'who as a comparative stranger, had unwittingly invited some discordant elements of Dereham society. Happily we are on such good terms with both sides as to be able, with a little tact, to keep things comfortable.' Small-town politics and the fact that everyone knew all there was to know about his neighbour meant there were innumerable rivalries and jealousies. 'No pastor in a town desirous of doing the church's work ought to expect an enviable freedom from trial' (4/9/55).

The coming of the railway to Dereham meant that the 1850s were years of rapid town expansion, with rows of new brick terraces appearing.

20 The railway station, from where Armstrong was a regular passenger, has changed little since it was built in the 1840s. He wrote in 1863, 'what wonderful things railways are and how time and space are annihilated by them'.

As a result, there were now new families to be visited. Here he found those employed by the railway company 'superior' to the agricultural labourers. The railways brought new industries and men Armstrong described as 'artisans', somewhere between labourers and tradesmen. Others, particularly those who worked in the two iron foundries, were 'a coarse and ungodly lot; very different from the aborigines of these parts'. They were not interested in the church and their children were unbaptised: 'They might as well be living in the backwoods of America' (30/5/54). Twenty years later, Armstrong was visiting 'a new quarter of the town recently built' which was occupied by 'strangers, too many of whom are dissenters' (1/7/74).

A group that Armstrong condemned for their meanness was the farmers. A plan to provide piped water and sewage in the town failed because they were not prepared to pay higher rates (21/9/54). Referring to the farmers of Hoe, he wrote, 'The old English farmer is generally ignorant, mean and obstinate.' When describing the churchwarden farmers attending a visitation service in Litcham, he commented on their 'coarse and singularly unintellectual countenances'. Armstrong was probably referring to the small farmers, many of whom were 'little masters who were often worse off than the labourers on a large farm' (16/11/53). In Hoe, however, Armstrong found most of the farmers 'rich', and even they were different from the seventy or so farmers with whom Armstrong took lunch at a ram sale. They were 'of the sort that Norfolk alone can show. Some of them farmed 1,000 acres and they were intelligent and advanced men' (25/8/58). In this category was the progressive Mr Hudson of Castle Acre, whom Armstrong met on a train to Norwich. After he had left the train at Wymondham to go shooting, Armstrong's fellow passenger, another 'princely Yeoman', explained Hudson's background. He had begun as a postilion and had managed to save £100 a year. He then married a wealthy widow, 'by whom he had access to a fortune', which allowed him to take on a large farm at Castle Acre. 'Though still an ignorant man, he is worth £100,000!' (19/12/56).

At the bottom of the social scale were 'the poor', whom Armstrong barely understood but regularly visited as part of his pastoral duties. His annual visitation began after Michaelmas and took until Christmas. He found the poor apathetic and reserved: 'They seem all alike.' His lack of understanding is illustrated by a diary entry for November 1854 following mention of his sermon praising the ability of the poor to 'make do and mend': 'It is astonishing how the poor contrive to live' (26/11/54). He was struck by the amount of insanity to be found amongst them and thought the solution should be the provision of 'more amusements to relieve the monotony of toil', but went on to write, 'We cannot wonder at the poor being heavy and dull when their superiors are not much better' (7/12/53). This opinion was strengthened when he was asked to write a letter by a poor woman to her grandson in Australia. She could think 'of nothing to say although she had not seen him for years – an instance of the undemonstrable stolidity of the poor' (1/4/68).

Augustus Jessopp shared this view of the poor. He also described them as having a 'dullness that seems to steep their lives in a leaden hue'. They 'have not much love to give, they are suspicious of others' motives, the men have a certain shame in expressing admiration and they have a large fund of sullen hatred'.[13] Armstrong described 'a sad case' of a type he frequently had to deal with. He had a request from an employer that a servant 'with child' should be taken back by her family. However, her father was already living with another daughter who was 'kept by a merchant of the town' and so had no room (27/2/61). Of his visitations to the poor in 1861 he noted that cleanliness was improving, but that there was no decrease in illegitimacy: 'the girls see nothing sinful and mothers apparently conniving' (2/11/61). In February 1864 he visited a dying young woman on Etling Green, 'the victim of field work – a disgrace to this country' (6/2/64).

His visits were sometimes enlivened by meeting 'unusual' people. In November 1861 he described meeting a very poor 'pious old Baptist local preacher'. He was a teetotaller, very poor and lived alone with his Bible for company. 'Gave him a trifle' (11/11/61). Later he encountered a 'little schoolmaster', well educated, with a good knowledge of Latin and Greek, 'probably a Baptist – an extraordinary person and a change from the ordinary, undemonstrative people one meets in the course of a parish visitation' (7/2/64).

In his diary Armstrong described examples of the elderly living in shacks, and destitute, abandoned wives, often with disabled children, whom he praised for their fortitude and 'contentment' in the face of misfortune: 'these instances are the true triumph of the cross of Christ' (1/9/53). At Etling Green there were dirty and dilapidated cottages where typhus was present: 'The landlord, being poor and ignorant, unlikely to do anything' (22/8/54). Armstrong was frequently struck by the contrast between the exterior and interior of the cottages he visited. While the gardens were full of flowers, inside was misery. In one instance there was a dying man in a 'close upper room', a child with a broken arm and a recent bride in great distress because her husband had joined the army and gone to war in the Crimea' (28/7/54). While most of the poorest cottages were to be found in the outlying hamlets such as Etling Green, some of the worst conditions were near the church, where some of the poor now lived 'consequent on the pulling down' (for the building of the Corn Hall?) 'of their previous places of abode'.

In December 1853 he drew up a list of forty families of 'aged and deserving poor' who would be eligible for soup from the vicarage soup kitchen 'at periods during the winter'. The winter of 1853/4 was particularly severe and Armstrong could 'think of nothing but the privations of the poor'. A thin harvest, the fear of war and the weather meant that provisions were scarce and expensive. Prices were still high in 1855 and the vicarage soup kitchen again operated through the winter. In the winter of 1860 there was a weekly soup kitchen for forty 'as usual'. In January 1856 Armstrong was distributing meat tickets to all the families on Etling Green, leaving his 12-year-old daughter to teach a class at the school (28/1/56). A meeting in January 1861 discussed whether any steps should be taken to 'alleviate the prevailing distress', but it was agreed that the available charity money was enough for the time being (23/1/61). Although there were no mentions of the vicarage soup kitchen after the 1860s, extra coal and meat tickets were issued in the bitterly cold winter of 1878/9 and Armstrong feared for the welfare of the poor. In December 1879, in deep snow, he was taking coal and bread tickets in his sledge to the outlying cottages 'too far for District Visitors to reach' (13/12/78).

He was describing the class-ridden society in which he lived and in which it was the duty of those who were better off to support those at the bottom of the pile through individual charity. The suggestion that there was anything wrong with a society that allowed such poverty to exist would have been alien to him.

Town governance

There was one area where some central control was needed and that was public health. On 8 October, the Dereham Health Board ('which I was instrumental in forming') met for the first time. The members were divided into three groups to inspect the town. 'I was astonished in this, one of the prettiest and cleanest towns in England, to find such fearful nuisances at the <u>back</u> of some of the houses. Attempts at pig and cow keeping in a town must be injurious and added to the defective <u>surface</u> drainage must be pestiferous' (8/10/53). A year later the Board of Health called a Vestry meeting to consider the installing of a drainage system and piped water. The attendance was so large that the meeting had to be moved to the Assembly Rooms, but there was no agreement. The farmers who lived outside the town, and therefore would not benefit, refused to pay the increased rates necessary.

The real water-borne cause of cholera was still not understood. The debate was over whether it was something in the air or in noxious vapours from the earth. Armstrong was made chairman of a new Sanitary Committee set up following the Nuisance Removal Amendment Act of 1855 specifically aimed at overcrowded housing and the regulation of industries such as tanneries and gasworks (opened in Dereham in 1836) which emitted noxious effluent and fumes.

Armstrong also interested himself in the movement to build a corn hall. The first meeting was in November 1853 and at a Vestry meeting in December it was agreed that the Shambles (individual butchers' stalls) beside the Market Place should be pulled down to make way for the hall. However, things did not go smoothly as two rival companies were involved. One scheme blocked the existing thoroughfare, but provided a better alternative one. The five or six owners of the butchers' stalls had to be bought out, together with the ground occupied by the porch of the Red Lion Inn and further pieces along the Market Place. A permit to build was obtained by the Corn Hall Company supported by many in the farming interest and included Lord Sondes of North Elmham, the Earl of Leicester of Holkham, Lord Hastings of Melton Constable and Lord Suffield of Gunton. A second company (the Corn Market Company) took the first to court over blocking a public right of way. 'Wine, horses and women are all sinful ways of spending money, but

NEW CORN-HALL, EAST DEREHAM.

21　Dereham Corn Hall, opened in 1856, following a great deal of controversy.

"law" the most foolish of them all' (1/7/56). Meanwhile, the impressive building, with its classical façade topped by a statue of the agricultural improver Thomas William Coke, was completed at the end of 1856 at a cost of £1,800, and in January 1857, it was officially opened for business with fifty semi-circular merchant's stands. On 11 February at 5 p.m. there was an inaugural dinner attended by 250 guests. Lord Sondes took the chair and the event was attended by Lord Leicester and other members of the aristocracy, as well as the Lord Lieutenant, the Mayor and Sheriff of Norwich and four local MPs. Armstrong said grace and returned thanks on behalf of the bishop and clergy, declaring that the Corn Hall would be a great improvement for the town. He stressed the identity of farming and ecclesiastical interests and appealed to farmers to help the clergy in their efforts to improve the physical, moral, spiritual and intellectual good of the labouring classes. 'I hope the time is fast disappearing when the labouring man will not be looked upon as so much blood and muscle out of whom it is necessary to squeeze a certain amount of work.' He spoke of the need to improve the moral and physical condition of the labourer and praised a farmer he had met who was taking his men to Lowestoft for a day as a way of creating good relations.[14] Afterwards one of the MPs told him he had made a 'darned good speech'. However, Armstrong was not taken in by this flattery and thought the MP was merely after his vote. The evening ended at 10 p.m. In the background the Corn Hall law case was rumbling on and dividing the town. The case finally went to court later in the year and half the town were called as witnesses for one side or the other, 'stirring up the mud in our little tea cup' (22/7/57). The row even affected the election of churchwardens at the Vestry meeting in April 1858. Mr Drake 'has suffered his partisanship over the Corn Hall to obstruct church work' and as a result Carthew and Hyde (of Moorgate) were elected and Drake lost his position. The town dinner in May of 1858 was ill-attended because the argument was still dividing the town, but finally in June news came that the case had been settled (2/6/58). It was agreed that a public right of way had been blocked, but that the alternative provided was an improvement on the old one and so the Corn Hall would not be pulled down. The church bells were rung, much to the annoyance of Armstrong, who did not want to be seen as taking sides in the argument.[15]

A topic that was bound to arouse a great deal of interest in the town was the closure of the churchyard for burials and the establishment of a town cemetery. The discussion took place at a Vestry meeting in 1868 which was held, not as was usual in the church, but instead in the Assembly Rooms again because of the large numbers expected, 'which saved our beautiful chancel from the profanation of puritans and free thinkers with their hats on' (3/3/68). A Burial Board of nine was set up, five of whom were members of the Church of England and four dissenters. To Armstrong's pleasure, the board members worked well together. There were to be two chapels in the cemetery, one for the Church of England and the other for dissenters, and the plans presented by the Norwich architect John Browne were accepted unanimously by the Board in January 1869 – 'a very beautiful design' (21/1/69). In December 1869 the new burial ground was consecrated by the bishop.

As there was no one equivalent to a resident squire in Dereham, Armstrong was often called upon to mediate in local disputes. For two nights in December 1855 there were no street lights because of an argument with the gas company. This he resolved, pending a meeting arranged for five days later which he chaired, when an extension of the street lighting was agreed (17/12/55). Further extensions were agreed in January 1857, when there was also a meeting to discuss the straightening of the road to Quebec Hall, something objected to by Armstrong, who enjoyed walking along the curving lane shaded by trees (1/1/57).

In May 1875 he attended a meeting to fix the names of streets in the town. He was concerned that both St Withburga and St Nicholas should be recognised. A lane near the church became St Withburga's Lane, while the patron saint of the church was acknowledged in a small terrace of new housing off Theatre Street.

Although there were many aspects of town and public life in which Armstrong was involved, he felt that the role of a magistrate was not compatible with the duties of a clergyman. The rector of Watton came in for particular criticism: he spent all his time as a magistrate or playing cricket (25/9/54). Most of the clergy magistrates were drawn from the gentry class. Forty-one of them lived in houses grand enough to be classed as 'seats' in White's *Directory*. Nine of them were also Deputy Lieutenants. Although many of the names are those associated with county families, parsons were often appointed in areas where there

22   Designed by John Brown in 1869, this ornate archway linked the two chapels, one for members of the Church of England and one for dissenters, at the new Dereham cemetery.

were no resident gentry.[16] In 1837 31.5 per cent of Norfolk magistrates were drawn from the clergy, but by 1883 the percentage had dropped to 17.2, indicating a decline in their influence on the Bench.[17] By 1916 there were only nine clergy magistrates and these included well-known county names such as Fellowes, Ffolkes and Lee-Warner.[18]

Much of a magistrate's work was mundane and Armstrong felt it a waste of clerical time. In 1854 he had to attend a court on the question of the ownership of a drain on the glebe.

> Two of the magistrates, well known to me, were clergymen. I could not help thinking they had mistaken their vocation. They were not distinguished by any clerical dress and here they were discussing sewers with the keenest and liveliest interest while one of them has a large parish with no school and the other two with only one Sunday service in each although having a curate! (12/10/54)

The duties of the magistrates ranged far beyond sewers; before the County Council Act of 1888 they were responsible for much of the county's administration. Their major task, however, was the enforcing of law and order and meting out justice. In June 1851, John MacKenzie, a ropemaker from Edinburgh, was found guilty of stealing an umbrella from Armstrong and three pairs of boots from the Revd Joseph Thompson at his Guildhall school.[19]

Armstrong had a low opinion of magistrates in general. Having visited the jail at Swaffham he was horrified by the cells for solitary confinement, one of which was completely dark. 'To me it seems very incongruous that such eccentric and ill-informed men as some of the county magistrates are, should have the power of sentencing prisoners to such an awful penalty as solitary confinement' (5/10/74). The Colkirk-born Cambridge scholar William Heitland commented that clergy magistrates were often the most harsh, contributing to a 'sullen discontent' towards the church.[20]

It was in the magistrates' court that the clergy encountered 'the gritty secular world of the labouring poor' and in some it awakened a social conscience. Significant is the Assize Sermon preached in 1876 by the Revd Henry Ffolkes, himself from a gentry family, in which he suggested that there might be a link between crime and poverty, and that this should be taken into account by magistrates.[21] Whilst this may have awakened some sort of sympathy, the clergy were as harsh as their fellow magistrates in the enforcement of the game laws.

Beyond Dereham

National events did occasionally impinge on Dereham. The declaration of war against Russia in the Crimea in October 1853 meant that there were preparations for hostilities in the town and news arrived that troop ships had reached the Black Sea. At the end of March 1854 the militia paraded in the Market Place. In October of the same year news of the battles of Sebastopol and Alma reached the town and Armstrong recorded that there were many Norfolk officers killed 'and county families plunged into grief' (12/10/54). News of Balaclava, with its 'great slaughter', reached Dereham on 20 November. In the following months he was busy collecting for Lord Sondes' Patriotic Fund to help widows and orphans of dead soldiers. News from the Crimea continued to be bad. In February 1855 Armstrong recorded:

> Affairs in the Crimea are wretched! The government at home is broken up and reconstructed ... The Duke of Newcastle, Lord Aberdeen and Lord John Russell retire from the cabinet. It is on this trio that the popular voice visits all the disgrace of the war. At Sebastopol our men die at the rate of hundreds per diem; through disease, exhaustion and neglect ... they are more like Eskimos in their wigwams than the fine soldiers of our army. (7/2/55)

Later in the month he quotes in full a soldier's letter sent home to one of his parishioners describing the slaughter at Alma and conditions at Sebastopol and expressing the view that the war would be a long one. In March his servant, Ray, who had been with him since Little Stanmore days, enlisted. Armstrong felt it his duty to support him in this, although he had grave doubts about the management of the war.

Finally, on 30 April 1856, the war came to an end and the church bells were rung. On the fourth of May there was a thanksgiving service in the church, which was poorly attended, something that did not surprise Armstrong, there being little enthusiasm for such 'national occasions'.

23 This photograph of Dereham Market Place shows the celebrations for the queen's golden jubilee in 1887. The scene must have been very similar to the festivities at the end of the Crimean War thirty years before.

Armstrong was critical of the modern 'trashy' words provided by the archbishop for the thanksgiving service, which he did not receive in time to practise. Some felt that the army was now much better organised and equipped and that it was a pity to have made peace. 'Such people can hardly be aware what miseries attend this scourge [of war], both at the scene of action and also at home.' For instance. at the height of the siege of Sebastopol, 3,000 Russians were said to be dying daily. 'Another year's war would have made thousands and tens of thousands of wives widows and children fatherless <u>and for what?</u> To prop up an infidel, imbecile and used-up Empire' (4/5/56). A second day set aside for celebrations, 29 May, with a church service followed by a schools' parade with a band, then 600 sat down for a tea in the Market Place, after which there were games and 'dancing on the moor'. 'I consider dancing should be encouraged amongst the lower orders as a polite and humanising exercise' (29/5/56). The evening ended with a firework display. The firework display in London had a rather unfortunate consequence for Armstrong's friend Mary Hales, who was staying there at the time. She was knocked unconscious by a rocket stick and was only revived with the help of 'galvanism' (electric shock treatment) (6/6/56).

To Armstrong's relief Ray did return safely and called at the vicarage while one of the Challice nephews was staying:

> My old servant, Ray, returning from the Crimea, my little nephew informing me in my dressing room that a soldier in the kitchen had been seen to kiss the cook. It was but a sisterly gesture as all the women kissed him when he left. ... He wore his Sebastopol medal and was quite the lion all day.... He seems much improved by the various scenes of life he has gone through and says the army, though glad of the peace, would have liked a finishing tussle with the Russians this summer. (15/8/56)

The following year news of the Indian Mutiny reached Dereham and shocked Armstrong. A service in aid of a fund to help the sufferers in October 1857 raised £20, more than given to any other charitable collection.

In 1862 the town was moved by the news of the closure of all the cotton mills in Lancashire, caused by the interruption in the supply of cotton from America because of the Civil War. A meeting to provide support for the factory workers was organised and £250 was raised, partly as a result of Armstrong's house-to-house collecting (1/12/62). The Franco-Prussian war, the defeat of France, the deposition of Napoleon III and the following chaos in Paris in 1870 shocked Armstrong and Dereham society. The ladies were busy making bandages for soldiers.

In 1873 there was more excitement in the town over the election of the two churchwardens than over that for the Member of Parliament. Traditionally, there were two wardens, one the vicar's and the other the people's warden, and all ratepayers had the right to vote. Armstrong always dreaded Vestry meetings and the election of the people's warden, but usually managed to manipulate things in his favour. While Armstrong's friend George Carthew remained as vicar's warden, it was the election of the people's warden that caused all the interest as it became a clash of interests between dissent and the low church and Armstrong's high church views. In the end it was Armstrong's friend and supporter, Mr Everington of Dillington Hall, rather than the 'low church radical', Thomas Gidney, the ironmonger on the Market Place, who was elected. He replaced Mr Hyde of Moorgate, who 'had always worked against me' (14/4/73). Later in the year Mr Hyde died. Armstrong conceded that he 'had done some good in the parish', but 'was a dictatorial character'. His 'great energy and capacity for business meant he was respected rather than loved' (13/5/73).

Despite continuing to play a leading role in the town's affairs, Armstrong was not universally popular. Although he claimed in his diary that the low church members of his congregation were gradually coming around to his way of thinking, there were still those dissenters who remained antagonistic, as the breakaway Benevolent and Mutual Improvement societies showed.

The 1870s saw the rise of Joseph Arch's union (see p. xx) and with it vocal radicalism. The year 1874 saw even greater trouble, fermented, according to Armstrong, by union members, at 'the most rowdy and uproarious meeting ever assembled in Dereham'. The question was the enclosure of Rush Meadow, which had recently been common ground where the poor could collect fuel and graze horses. The trustees (the vicar and churchwardens) proposed letting the wettest part to a London grower of watercress for £40 a year, the income to be used for coals for the poor. The withdrawal of commoning rights led to an outcry from the poor, especially those who had taken advantage of the grazing. 'We found the room [St Nicholas Hall] full of roughs and the chair taken by an active dissenter [Joseph Warren] who was perfectly incapable of keeping order.' When the meeting broke up, Armstrong retreated from the mob to the Reading Room, from where he managed to get safely home (18/3/74). Mr Everington, who was regarded with suspicion as he was suspected of wanting the land for himself, drove through the town as the meeting broke up. His horses were frightened and it took some time before they could be controlled. Both the *Norfolk Chronicle* and the radical *Norfolk News* reported that very few of those at the meeting were commoners and when those with a grievance were called forward, no one responded. The general hub-bub meant that neither George Carthew as churchwarden nor Armstrong could get a hearing, 'the interruptions and noise being worse than ever before heard in Dereham'. When the motion was put, the letting of the meadow was unanimously defeated.[22]

The 1870s and 1880s were to see many changes in Dereham as its industries developed, the population rose and new social attitudes emerged, sometimes questioning the established order. All of these developments were to play a role the later years of Armstrong's ministry.

Notes

1   *Manual of Clerical Work by Various Writers*, 1888, 127.
2   A. Russell, *The Clerical Profession*, 1980, 119–20; Samuel Best, *Parochial Ministrations*, 1839, 95.
3   Quoted in B. Turner, *The Victorian Parson*, 2015, 137.
4   NRO, PD86/146.
5   NRO, PD86/89.
6   *Norfolk News*, 29 October 1859.
7   *Norfolk Chronicle*, 12 March 1859.
8   *Norfolk Chronicle*, 6 March 1858.
9   W. White, *Norfolk Directory*, 1864, 934.
10   *Norfolk Chronicle*, 23 November 1867.
11   L. Woodward, *The Age of Reform 1815–1870*, 1962, 178.
12   *Norfolk Chronicle*, 12 July 1862.
13   N. Hartley, *Augustus Jessopp, Norfolk's Antiquary*, 2017, 208.
14   *Norfolk Chronicle*, 14 February 1857.
15   N. Boston and E. Puddy, *Dereham: The Biography of a Country Town*, 1962, 85–8.

16 R. Lee, *Rural Society and the Anglican Clergy, 1815–1914: Encountering and Managing the Poor*, 2006, 105.

17 Ibid., 107.

18 *Kelly's Cambridgeshire, Norfolk and Suffolk Directory*, 1916, 15–17.

19 *Norfolk Chronicle*, 21 July 1851.

20 W.E. Heitland, *After Many Years*, 1927, 22.

21 Lee 2006, 105.

22 *Norfolk Chronicle*, 21 March 1874; *Norfolk News*, 24 March 1874.

III

Family and Friends

Eight

Family Life

I verily believe that few lives have been so even and uneventful and therefore so uniformly happy as mine. (1/1/63)

Armstrong moved to Dereham in early October 1850 with Nellie, and his two daughters, Helen, aged 6, and Louise (Lilly), aged 2. Within a few weeks his first son, John, was born. A further son, Herbert (Bertie), in 1853, and daughter, Gertrude, in 1855, were to follow. As a thanksgiving for the safe birth of his son, he presented a Bible to the church to be placed on the eagle lectern. While he was dedicated to his parish work, Armstrong was also a family man; he had felt isolated from his relations when at Crowle. Dereham was somewhat nearer, being 100 miles from London, and the developing rail network made family visits much easier. He was particularly close to his father, whose opinion he always valued, and they exchanged weekly letters. In 1853, he felt that as his high church practices were becoming accepted in Dereham, he was in a strong enough position to introduce daily services in Lent and carry on with them thereafter. However, before embarking on this innovation, he was anxious to have his father's approval and wrote to ask his opinion. His reply was very diplomatic, saying that his son should do what he felt was right, but also that he should proceed with caution, partly because of all the extra commitment he was letting himself in for. When he was sorting his father's papers after his death, Armstrong found that all his letters to his father had been carefully saved. Sadly, they do not now survive.

In May of the year following the move to Dereham, his parents came to stay and were pleased with all they saw. This may have been the first time that they met their grandson and Armstrong's pride in the boy was partly due to the pleasure he knew an Armstrong heir would give his father. The next month he stayed with them in Southall and went up to London to see the Great Exhibition. In November he went to see his parents' new home in Wimpole Street, and to see the lying-in-state of the Duke of Wellington and watch the funeral procession. In March he went back to Crowle to see his brother-in-law, William Duncombe, now installed there in his place. This journey had to be undertaken by road, and while the route was across the flat fens, the wonderful spires of the fen churches, the cathedrals of Ely, Lincoln and Peterborough and the monastic ruins of Crowland and Kirkstead created interest. At Crowle he found William well settled in his own parish.

Family holidays

All his life Armstrong enjoyed travel. In many ways a Londoner at heart, visits to his parents and his wife's family at Lagley were a relief from the 'monotony of toil' and small-town life. After the Easter services in 1852 Armstrong took his family to London to stay with his parents while building work was undertaken at the vicarage. They were away for a month, during which they went with his sister's children to see the sights of London. There were trips to Canons Park to visit Lady Plumer, described by him on her death in 1857 as 'a kind friend' and 'an excellent remnant of the old school of George III' (27/11/57). At his old parish of Little Stanmore he was greeted with enthusiasm, but he was disappointed to see that his successor had not 'given much time to the work of the ministry' and numbers in the school and attending church had decreased. He also returned to visit old friends at Harrow and worshipped at various London churches. He spent time in Oxford with his father exploring the colleges, and back in London there was the exhibition at the Royal Academy to see. While at Southall they visited the Duncombe family at Lagley. Nellie's father had been a cause for concern, but was now recovered and so 'happiness and peace' returned. There was also time for fishing with his brother-in-law. Armstrong preached several sermons while away and kept in touch with affairs in Dereham. The round of visits over, the family returned home to their enlarged vicarage and in time for the opening of the restored chancel on Whit Sunday.

These month-long visits to London between Easter and Whitsun with the family became an almost annual event. Time was spent both in London and Lagley. There were plenty of visits within London, 'our nurse being a country girl had never seen London before' (24/5/53). Dinner parties at his parents' with their London business friends, where the conversation was all of 'mines, railways, and other money-making projects', did not interest him; the Royal Academy and the opera were much more to his taste. A performance of *Judas Maccabeus* at the Crystal Palace was 'most impressive'. And a visit to London was never complete without a trip to the baths – 'a cheap luxury'. Ten years later the need for a hurried visit to Dereham saw him catching a train in London at 8 a.m. and arriving in Dereham at 3p.m.: 'It is only by such practical examples that we understand what wonderful things railways are and how time and space are annihilated by them' (19/5/63). Thanks to the railways and improved passenger ferries, Armstrong and his father spent a few days in Boulogne in 1853.

Later that year the Duncombe family from Crowle came to Dereham to stay for a month and again there were plenty of outings, as well as some quiet days fishing with William. On one such day at Castle Acre, 'during our hedgerow dinner in sight of the church and ruined castle, we fell into conversation with a gingerbread maker on his way to Harpley Fair. He told us he had no home beyond his cart and baked his nuts in the bakers' offices in the various towns he went through' (22/7/53). William did his share of preaching while in Dereham and Hoe and a pleasant time was had by all.

The 1854 London visit was overshadowed by news of the lack of progress in the war in the Crimea and of the lengthening casualty lists. There were 'an unusual number of black armbands'. He took his elder daughter to see the queen and the state opening of Parliament and went with his father to the Haymarket theatre to see the dancing Spanish girls. 'Alas, alas, how sad it is that so much that is beautiful should be closely allied with sin.' A late-night party resulted in them all being very 'seedy' the next morning (12/6/54).

As the children grew older, there were more attractions to be visited in and around the capital. Windsor Castle, with the royal stables, was a favourite with the children, who were fascinated by the miniature ponies ridden by the royal children. Kew Gardens, Hampton Court and the Tower of London were all included. There were circuses where trapeze artists 'flew like a bird', pantomimes and a tightrope walker at the Crystal Palace, now moved to Sydenham: 'the dreamy delicious feel that comes over one in the fairy scene' (15/7/60). There were several visits to the international exhibition at Sydenham, which Armstrong thought was not as impressive as the Great Exhibition of 1851 for which the palace had originally been built. Armstrong's interest in art meant that the Royal Academy exhibition was never missed, and in 1860 he noticed that a portrait of Mrs Collinson of Bilney was exhibited (3/7/60).

In May 1857 Armstrong took Helen to London for ten days. His sister, Annie, was also staying with his parents, and he found her looking very ill. By this date the financial affairs of her husband, Dr John Challice, were causing worry and domestic troubles. Annie had become a popular novelist in her own right and was recovering from the strain of finishing her latest book, *The Sisters of Charity*.[1] Whilst in the capital he went to hear Gordon Cumming, a noted big-game hunter, whose trophies had been displayed at the Great Exhibition of 1851. Although by 1857 it was nine years since he had been in Africa, he continued to capitalise on his adventures by putting on displays.[2]

> The room was surrounded by the most wonderful horns and skins of every animal inhabiting South Africa and the hunter who is in Scotch costume and stands between two elephant tusks, explains his sport by means of very good panoramic pictures. Fourteen elephants, a few lions and shoals of buffalo and antelope are an ordinary fortnight's spoil, to say nothing of rhinoceros.

Armstrong was not impressed by the native dancers and musicians who formed the second part of the evening's entertainment.

> More degrading specimens of mortality I never beheld – their guttural noise, shrieks, yells and maniac movements being painful to behold ... scarcely superior to the beasts that perish. The exhibition was very instructive. (16/4/57)

As well as the London visits, there were also trips to the seaside with the family. Yarmouth he regarded as 'a coarse, rough place' and preferred Lowestoft, 'decidedly the best East Anglian watering place' (5/10/69).

'A seaside life is a lazy one – reading, smoking, sketching, bathing and the like.' Needless to say, Armstrong also found time to write a few sermons (4/10/54). In spite of his dislike of the place, in the summer of 1856 he took the family to Yarmouth for a fortnight. The house needed decorating, the children were recovering from whooping cough and Nellie had not been well and needed a change. Armstrong liked to keep moving and seeing new things, so it was not his idea of a holiday, though the children and Nellie enjoyed it. He was prepared to admit that the Winter Garden had a 'semblance of good taste, but vulgarity reigned supreme'. Probably the highlight for him was preaching in the church to a congregation of 3,000 (20/7/56). The following year he took his wife and children to Yarmouth and then came home, 'pressure of work and my conscience forbidding me to go'. Instead of holidaying he intended 'putting his bachelor existence to good use' (22/6/57). In 1862 they spent nearly a week in Yarmouth, but this time his wife did not enjoy socialising. Armstrong himself was most impressed by the sight of 'the thousands of people pouring out of different places of worship and promenading' (20/8/62).

There were, however, times when a quiet day out with his family was what Armstrong enjoyed. 'What is so delightful as vagabonding? You take your wife and child, a telescope and a country map in your phaeton, start where you please and return when you please. To a lover of the picturesque and the man of independent feeling, this is exquisite' (31/8/52). In this way they went to Cromer, returning the following day. A few years later he took a day off to drive the family to neighbouring Bawdeswell: 'not a feature of the landscape escaped me on this glorious day' (16/4/55).

One of the activities Armstrong enjoyed with his father was their travels together and sharing the new experiences which went with it. This taste for travel dated back to his visits to the Channel Islands and France as a child. With his father he went on a continental tour after he left Cambridge and later there were visits to the north of England, France, Germany and a Cook's tour to Ireland and North Wales.

In the autumn of 1856, they took an extended trip to Ireland, this time to see Armstrong's friend who was now Dean Bull with responsibility for Carrickfergus and surrounding villages. The journey by rail to Fleetwood, 'an unfinished kind of watering place', took them through the 'endless factories of the industrial districts', which he found very depressing. From Fleetwood they took a ferry to Belfast, where he was horrified by the poverty and ragged condition of the people. From there they travelled to Carrickfergus by train and were impressed by the beautiful scenery, the fine estates either side, as well as Dean Bull's house and the local scenery. In their wanderings in the area they were only too acutely aware of the deprivation resulting from the potato famine of only ten tears before. Their travels took them to a farmhouse 'where two splendid Irish girls were making triangular cakes, brushing the flour off with a goose's wing and baking them on a plate suspended over a fire. Their mother was sitting moodily be the fire, evidently in decline' (1/10/56). Armstrong was shocked by the lack of 'church work', the 'main thing being to hate the Pope and enjoy yourself'. The dean's establishment and estate were very impressive, 'large enough for a man of £10,000 a year'. His time seemed to be mainly spent in social visits, field sports and entertainment. Armstrong and his father enjoyed meeting Irish society, as well as walks in the hills, through the woods and by the sea, where they saw large numbers of sea birds. While there Armstrong preached several sermons and helped take services in what seemed to him very 'puritanical' churches. There was also a visit to the Giant's Causeway which involved a hazardous journey and several changes of vehicle to get there. After a fortnight they returned to Belfast, noting the 'palatial palaces of the mill owners who might be seen in elegant equipages or on well-bred Irish nags returning from "business" for dinner'. The return ferry was miserable because of the storms and they were relieved to see the buildings of Liverpool come into view. Together they travelled on to Crewe, where Armstrong's father left to travel to London and Armstrong to Peterborough and then Dereham, where he 'embraced his dearest wife and children almost resolved never to leave them again'. 'One of the many delights of travel is making us more pleased than ever with our lot at home' (19/1/56). A week later, 'while dining with gentry on iced champagne and hot house grapes my thoughts reverted to Alice Semple making the oatcake by the loch and the coarse food of Ballycarry. What a responsibility does wealth entail!' (21/10/56).

Armstrong was very much a Francophile, taking a great interest in French affairs. He was an admirer of Emperor Napoleon III and was as horrified as others by the defeat of France in the Franco-Prussian war of 1870. On his visits to France he admired the architecture, stained-glass windows and decoration of the French churches and the fact that they were kept unlocked, unlike English churches at the time.

When he first arrived in Dereham Armstrong went through the burial register and was intrigued to find an entry for 1799 referring to Jean De Narde, a French prisoner of war who along with others had been held overnight in the bell tower of the church. He attempted to escape and was caught along the road near Scarning, and when he refused to surrender was shot and killed. He was buried in a 'remote corner' of Dereham churchyard. Armstrong's real empathy with the French is shown by his concern over the young Frenchman and desire to locate and mark the site of the grave with a memorial. It was several years before he carried out his wishes, but for ten days in September 1857 he acted as guide and interpreter to two friends, Mr Cooper and the Revd William Wollaston, and his father on a ten-day trip to Paris. They saw all the sights and particularly enjoyed the botanic gardens. Together they must have discussed the idea of a monument to De Narde, because the following year the *Norfolk Chronicle* reported in March that the 'vicar and two other gentlemen' were responsible for putting up the gravestone.[3] In fact it had been erected on 18 February and on the 22nd Armstrong wrote to the curé of St-Malo, where De Narde's father had been a notary, to report that the cross had been erected, saying that the parishioners were ashamed of the manner of the young soldier's death, and to ask that any relations could be informed. He ended with the hope that the alliance between the two countries would be long lasting (22/2/68), all of which went well beyond the call of duty, but instead shows a genuine horror over the war with France hardly more than a generation before.

As the years went by, his devotion and anxious concern for his family continued to be reflected in his diary. On his tenth wedding anniversary he wrote that they had been years of 'undiluted happiness'. Elsewhere in his journal he mentions the occasional disagreements between himself and his wife when relations with her family were at a low ebb. The reasons for these cooling of relations with the Duncombes are unclear, but probably date back to the fact that Nellie's father refused to contribute to buying the Little Stanmore living for his son-in-law. After

In Memory of
JEAN DE NARDE
SON OF A NOTARY PUBLIC
OF ST MALO
A FRENCH PRISONER OF WAR
WHO HAVING ESCAPED
FROM THE BELL TOWER
OF THIS CHURCH
WAS PURSUED AND SHOT
BY A SOLDIER ON DUTY
OCT. 6TH 1799
AGED 28 YEARS

HUBBARD   DEREHAM

24   De Narde gravestone, erected in 1868 by Armstrong.

the death of his father-in-law in 1856 there were further unpleasant exchanges over the will and the portion due to Nellie which continued to rumble on up to 1870.

Armstrong's children

His deep-seated affection and anxiety for his children is shown when he records in February 1853 his feelings when the 9-year-old Helen went away for the first time with a family friend to stay in Wroxham for a fortnight. 'The feelings elicited were new and strange' as they waved goodbye to the child and her companion (28/2/53). Armstrong always hated partings and was always depressed when his parents went back to London. On one occasion his feelings on their departure were so acute that he wrote, 'were it not for my anxiety about my sweet children, how gladly, notwithstanding my many blessings would I flee away to be at rest'. 'In Heaven there will be no more parting.' He complained of a 'frail constitution' and reflected that 'If I had heavier trials, perhaps I would be less sensitive to lesser ones' (18/9/54).

In September of the same year he gave a detailed description of the children at that time. Helen, always to be his favourite, was 9, 'tall and amiable', Louisa was 5, 'a little rosy fat thing with beautiful eyes', 'not quite so amiable', but still 'a dear little thing', Johnny was 3 'and a little spoilt', but intelligent and with a winning way of speaking, while little Herbert was 14 months old and 'the flower of the flock'. The following January there was a party at Necton Hall attended by both gentry and clergy to which he took his wife and 'dearest Helen'. 'It was quite a new feeling I underwent seeing my daughter (now ten) dancing at a large ball' (19/1/54). Later in the year he was 'moved to tears' by Helen's singing (11/4/54). He described her as 'a pure and holy being of a better world – truly the most loving and sweet child [with a] knowledge and appreciation of spiritual things' (12/7/54). He described his son Johnny on his fourth birthday as 'a delicate, timid and loving boy; very different from his brother' (18/10/54). In February 1856, when Helen was 12, he described her as 'tall, thin, affectionate, but no application as to the acquiring of knowledge'. Louise at 7, on the other hand, was 'very quick in learning', but 'could be wayward'. By his fifth year Johnny was 'loving, shy and inclined to be sly' while Herbert was a fat and robust 3-year-old.

They all played well together, were obedient and were easily amused' (12/2/56). By 1858 Helen was described as 'a treasure. So amiable, so intelligent' and he gave her a box of drawing materials (16/1/58), and in 1864 a paint box 'in recognition of her great talent in drawing' (8/12/64). She was a frequent companion when he went to exhibitions at the Royal Academy on his visits to London. Louisa's talents were musical and 'out of the common way' (31/3/58), but by 1859 it was Helen who was described as 'dancing and playing admirably' (30/11/59).

The 1850s saw the expansion of photography and in 1856 he went to Norwich with his friend Mary Hales to have his photograph taken. He did not like the result: 'photography a good cure for vanity' (26/4/56). The following year he had a photograph taken for his wife, a copy of which he tinted for Mrs Wollaston, 'who greatly desired such a souvenir' (29/4/57). Later a travelling artist took excellent likenesses of the children at 1s (5p) apiece (18/8/57). In the winter of 1861 he noted that the photographer was not taking pictures again until the spring because of the foggy atmosphere There are no directory entries for photographers in Dereham at this time, but by 1864there were seventeen in Norwich,[4] where the many factory chimneys would have contributed to the polluted air. Later the same year he started his photograph album. More full-length photographs of the boys together and Helen on her own were taken 'very successfully' and twenty-four cards made for £1 (26/2/62).

At Christmas 1857 Armstrong organised a magic lantern and 'snap dragon show' for his own children, but 'a selection from the National School were also admitted' (25/12/57). Snap dragon was a game whereby raisins were put in a dish of brandy which was then set alight in a darkened room. The game was to remove the raisins without getting one's fingers burnt.[5]

Although deeply committed to his church work, he also was strongly aware of his family duties and often felt the conflict between them. He records spending an hour 'storytelling with my darlings after dinner' (8/12/56). After enjoying a spring day with his four children in 1857 he wrote, 'Perhaps I do not spend as much time with them as I should' (23/3/57).

Like all children, the younger Armstrongs suffered from the usual round of childhood diseases, but these could prove more serious than

a

25a, b   Armstrong (a) in
middle age and Nellie, his
wife (b), probably painted by
Armstrong or Helen.

b

MRS ANN REBECCA ARMSTRONG

they do now. At Christmas 1857 they were all in bed with measles, 'but their confinement mitigated by a box of very expensive presents from Grandmama Duncombe' (25/12/57). There were also childhood tumbles. Eight-year-old Johnny fell off a loft ladder on to the stable floor. Although he was concussed there was 'no permanent damage' (24/7/58). Later in the year he was made a member of the choir, and seeing him dressed in a surplice and walking in the procession, his 'meek little face' moved Armstrong greatly (18/10/58).

As the children grew up, so their entertainment changed. From 1859, when Helen was 15 and Louisa 11, an evening party for the children was regularly given in January. Thirty-five young people were invited in 1859. They were all the sons and daughters of 'first-rate Norfolk Yeoman'. The party lasted late into the evening and they were kept up 'until the early hours' (10/1/59). A similar party in January 1860 was attended by fifty and went on until 2 a.m.: 'these sorts of parties go somewhat against my ecclesiastical conscience' (10/1/60). In June an evening party was given for Helen. 'As the beaux, as usual in country parties, were in the minority and were over juvenile – lost in fact in a perfect sea of floating muslin – I had to dance a good deal and kept up the *valse à deux temps* for a long time' (26/6/60). In 1867 snow prevented the party being given in the Christmas season and it was put off until April.

Music would have been an important part of family life. Nellie played the harp as well as the harmonium in church. Both girls played and sang. The family went regularly to London and local concerts. In October 1860 Armstrong described going to a performance of *Messiah* in St Andrew's Hall in Norwich to which he took Helen and her friend. The music was 'grand' and the oratorio beautifully sung, but it was the number of local aristocracy present that really impressed him. Only the bishop, who did not support the Norwich festival because of the dubious morals of some of the performers, was absent (22/9/60).

As the years went by and the children grew up, Armstrong enjoyed their company and sharing his work and relaxations with them. He would take Helen on his visits to schools and parishioners as well as a as companion on social calls and walks. In May 1854 he 'Walked to Hoe with Helen – lingering to gather the numerous wild flowers which grow on Norfolk banks – birds singing, leaves coming out, grass green, lazy cattle wending their way along – altogether a day that made one

HELEN

LOUISA MARION

26a–d The Armstrong children: (a) Helen Armstrong, born 1844, died b
1917; (b) Louisa Armstrong (Nelson) born 1848, died 1883; (c) John
Armstrong, born 1850, died 1924; and (d) Herbert Armstrong, born 1853,
died 1910. d

BENJAMIN JOHN

HERBERT DUNCOMBE

thankful one's lot was cast in the country' (14/5/54). He dreaded the day when Helen might be married and leave home.

When Johnny was old enough to have his own pony the two of them would go riding and to see the meet gathering for a day's hunting – occasions when Armstrong would feel a pang of regret for the many days in his youth when he had enjoyed the sport. In 1861 he took Johnny to see the meet at Gressenhall and in 1862 the young Bertie (now 11 years old) to see the hounds gathering at Elsing (23/1/61). Fishing was another favourite pastime which he was increasingly able to share with his sons. In July 1861 he took the 9-year-old Bertie and 10-year-old Johnny fishing at Hoe, where they caught a quantity of perch and roach. The following year he took them trout fishing.

In September 1861, at the age of 17, Helen was launched into local society when she accompanied her parents to a dinner party at Letton Hall. 'We were glad her debut should be made at so good a house' where the 'unaffected simplicity contrasted with the manners of the would-be genteel' (18/9/61). The Letton dinners were, however, always grand occasions with powdered footmen, fine silver and Dresden fruit plates. The year ended as usual with the Dereham Assembly and the question as to whether Helen should go, 'but the high social position which the clergy hold in Norfolk makes that fitting, which would not be so every-where'. All the best families were there. Lord Sondes 'made himself affable and his lady as imperious and exclusive as ever' (12/11/61).

The education of his children was a great concern to Armstrong. In February 1858 they were all in school and the house seemed empty, but the following year the boys were sent to study with Mr Hillyard, Armstrong's new curate at Hoe, because 'there was no school in Dereham to which I would like to send them and they are too delicate to be sent to boarding school' (31/7/59). There were in fact four Dereham schools for boys listed in the *Norfolk Directory*, one 'the Guildhall School', run by the Revd Joseph Thompson, which might have been thought suitable,[6] but Thompson was one of those who had objected to the changes Armstrong was making to church services, and so his school could not be considered. Mr Hillyard's tuition did not last long, as he found that he could not make a living on his curate's stipend at Hoe and by taking in pupils, so he resigned. For a while they were taught at home and Armstrong bought desks for them which were put in his study. The girls went to a day school for girls in Dereham and in 1861, at the age of 17, Helen left.

In April 1861 the boys moved to Mr Aldis's School in Norwich Road.

This school is not so good as it ought to be for my boys, the school being chiefly for the sons of farmers and the better sort of trades people, but it will do for about a year <u>and besides which there is no other.</u> (16/4/61)

In March 1862 he visited Christ's College at Finchley, founded by the Revd Thomas White in 1857. Fine new buildings with accommodation for 150 boys were opened in Hendon Lane in 1860 and Armstrong was suitably impressed, although the thought of parting with his sons was painful. By the summer he was teaching them at home again and in September he took them to Finchley, much to the distress of their mother; 'Dear boys, they are tender delicate and affectionate' (12/9/62). The experiment was a disaster. They were miserable and refused to eat and a week later he fetched them and brought them home to attend Joseph Thompson's school, which he now regarded as a 'a good one', although Thompson had not always been the best friend to me', and where they were happy (24/9/62). In fact so happy was he with the school that his friend William Duncombe then brought two of his children to join the boys there. At Christmas 1863 they came home for the holiday, 'much grown and improved' (20/12/63). In 1869, well after the Armstrong boys had left, Armstrong was surprised to hear that Joseph Thompson was selling his school and leaving the neighbourhood. By 1864 Armstrong was already thinking of suitable careers for the boys. He took Johnny around the Cambridge colleges, hoping to encourage him to enter the church, 'but he was not keen' (17/1/64).

In the spring of 1865 he was tutoring the boys at home again and preparing them for Bury St Edmunds Grammar School in Northgate Street. The headmaster, the Revd Mr Wratislaw, was assisted by the Revd Mr Statham as second master, as well as teachers of mathematics, English and French.[7] They left home for Bury in the autumn. The following autumn they were confirmed in Norwich, and in January 1867 they all went to a ball at the Barnwells in Mileham, 'Johnny wearing a dress coat for the first time' (5/1/67). By 1869, however, it was agreed that John would enter the church. He left home for Caius College in the autumn of 1869, and completed his degree three years later. Armstrong went to Cambridge for his graduation on 10 December 1872, and was relieved that he was now set for a career in the church. The following year he passed his examinations for deacon's orders and was ordained in Christchurch, Oxford in December, taking up his first curacy at Thatcham in Berkshire.

While Johnny was destined for university, Herbert was not so academic, and the civil service or 'merchant's counting house' in London was thought more appropriate. In February 1868 Armstrong was in London looking for a suitable opening. Armstrong's father, who was a director of the Metropolitan Railway, managed to secure a post for Herbert in their offices, and in October Armstrong brought him to London. Sixty pounds a year for a working day from ten until four seemed a very good salary for a boy of 16. He was to live with his grandparents, aunt and Challice cousins at Wimpole Street (Dr Challice had died in 1863). Armstrong was worried that he might find life there with his elderly grandparents restrictive and felt the Challice boys might be a bad influence. Herbert might also feel caged in London after the freedom of the countryside. Armstrong did not see Herbert's work with the railway company as the beginning of a commercial career, but thought him more suited to the army. He made enquiries and Herbert finally sat the examinations for an army commission. Armstrong was worried that his son might not be suitably prepared, but all went well and he passed in August 1870. He remained at the railway company until there was a vacancy and Armstrong continued to worry about him. He heard that his son was getting into debt and he noticed a 'certain roughness of manner'. The Challice boys were argumentative and quick-tempered, 'which bodes ill for their future'. 'London seems more shamelessly wicked than ever' (17/11/70). In 1872 he exchanged parishes with a London parson for a month so that he could be with his very frail father in Wimpole Street and laid down 'some stringent rules for the young men who lived there' (the Challice boys and his son) (15/4/72). In January 1873 Herbert took up his first regimental appointment as a sub-lieutenant with the 97th Foot in Dublin, 'a very respectable, though not crack regiment' (27/1/73). A couple of months later he was in London with Herbert to buy his uniform and on 18 April he was put on the train in Dereham to travel to Dublin. His father was naturally fearful, although admitting, 'it was time he was employed. He will be 21 in July' (18/4/73).

The girls, too, were growing up and he was surprised in the winter of 1868 to have a request from Arthur Nelson to be a suitor for Lilly: 'This is quite a new feature in my life!' However, he had to refuse. Lilly was too young at 19, Arthur had no profession and his father, rector of a small Wiltshire parish, was not well off (12/12/68). Now that the girls' education was over they spent much of their time at home helping with parish work and accompanying their parents to dinners, garden parties, often with croquet being played, and archery matches. Armstrong himself became 'a member of the archery club for the sake of the young people' (27/8/72). They also went to stay with more distant friends (often the families of fellow clergymen) for short periods.

Nellie and Annie

Although Armstrong's children feature regularly in his diary, we know little of his wife, Nellie, who is always described as 'devoted' and 'amiable'. In January 1854 he mentions that he had restrung her harp and there is a small watercolour of her playing it. On their thirteenth wedding anniversary he wrote in his diary that he was thankful for such a good wife, describing her as having every qualification for a husband's happiness, 'being very considerate, unselfish and affectionate with a quiet, dignified and unaffected manner', although she was perhaps too 'engrossed in nursery matters and over indulgent to the children'. He continued, rather patronisingly, 'There may be others more brilliant and more beautiful, but a better [wife] it would be impossible to have' (30/8/55). She was described as dressing 'handsomely in black velvet and old lace with one or two good ornaments' (13/5/55). This rather sombre appearance may have reflected her character. In 1859 he described her as 'self-denying' and 'rarely experiences much pleasure' (30/11/59). In 1857 we hear that she ran a parochial library in the church containing story books and biographies as well as religious titles (15/11/57). Although the impression is that she lived very much in the shadow of her husband, she must have taken a great interest in the affairs of those around her. In March 1858 the household was disrupted because of 'a disappointed love affair in which my wife had been a chief agent (a bad trade)'. Nellie shared her brother William's enjoyment of fishing and occasionally Armstrong went fishing with her at her childhood home of Lagley (13/5/58). The fact that Armstrong took a rather jaundiced view of weddings, writing that he disliked them – 'I would rather attend a funeral' (7/2/54) – his frequent references to his 'first love' (now Mrs James and married to the Revd Robert James) and his obvious attraction to Mary Hales (see Chapter 10), along with his enjoyment of his 'bachelor existence' when his wife was away, suggest that the marriage may have lacked romantic sparkle. Much later, in 1883, he recounts a visit to Lagley church where their marriage had taken place and giving his wife a kiss 'before the altar to assure her I do not regret the compact we made then' (26/9/83). This rather negative entry is hardly an enthusiastic endorsement of a long and happy marriage.

Relations with Nellie's family were strained from time to time, probably beginning with Nellie's father's refusal to contribute towards the purchase of the patronage of the Little Stanmore living as part of Nellie's marriage settlement. His meanness with money Armstrong attributed to the fact that he 'had to make his own way in business as the inheritance all went to his brother who spent it all and then came to rely on his brother.... Money earned and money inherited differ in the estimate of its owner' (27/2/56). In later years her father suffered from bouts of insanity, a great worry to the family. Nellie was summoned to Lagley on 12 February 1856 as his death was imminent, but he was dead before she reached him. 'Being miserable in mind and health for some years, such a release can hardly be a matter of regret' (12/2 56). The funeral was on the 18th and Armstrong joined his wife for the occasion.

One of Armstrong's great sadnesses was that his close childhood relationship with his sister Annie did not continue in his adult life. Her marriage to Dr Challice was dogged with financial worries, mainly brought about by poor investments. These included various hotels, the Metropolitan Railway and Turkish baths. Armstrong's father frequently had to bail Challice out to prevent his bankruptcy. This all led to a cooling of relations within the family. His father wrote that 'the profits of his [Challice's] profession, added to our allowances should be sufficient to keep her [Annie] and the children in perfect respectability and independence'. Instead, a third of Annie's father's income went to support the Challice family. Armstrong was to take a great interest in the progress of their children and they were frequently invited to Dereham to stay. On the family's London visit in 1854 they took 'the intelligent little nieces' out for the day and then returned them to their parents, where they found Challice, 'in spite of his pecuniary problems, writing a long letter to [Prime Minister] Palmerston on sanitary reform' (27/4/54). He was always critical of his sister's extravagance and when he visited the family after his father-in-law's funeral he found the children dressed 'too showily – as is their house and way of life'. The next day, however, he found Annie more her old self, 'natural, charming and full of talent' (18/2/56). In December 1856 her eighth child was born and Armstrong was concerned as to what would 'become of them in later life – but this happily does not worry the parents' (10/12/56). When he visited her in June 1858 she was affectionate but 'as peculiar in dress and manner as ever' and he wished she was 'quieter and less dramatic' (7/6/58). A ninth child was born in April 1859, but by now Challice was a deputy coroner for Middlesex and there was hope that their finances would be on a surer footing. Annie now had grand ideas, dressed in a 'quasi oriental fashion' and talked expansively of parties and the books she was about to publish. Armstrong wished 'that she was more real and less exaggerated' (4/7/60). The following year, however, Challice was ill and his finances again insecure as his illness meant he lost patients. Armstrong and his father once more attempted to sort out his affairs and found them in a worse state than they had expected.

Annie's eldest child, Johnny, was Armstrong's godson and he followed his progress with interest. He became a naval cadet in April 1859 and passed his midshipman examination in October. Armstrong gave him his regulation dirk, belt and pistol, 'not exactly the gifts from a man of peace and a godfather!' (25/10/59). In November 1860 there was fear that he might have to leave the navy because of his deafness, but the following month he sailed for the West Indies. In January 1861 he was back in Portsmouth. Presumably he continued to be at sea with regular spells of leave. By 1869 he was a lieutenant and arrived in Dereham to visit his godfather 'on a bicycle'. Armstrong regarded him as 'selfish, dictatorial and neglectful of appearances' (28/7/69). In 1870 he sailed from Portsmouth on HMS *Volage*, but seven years later he returned from New South Wales 'hopelessly insane' (17/8/77) and was placed in the Naval Hospital in Yarmouth, where he lived for the rest of his life.

Johnny's brother, Roger, was also a problem. The wild life he led meant that he was nearly killed by a hired horse in August 1866. Armstrong hoped this would wake up his sister to her duty as a mother, but instead Roger was sent off to New Zealand to make his way there. The younger children were frequently ill and the burden of looking after them often fell on their elderly grandparents, which was a concern for Armstrong, who had little patience with his sister.

Armstrong hated the coolness of relations both with his sister and his wife's family and a red-letter day was when they all met for dinner at his parents' in Wimpole Street. 'I was so thankful that I danced' along with the others (13/7/62).

Later in the year Challice's investments for once paid off and he came into a large sum of money, with which he took a fine, fashionable house which they furnished lavishly and then took a holiday in Italy. Armstrong visited them on their return, when he found Annie 'as full of self love and effect as ever. It makes my heart sad to see such exaggeration and unreality' (13/4/63). A month later, just as they were happy and prosperous, Dr Challice died suddenly and as his father was becoming old and less able, Armstrong felt the responsibility for the family falling upon himself. After the death of her husband, Annie's fortunes inevitably declined, and much to Armstrong's consternation she planned to move to Geneva. This would leave him alone to support their ageing parents. This plan appears to have come to nothing. She continued to live with her children at Wimpole Street with their parents, where for several years she refused to leave her room or face the world, while her children were the responsibility of their grandparents. Later in the year young William Challice was offered a place in a government office at £90 a year, which must have been a relief to the family. By the end of 1864 they had left Wimpole Street and were back in their Southall house. Annie was again writing 'and full of high-flown fantasies' (31/12/64), but still keeping to herself. By early the next year they were back in Wimpole Street, and when Armstrong visited in June 1866 he only saw Annie once as she kept to her room. After a long illness, their mother died on 17 May 1869 and was buried in Highgate cemetery. At last Annie began to emerge and joined the family for dinner, 'a great improvement after her long seclusion' (31/5/69). Relations between brother and sister remained strained 'on account of her vanity' (23/5/70).

Annie had already proved herself to be something of an author. She had published three novels: *The Village Fete* in 1847, *The Laurel and the Palm* in 1852 and *The Sisters of Charity* in 1857. Armstrong read her novels with a critical eye. In June 1859 the two-volume *The Wife's Temptation* was published and while Armstrong agreed that his sister was 'very talented' he found it a 'distressing tale to read'. None of the characters was Christian and the book contained 'sneers and sly hints at the clergy'. The highly 'gothic' style of writing which contains over-blown death scenes and reconciliations makes the book difficult for the modern reader to read. Armstrong much preferred her 'simple if less talented' story about a village fête, which was much more calculated to 'do good – which should be the aim of every author' (6/6/59). Later in life she turned to French history with *A History of the Court of France under Louis XV* (1861). For this she made original use of documents in the British Library that had not been consulted by earlier researchers and the book received good reviews (8/9/61). Later came *French Authors at Home* (1864) followed by *The Illustrious Women of France* (1873), about pre-revolutionary France.

In 1872, when Annie was working on *The Illustrious Women*, she was taken in by a man claiming to be the 'Duc de Roussillon', who offered to help her in return for 'considerable sums of money'. Annie refused to accept that his claims might be fraudulent and said she would rather leave the house than be forced to give up the friendship. Armstrong then met a General Blunt, 'chairman of a society for the detection of such miscreants', who said he was aware of 'several similar cases against him'. Armstrong agreed to pay a private detective. Lawyers were consulted, Armstrong remained firm and eventually Annie relented. Again, he put down the cause of the whole 'unhappy affair' to her 'vanity' (30/12/72–6/1/73).

Life at the vicarage

Armstrong could afford a gentlemanly lifestyle. In his early years he kept a riding horse as well as one for the trap, several servants, including a nurse for the children, and, for a while, a governess for Helen. He complained about how difficult it was to get his servants, 'three comely maidens', to church. (28/9/54). In May that year he did his accounts and found that he was just living within his means. However, he expected heavier taxation to pay for the Crimean War and feared that retrenchment might be necessary, which could involve giving up his footman. 'Honesty, independence and personal peace demand this' (18/5/54). The following year income tax was doubled and he noted with alarm that his expenditure was exceeding his income, so he 'discharged his manservant, turned the nag out to graze and gave away the unprofitable hens' (9/8/55). In 1856 he records his staff as a gardener and wife, cook, nurse and housemaid. Income from tithes was low that year. He missed his horse, but it meant that instead of going for relaxing gallops, he spent time looking after the garden and going on local visits. When she was away, he had the use of Mary Hales's pony for more distant calls. At the end of his spring visit to London in 1857, his father took pity on him and gave him £25 towards the purchase of a horse (18/4/57). By the end of the year his finances had improved enough for him to be able to hire a manservant again. The household now needed to spend less on maidservants, as the children, now ranging in age from 13 to 5, were 'old enough to look after themselves'. Finally, in May the following year, now that he had a servant to look after it, he bought a 5-year old thoroughbred for £30, 'a very handsome and beautiful goer'. He was determined never to be without a horse again (29/4/58). 'What could a parson of a large country parish do without a horse?' (14/5/69). By the late 1860s Armstrong was again worried about money, perhaps because of the expense of sending Johnny to Cambridge. He was refusing dinner invitations because he could not afford to return the hospitality. 'We cannot afford parties, our expenses so much increased' (9/12/68). In February 1871 he felt able to entertain again and gave a dinner party for both old friends to whom they owed a meal and newcomers to the parish. The guests included the Bulwers of Quebec Hall and the Collinsons of Bilney, as well as some new names. The census for that year shows him keeping a cook, a parlourmaid and a housemaid.

Socially, because of the aristocratic links of his wife, Armstrong moved in county circles. As well as being guests at Quebec Hall, they dined with several of the local landowning families such as the Brampton Gurdons at Letton, Colonel Mason at Necton and the Haggards at Bradenham. However, he did not always enjoy these occasions. Of a dinner at Letton he wrote, 'As is generally the case with grandees, no opportunity presented itself for intellectual conversation.' He was rather shocked to find that a brother of Mr Gurdon's was the incumbent of four parishes near Dereham. Again he confided in his diary: 'Dinner parties are endless and there is always a good reason why we should not decline.' However, he did enjoy hosting dinners and he thought early September was the best time. The fruit, poultry, fish and game were at their finest, there were plenty of flowers for decoration and everyone who lived in the country was likely to be at home. The weather was often favourable and, importantly for him, the evenings were not too long (8/9/54).

Purely social engagements he found difficult: 'after-dinner conversation is so wretchedly small and commonplace' (1/7/54). 'The sad idling of time, in country re-unions' he found particularly trying. 'People have no right to twaddle a precious morning away at bagatelle or insipid and profitless conversation', he wrote of a luncheon party at Quebec Hall. He left just as the guests were 'beginning the pros and cons as to whether or not the weather was fitting for a drive' (11/2/58). At a 'gentlemen's evening party at my curate's I was sorry to see that cards were the order of the evening' (9/1/54). He described a particularly difficult party at which

> Smith of Brisley was repulsed by Mary Hales who flirted with E. Hastings to provoke him. E. Hastings did not know what to make of it. Mrs Cooper was annoyed because the bachelors took no notice of her daughters and Mrs Brooman was upset because Mary Hales sung better. How I wished myself away. (10/7/57)

However, garden parties, which he claimed were now becoming fashionable, were different and more enjoyable.

In October 1853, while visiting Duncombe in Crowle, where fishing with his friend was the main relaxation, he 'often thought during our visit that I was fearfully wasting time'. He also wished his friend, 'my amiable, charitable and well-intentioned brother-in-law might be imbued with more ecclesiastical spirit' and took his calling to the church more seriously.

On the first pages of his diary Armstrong revealed that he had few hobbies outside his profession: 'the architecture of churches and the composition of a sermon afford me the greatest delight'. However, the diary does give us glimpses of other pastimes. Perhaps that most frequently mentioned is fishing, particularly with his close friend, William Duncombe. On 30 August 1853 he spent much of the day gardening, 'an occupation of which I am very fond'. In September he was organising the cutting down of trees in the shrubbery. The warm weather in December 1857 meant that 'a pretty bouquet from the garden adorns the dining room table' and strawberries were being picked (6/12/57). In June 1859 he was busy in his greenhouse, an occupation 'I have now taken up and find great delight in. I have already made a grand show' (14/6/59). He regularly gave what he called a 'haymaking party' to which he invited friends to his 'hut in the wood', which was festooned with flowers with carriage lamps set amongst them. Tea and strawberries and cream were served with wine, and cigars for the gentlemen (24/6/59).

It is not clear how much interest he took in farming his 50 acres of glebe. Twelve acres of this were taken up by the 'Homestead, yard, garden, orchard, and pastures'. As well as this there were 15 acres of pasture and Scarning meadows, which were in hand, while 10 acres along the Norwich road were let.[8] By July 1857 some of the pasture was let and Armstrong went over the land with his new tenant, while some meadows were still kept in hand. The fencing between the tenant's fields and the shrubbery must have been poor, as two of his horses died as a result of eating yew in the vicarage grounds (2/8/58). There is mention in his diary of ejecting sheep from the lawn in the autumn of 1856. In May 1860, 'Helen and I sold our sheep for £5.... Their frequent invasions into the garden and fear that they might destroy the bedding plants was why they were sold.' Armstrong quoted the saying 'A man will have trouble if he keeps sheep' (19/5/60). Hay was made every year. In July 1854 he gave his haymakers a party. Supper was taken on a table under the trees and they smoked and sang songs until after nine. A couple of years later a similar event is described. 'The evening was spent in songs and polkas, while the aged smoked in silence.' It ended with the singing of the national anthems of England and France. 'What pleasure is so great as making the poor happy?' (2/7/56). The choirboys could then have their first game of cricket on the newly mown grass. In June 1869 he returned early from the volunteer's camp at Hunstanton 'to superintend the stacking of the hay' (26/6/69). He noted with satisfaction that the contents of Christmas hampers he sent to London at the end of 1857, including the 'hampers themselves were the production of our own premise' (6/12/57). There were two basket-makers in Dereham at the time who could have used rushes or willow from the waterside meadows below the vicarage to weave the hampers. It also suggests that he was keeping a few turkeys. Much of the glebe was certainly wooded. In the autumn of 1857 he felled 132 trees; the same year he had a bumper crop of apples and was able to send them to the school. Each of the 170 children had as many as they could carry away. A mid-nineteenth-century plan drawn when some glebe was exchanged for a small piece in Scarning shows the gardens surrounded by a belt of trees and a small ornamental pond, presumably filled by a spring and flowing out into the Scarning river. The outbuildings of the vicarage included a cart house, fowl house, bullock shed and boxes, as well as a cow yard, but how much they were used by the vicar is unclear.[9]

Armstrong's main relaxations were reading and a quiet smoke with a friend. He read a wide range of books, including the novels of Dickens, Thackeray, the Brontë sisters and Mrs Gaskell, and the autobiography of Sidney Smith as well as travel and history books. 'What a privilege and comfort is to be found in literature.' (21/1/55) A much-anticipated lecture by Thackeray given in Norwich in May 1857 proved to be rather disappointing. While in London a couple of years later he attended a reading of *Little Dorrit* and contrasted Thackeray's 'genial' face with the 'look of ill-temper' about Dickens (17/1/59). When he heard that Anthony Trollope, another author whom he much admired, was staying at the King's Arms in Dereham, he made a point of calling on him (24/9/63). He described the perfect end to a busy day and working evening: 'finished off the evening with a pipe and *Vanity Fair*' (12/11/57). Relaxation with a pipe was one of Armstrong's greatest pleasures. Sometimes he enjoyed this alone in his study, but occasionally it would be with one of his closest friends, Dr Hastings. 'There are very few parishioners with whom I am on smoking terms' (22/6/58).

Outdoor pleasures such as an energetic gallop were also enjoyed. An evening's fishing allowed him several hours beside a peaceful river. In

October 1854 he took up watercolour painting again, allowing himself an hour a week of lessons with his organist. In this he was following the tradition of better-known clerical artists such as Edward Daniell, who had sat at the feet of some of the famous artists of the Norwich School of painting in the earlier years of the nineteenth century.[10] 'Every spring brings the desire to catch trout and every autumn the desire to copy nature. I take my frame into the field and paint away' (11/9/55).

1855: A year in the life of Benjamin Armstrong

Typical of the early years of his life in Dereham, with its highs and lows, was 1855. It began with the usual round of social engagements and a dinner at Quebec Hall. By the morning of Sunday 7 January, when Armstrong set off to church to give his sermon on the subject of the Magi, it was clear that his wife was about to go into labour and that evening, before the monthly nurse had even arrived, a baby girl was born. At 37, he was now the proud father of five children. 'It seems a great jump from four to five. I feel quite patriarchal at being head of such a large family' (7/1/55). The next day he was busy writing letters to family and friends informing them of the new arrival and particularly to his two close friends, Mary Hales and Lady Plumer of Canons Park, whom he wished to be sponsors at the baby's baptism. There followed the customary month of confinement while his wife rested away from the family and so Armstrong lived a 'bachelor existence'. He enjoyed the peace of his study surrounded by his books. His friend and church-warden, the antiquarian George Carthew, dined with him and 'much as I delight in the society of my dear wife, my bachelor life is not insupportable' (12/1/55). On 7 February, Nellie finally joined the family and was 'churched', when thanks were given for the good health of mother and child. There followed a family celebratory dinner. On 9 March the new baby was baptised Gertrude Mary followed by a dinner party. Later in the month little Gertrude was a cause for concern when she developed a 'congestion of the lungs' and it was doubtful whether she would survive. Armstrong wrote rather callously that it would be 'easier to part with her now than when she has entwined herself more in our hearts' (21/3/55). However, she was out of danger by the end of the week. The year continued very much as usual: there were visitors and partings, lectures at the Institute, the schoolchildren to be catechised, sermons to be written and the poor and the sick to be visited. In June his friend William Duncombe and wife invited themselves to stay, 'he being used up and out of order with his work (as I am!)' (29/6/55).

In July 'Wife, five darlings and two nurses' took the train to London for the annual visit to the Armstrong parents. There was a boat trip on the Thames, which although pleasant, was spoilt by the stench of the river – 'It is a pity the Thames is a sewer' (11/7/55) – visits to the Royal Academy, Crystal Palace on its new site, the theatre, dinners including one with the Marquis of Salisbury and London magistrates (of which his father was one) and a garden party: 'Though the company was not aristocratic and the letter H was frequently ignored, there was everything that a kind heart and great wealth could provide' (24/7/55). The money worries of his sister and Dr Challice continued to be a problem and cast a shadow over the otherwise happy time. In the autumn Armstrong indulged his love of travel with his father by taking a Cook's tour to Ireland and North Wales. The Leicester firm guaranteed to take him from Dereham station and back for 42s (£2.10), which seemed an opportunity too good to be missed. They left on 17 September, returning on the 26th, having visited Dublin, and on the way back, climbed Snowdon, 'armed with a guide, a bottle of brandy and an Alpen stock'.

But even the quiet and ordered life of a clergyman could be interrupted by domestic disasters. Within a few hours on 9 November Armstrong was interrupted by news that the well had fallen in, the pump was out of order, the chimney on fire, the coals 'out', the tax collector in the study 'waiting for you' and 'Bertie had nettle rash' (9/11/55).

The autumn brought its usual round of social engagements and he wrote on 19 November, 'Have been dining out too much of late to suit either my health or inclination.... Fortunately it has not hindered my work, from which one derives more lasting satisfaction than from worldly gaiety and excitement.'

The build-up to Christmas was a particularly busy time of year, and was especially pleasurable this time because for the first time Armstrong's parents were to join them, and even though, at 11 months, baby Gertrude was too small to understand the importance of the day, it would be her first Christmas. His parish duties involved the distribution of 400 loaves, a clothing charity to be cashed up and tickets to be distributed, Christmas dinners to be given, stipends paid to schoolteachers, the church to be tastefully decorated with wreaths and music practised. On the domestic, front turkeys had to be sent to London friends. In preparation for the arrival of their grandparents, the children had got up a 'Christmas tree glittering with cheap presents for all'. Armstrong's father recorded in his diary that the Christmas tree 'was lighted for the amusement of the children and presents were distributed by my dear son with very pretty appropriate speeches, first to my dear wife and myself and then to his wife and children and Mr Kinsford, the curate'. Twenty-four school children came to sing and were all given a present from the tree. The next day a note of anxiety appeared in the diary as Armstrong wrote that baby was unwell and by the 27th this was causing concern as she was having difficulty breathing. The worried parents called Dr Hastings, who reassured them that the child was out of danger. The 28th was the Feast of the Holy Innocents, and Armstrong's sermon was on that theme. Reassured by the doctor's prognosis, Armstrong and his father went for a drive but on returning were told that that Gertrude was rather worse, so the doctor was called again. Dinner was a melancholy meal, and the doctor now warned the family to 'expect the worst'. By half past seven the baby was dead. 'The poor dear mother was almost inconsolable and we all retired for the night stupefied with excessive grief.' Infant mortality was a sadly regular occurrence in mid-Victorian Britain, and the nursery may have been a distant place, rarely visited by fathers, but that did not lessen the blow to individual families. Most of the caring for small children in well-to-do families was left to nurses, and in this case, the 'poor nurse ... could scarcely have been more grieved if the babe had been her own'(29/12/55). Armstrong himself set an example of resignation and his father wrote, 'it then occurred to me how feelingly my dear son had alluded to the probable happiness and bliss of the departed Innocents in his Lecture this morning, not knowing his own sweet babe would be added to the Angelic Band ere this sad day passed away'.[11] The cause of death was said to be a chest infection brought on by the cold easterly winds and severe weather, made more severe by an underlying lung 'defect'. The Christmas festivities, begun so joyfully, ended sorrowfully. Armstrong's father had to return to London, but not before he had called on the local families such as the Lee-Warners at Quebec Hall

27   The cross put up in the churchyard as a memorial over the grave of Gertrude Armstrong, who died at 11 months in 1855. Armstrong, his wife and Louisa are all buried near it.

and Mrs Gooch at Hill House to save his son the ordeal of spreading the news. Meanwhile Armstrong was busy writing letters to those further afield. His mother stayed on and both she and her son did their best to comfort Nellie. Until 2 January the coffin was open for the household to take a final look at the child, 'with fresh white chrysanthemums like a halo around her head'. The coffin was finally borne to the church-yard by four schoolgirls dressed in white. The service was performed by the curate, and as was the custom, none of the women or children was present, so Armstrong was the only mourner. 'I left my darling in the cold churchyard.' The grave was at the east end of the church, past which the parson would walk each day.

By 3 January he had plunged back into work, hoping to find relief in the usual round of duties as a new year began. On 7 May 1856 Armstrong erected a tall Gothic cross in the churchyard to mark Gertrude's grave. As it was the first such cross to be erected, he was afraid that the low church supporters might object and vandalise it, seeing it as a symbol of popish idolatry, but happily this did not happen.

It was not long before further sadness hit the household with the death of Nellie's father, William Duncombe, and, with it, disputes over his will.

Notes

1   By then she had published *Sisters of Charity* (1857) and *The Village School Fête* (1847).
2   C. Armstrong (ed.), *Under the Parson's Nose*, 2012, 320.
3   *Norfolk Chronicle*, 6 March 1858.
4   W. White, *Norfolk Directory*, 1864, 319.
5   Armstrong 2012, 320.
6   White 1864, 938.
7   *Morris's Commercial Directory: Suffolk*, 1868, 258.
8   NRO, DN/TA/267.
9   NRO, PD86/83.
10 J. Thistlethwaite, 'The Etchings of Edward Thomas Daniell (1804–1842)', *Norfolk Archaeology* **36**, 1977, 1–22.
11 Diary of Armstrong's father, also Benjamin (I am grateful to David Armstrong for giving me this information).

Nine

Friends

During his thirty-eight years as vicar of Dereham, Armstrong gathered a wide circle of acquaintances around him. He was a regular guest at dinner, luncheon and garden parties in the neighbourhood. He was well aware of the importance of rank and always noted the names of the more aristocratic guests when he went out. Dinners with the Brampton Gurdons at Letton Hall always impressed him. When Helen was launched into local society he was glad that it happened at a dinner party at 'so good a house' (18/9/61). The family knew everyone at the Dereham Assembly, which was always attended by the best families (12/11/61). However, he had few close friends. The local doctor, Horace Hastings, was one of the closest with whom he was on 'pipe-smoking' terms.

A second local friend was George Carthew, solicitor and antiquarian, who was his churchwarden for nearly twenty-five years. Articles by Carthew appeared regularly in *Norfolk Archaeology* from 1849 and his three-volume study of the parishes within Launditch Hundred was published in 1879. His lecture to the Institute on 'The Town We Live In' (18/4/55) was published a couple of years later. On his death in October 1882, Armstrong described him as 'my old friend. When I first came he was the only intelligent churchman in the place, and though my position was a very difficult one in those days, he always supported me. He was a great archaeologist and a man of considerable taste' (21/10/82).

Another antiquarian friend of his later years was Augustus Jessopp, who became vicar of Scarning in 1879. When dining at the Scarning vicarage a few years later he described the conversation as 'amusing and instructive as it always is there' (20/7/82). In 1883 Jessopp and his wife were frequently listed among Armstrong's dinner guests. Armstrong found it difficult to give dinner parties which included both 'town' and

28 The local doctor, James Vincent, who died 1888, was hardly a friend and was described in 1873, along with Mr Hyde and the lawyer Mr Cooper, as 'always working against me'.

'country'. Jessopp was in the country category, but on one occasion some of the guests ('although all professional') were from the town. 'Consequently they did not amalgamate as well as we could wish. This absurd distinction renders it difficult for a town parson to give a party whereas the country parson has no town parishioners to pay attention to' (17/1/82). In 1884 Armstrong recorded taking Helen to dinner with the Jessopps and described their host as 'a clever man who has recently written some articles in reviews called Achadie [*Arcady*] comparing the rustic poor now and forty years ago and are not favourable to their present condition not withstanding school boards'(17/11/84). It is dinner conversations on such subjects that would have attracted Armstrong to Jessopp as someone with whom serious topics could be discussed. It is also possible that it was Jessopp's antiquarian enthusiasms which encouraged Armstrong's son John to become interested in the subject.

Amongst Armstrong's county friends were the Haggards of Bradenham Hall, with whom he occasionally enjoyed a day's shooting. In 1856 Armstrong described William Haggard as a good churchman, a true squire with an agreeable wife and six sweet children (7/3/53). They were regular guests at Quebec Hall, and William Haggard was a captain in the local militia in which Armstrong was also involved. Armstrong described his 'thriving pair of moustaches which the infantry now wear as well as the cavalry' (21/1/55). Elsewhere, however, he is described as bearded, forceful, opinionated and short-tempered. Armstrong would have approved of his reading family prayers every morning and occupying the squire's pew every Sunday, checking on the latecomers.[1] Haggard's bad temper and unpredictability are shown in his dealings with his parson, the Revd George Stone, who often called on Armstrong to talk over the problems he had with his squire, prompting Armstrong's comment, 'verily Squires love to have pre-eminence and I'm thankful there is not one in this parish' (24/10/57). Some of Captain Haggard's eight sons also feature in the diary. The eldest, William, spent time at the British embassy in Washington, where following in the footsteps of other sons of the gentry hoping to recuperate family fortunes by marriage, he met and married an American divorcee who was said to possess 'very large property'. The Armstrongs met her at a grand dinner at the Haggards' to which the county elite had been invited in order to meet the lady in question. 'She was a very "fast" specimen, and although young, was much rouged and frizzled and wore very little above the waist' (8/7/75). However, the marriage did not last long and she went back to America and married a third time. On a visit to Bradenham in 1882 Armstrong heard all the family woes. Not only had William's wife left him, but another son in the army had married without his father's permission. Jack, who had joined the navy, had given it up to join his younger brother, Rider, in South Africa, where he was investing all his capital in 1,000 acres to farm ostriches for their feathers. This giving up of an honourable profession such as the navy to take up trade was bound to anger their father. The instability of the colony at the time of the Zulu War forced the brothers to return with the loss of their money. As well as this Mrs Haggard and a daughter-in-law were both ill. With his own family problems at the time, Armstrong felt he could sympathise with Captain Haggard (12/1/82). Armstrong had met Rider in 1879 while he was home from South Africa on a visit. Rider was to become a famous author, first with his book *Cetewayo and His Neighbours*, published in 1882, about the relationships between the British, the Boers and the Zulus, and later for his many novels, the best known of which are *She* and *King Solomon's Mines*.

In November 1882 Armstrong gave a dinner party to which he invited 'old friends, chiefly County people', and the list of guests shows the types of people with whom he regularly socialised. They included the Haggards, the Bulwers of Quebec Hall, Henry Hyde, a local JP, and his wife from Moorgate, the vicar of Mattishall, the Revd James Du Port, and his sister and Mr Browne, all of whom, except Mr Browne, feature regularly in the diary.

Armstrong remained in contact with some of his university friends who had also become clergymen, as well as curates and clergymen from his previous and adjoining parishes. The Revd William Fothergill was a frequent visitor and godfather to Herbert and there were many heart-to-hearts before Fothergill finally joined the Roman Catholic Church (6/12/59). Another Cambridge friend was Dean Bull, who moved to Ireland where he was visited by Armstrong and his father. He died in 1886 and Armstrong recalled him as an 'eccentric fellow' (26/4/86). In later years Armstrong noted the deaths of friends in his diary, although few made an appearance earlier.

Armstrong's closest friend was his childhood companion and brother-in-law, William Duncombe. On Duncombe's death he described him in his diary as 'my earliest friend whom I have known since we were twelve and with whom over nearly half a century, I never had a quarrel, though our ideas of life and its duty differed widely' (2/11/80). When William came to stay, he would preach several sermons, but it was clear to Armstrong that he was not really cut out for a clerical life, preferring field sports and fishing, of which there was always plenty when he came to Norfolk. In June 1856 he moved to France for a couple of years with his family, leaving his parish in the charge of a curate. At the end of the year Armstrong wrote that they were still abroad, 'retrenching' and enjoying themselves at the same time' (21/11/56). On his return in 1860, Duncombe found the church and parish in a poor state. At this time their ninth child was born, although only five siblings were living (9/3/60). Later in the year William's father (Armstrong's father-in-law), William Duncombe senior, died and Armstrong attended the funeral in Ivinghoe church, the burial place of the Duncombes. His long periods of illness over the previous years meant his death was seen as a happy release. In the spring of 1861 Armstrong finally managed to get to Crowle to see his friend, now back in his parish. He was 'as gentlemanly and unclerical as ever', but there was 'a quiet happiness in their reunion' (2/4/61). Later in the year came the sad news that Duncombe's wife had died at the birth of their tenth child (30/9/61). In February the following year Duncombe came to stay for a few days. He was restless and trying to sell the advowson and leave Crowle. The next month Armstrong went to stay with Duncombe at Crowle and found him very miserable. He later heard that Duncombe had been made a magistrate in Lincolnshire, something of which Armstrong disapproved. In 1863 Duncombe came again to Dereham to leave two of his children to join Armstrong's boys at the Revd Joseph Thompson's school.

William Duncombe was in many ways an example of a type of cleric which was becoming less usual during Queen Victoria's reign. His parish had been bought for him by his father to provide him with a gentlemanly lifestyle, but he had little commitment to the calling and was happy to abandon the parish to a curate and live abroad for a long period. The death of his wife unsettled him further, and much to Armstrong's surprise his friend remarried the following year 'a widow with four children and not well off!' (22/7/65). A year later they were living in Bruges, where Armstrong visited him and his new wife (1/8/66). Finally, at the end of 1867 Duncombe sold the patronage, where he had been non-resident for much of the previous few years, and accepted a curacy at Merton in the gift of Lord Walsingham, living at Rokelles, a fine old house near Watton and so near his long-standing friend. However, he was no more settled there and at the end of 1869 he moved to Nottingham for a year but was back in Norfolk by August 1870, when Nellie organised a large picnic at Scoulton Mere, near Watton, and invited the Duncombes to it. 'I am getting too old for picnics. I prefer my food indoors' (31/8/70), commented Armstrong. During 1871 the old friends saw each other occasionally, Armstrong accompanying William to a sale of Lord Walsingham's famous flock of sheep, where 400 prospective buyers sat down to luncheon (29/6/71). Duncombe settled at Rokelles with his new wife, Charlotte, and her daughters and they were all frequent visitors to Dereham. In the winter of 1876, there was an extended visit during which Armstrong's curate, Mr Watt, courted Charlotte's daughter, Mary. On 9 December Watt proposed to Mary and was accepted. 'Then of course followed mysterious disappearances on the part of the females, slamming of doors, brandies and water, and all the usual concomitants of "declarations"' (9/12/76). By 27 January the engagement was off, 'the eyes of both being opened to the fact that they are entirely unsuited to one another' (27/1/77).

By 1879 Duncombe's sight was deteriorating and Armstrong would read to him when he visited (4/4/79). The following month they met in London, where Duncombe had gone to visit a specialist about his eyes, which were getting worse (14/5/79). The following year he was in London again, this time consulting physicians, but was dangerously ill with cancer in the gullet which meant he could not swallow and was getting weaker. 'Poor William's case is a hopeless one' (30/10/80). There were plans to take him back to Norfolk, but on 2 November he died before he could be moved (2/11/80). This was a sad blow for Armstrong, who befriended Charlotte and her children, who spent Christmas and New Year 1881 with the Armstrongs. In June the Rokelles house was given up and they again came to stay, planning to move to the continent 'for the sake of economy' (17/6/81).

The women in Armstrong's life

As we saw in the previous chapter, Armstrong remarked after going with his father to see some beautiful and elegant Spanish dancers 'how sad it is that so much that is so beautiful should be so closely allied with sin' (9/12/54). He was by no means blind to the charms of women, but for him it was accompanied by a sense of guilt. In January 1862 Armstrong recorded the names of three women whom he regarded as his closest female friends. They were Mrs James, 'his first love', Emily Plumer, the daughter of Lady Plumer of Canons Park in his old parish of Little Stanmore, and Mary Hales.

All their names appear frequently in the diaries. In the early pages there is mention of 'his first love, Harriet Palmer', often accompanied by twinges of regret. On his fortieth birthday he lists his many blessings, but his sadnesses included the death of baby Gertrude and the 'hidden grief' of his 'first love' (11/11/57). His relationship with her was as a very young man in his first year of studies at King's College, London, when the prospect of marriage was a long way off. They kept in touch and she later became the wife of a West Country parson, the Revd Robert James, and would write to Armstrong asking for the loan of sermons, which he was happy to send, along with his *Manual of Prayer*, in the hope that 'she will use it, there being something soothing in the knowledge that one once dear to you, presents themselves before the Throne of Grace with the same supplicant as oneself' (31/3/56). In 1857 he records receiving a letter from her; 'She always writes in an interesting rather tender way' (6/3/57). When he was on holiday in the West Country in the summer of 1859 he planned to call upon her in Exeter, but she was away: 'perhaps for the best' (12/9/59). Later, in 1865, he arranged a meeting for the first time in twenty-five years 'by appointment' in London accompanied by his mother, but she was not as beautiful as he remembered her:

> There must be something in first love, however we may deride it in after years, that should impart an interest to a meeting after a separation of 25 years! After many narrow escapes of meeting at intervals during all that time we <u>did</u> meet today.... Alas, time and illness have made such havoc on her beautiful face!

Her manner and expression had also changed:

> She had lost her girlish gentleness; instead she had the tone of an
> invalid. I was much shocked. (30/1/65)

They continued to correspond and she confided to him when her son
made an unsatisfactory marriage, but they never met again.

Lady Plumer, widow of Sir Thomas, lived at Canons Park when
Armstrong was the incumbent of Little Stanmore-with-Whitchurch.
She and her family were supportive of his high church views and his
work within the parish. Her name occurs frequently in the diaries. After
he left Stanmore he visited her whenever he was in London and she
was one of the sponsors at his daughter Gertrude's baptism. He kept
in touch with her daughters, Georgiana (born 1833), and particularly
Emily (born 1834), who often came to stay in Dereham and lived in
London for many years.

The woman with whom Armstrong had a long-lasting and close relationship was his 'dearest friend', Mary Hales. We know little about her
except that she was one of ten children of James, a Norwich solicitor,
and Barbara Hales, whose memorial stone is on the floor in the cloisters
of Norwich Cathedral. Three of her siblings died as teenagers, her father
in 1831 at the age of 48 and her mother in 1850, when Mary was 24. A
brother, John Hales, was a well-known doctor in Holt who donated a
window to Holt church. A sister was married to the vicar of Whinburgh,
the Revd William Grigson, whom Mary frequently visited, and there
was a clerical brother living in Yorkshire. She also had close friends or
relatives at Blackheath, where she sometimes stayed. How Armstrong
met her is not clear. He was already describing her as 'his dear friend' in
1854 when they were at a dinner party in London together which was
also attended by the duc de Roussillon, who 'hearing my dear friend
Mary Hales was well off, paid her some attention. I fear he is an adven-
turer' (28/6/54). He may well have been the same 'duc' who attempted
to extract money from his sister eighteen years later (p. xxx). By July
she was back in Whinburgh, staying with her sister. Armstrong claimed
that his particular interest in Mary was because she was 'an orphan
without a sympathising home' (16/4/55). He even considered offering
her a home in the vicarage, but thought that 'tongues would wag'.

She frequently joined the Armstrongs on their outings both in and around London when she was in Blackheath and in Dereham when she was at Whinburgh, and was treated almost as a member of the family. They corresponded regularly and she agreed, along with Lady Plumer, to be a sponsor for baby Gertrude (7/5/55). It is clear that Armstrong was very fond of her and that the feeling was mutual. In March 1855 she came to him to consult him about an offer of marriage she had received and about which he found it difficult to advise her.

> My dear friend, Mary Hales, came to consult me about an *Affair de Coeur* in which she is concerned, and in which the *coeur* is only on the gentleman's side. I suppose her ultimate decision will depend upon how far she really assents to the opinion that every woman *ought* to be married under any circumstances.

He hoped his advice was disinterested, but he felt that their relationship would change. 'That which subsists between a married man and a single woman however pure it may be, must be different. Her husband, even if accepted without the fullest affection, becomes her <u>all</u>.' He might even be jealous. The result would be 'an acquaintance rather than a friendship', seen by Armstrong as totally different. 'I fear I may lose my last friend as I lost my first love but how thankful I should be that my sadly sensitive disposition can find repose in the affection of my beloved wife and darling children' (7/3/55). He was much relieved when she refused her suitor, but did not seem to consider that his own wife could feel jealous in the same way as a prospective husband of Mary's might.

In the autumn of 1856 Mary took a lease on Heath Cottage in Dereham so that she could stay there rather than with the Grigsons and so become a regular attender at church. 'She comes chiefly for the benefit of my ministry', Armstrong assured himself (21/11/56), and she soon became a District Visitor. Armstrong spent a considerable time taking her round, sometimes with Helen, to familiarise her with her district. He admired the way she had furnished the cottage. He described her as 'admirable in dress and sprightly withall' (7/3/55), while his wife, 'dressed in black velvet and old lace with one or two good ornaments' (13/5/55), as we saw earlier, must have seemed dull in comparison. Very soon she was organised enough to give dinner parties to which Armstrong and his wife were invited.

It is from 1857, while she was living at Heath Cottage, that Mary features particularly frequently in the diary. On 1 January the Armstrong children, then aged between 13 and 4, were taken to a children's party there to meet the little Grigsons. Later in the month Helen went to stay with Mary for two days and on 1 February 1857 Armstrong records that Mary 'stayed all night' at the vicarage. She was taken by the Armstrongs to many of the social events in the area to meet local society. In March she stayed at the vicarage for a few days, and with 'Nellie's permission has given me a beautiful ring as a token of friendship' (11/3/57). She went back to her house a few days later, 'although finding it a sore trial living alone' (15/5/57). A week later they were in Norwich together, buying Mary a pony carriage, and the following week she came to tea. She regularly dined with the family and the curate on Sundays after evensong. In October she again complained of being 'desolate living alone' (16/10/57) and stayed at the vicarage for Christmas that year. She was well connected locally and the Ffolkes family of Hillington Hall were cousins. She stayed with the Cauldwells at Hilborough Hall for several days and then visited them when they moved to Wiltshire. In the census of 1861 Mary Hales is described as a 'landed proprietor' and she went to Armstrong for financial advice: 'Went through Mary Hales' affairs with her and showed that she was not getting enough interest.' She had also spent more on her new house than her income justified. 'However it is wonderful how she manages' (4/5/57).

When she had a dinner party she would ask Armstrong, 'as clergyman', to act as host (15/6/57). Even when the family went to London for their annual visit, Mary Hales would be there, 'enhancing the pleasure' (15/6/57), sometimes staying with friends at Blackheath and sometimes with Armstrong's parents at Wimpole Street.

Mary continued her tenancy of Heath Cottage until 1860, throwing herself into parish work, where she was 'a most energetic and working parishioner' (23/12/58). On one occasion 'Her kindness won the poor thing's heart', resulting in the reforming of a woman on her visiting list (20/11/56). Later in 1858 there was a further gift of a print of St Augustine to hang in his study (11/11/58). In Armstrong's eyes, Mary Hales could do no wrong. She was energetic, had a good dress sense, furnished her house in the best of taste and was lively company. He was undoubt-edly flattered by her admiration and attention. In June 1859 Armstrong went fishing at Bilney, something he frequently did, enjoying the beauty and tranquility of a summer evening. He caught a bream, laid it on water-lily leaves and gave it to Mary Hales on his way home (9/6/59). We do not hear of him making such a simple gesture of affection towards his wife, and what she thought of the situation is not recorded. Armstrong often described her as 'uncomplaining' and she certainly had a lot to put up with. She must have felt she was the dowdy vicar's wife with the responsibilities of the house, family and entertaining all falling on her. Armstrong, however, felt sure of his ground. He knew the importance of 'disciplining the affections'. It was the 'great secret of happiness and existence and the only safeguard against moral defection' (12/8/54).

However, alongside Mary's vivacious character there seems to have been a certain instability. As early as 1854, during the Crimean War for which she had enthusiastically collected money and bought flannel underclothes to send to the troops, she even considered joining Florence Nightingale's nurses, something to which Armstrong thought she was totally unsuited, commenting somewhat unkindly that 'she would soon be among the nursed' (8/12/54). In August 1859 she was on the vicarage sofa suffering from a 'depression of spirits'; shortly after-wards her brother came from Yorkshire to visit (5/9/59). She was an ardent admirer of Armstrong and his Christian mission and must have wished that their relationship could be closer. By 1860 she was 34 years old and may have felt she was heading for unfulfilled spinsterhood. There was a strange episode only half-explained in the diary when she wrote a 'long heart-broken letter' to Armstrong while he was in London about a broken engagement with E. Hastings, possibly the doctor's son (29/1/60). A few weeks later 'she broke her imprisonment' to stay with his parents in London. 'I am well pleased that she is under the protec-tion of those I love so dearly' (16/2/60). A few days later she wrote to Armstrong to say that now the match was 'quite off', an explanation would be demanded from Mr Hastings. 'Now if he was badly minded he has it in his power so to twist and controvert things as to do Mary and myself much injury, but I hope better things of him' (16/2/60). No more was heard of the affair, but perhaps they both realised the danger of their friendship, however innocent, and how easily it could be misconstrued. There was certainly a change of tone between them. Their relationship cooled and she became particularly restless. Within a few weeks Mary was back in Dereham, but planning to sell her house and move to join her brother in Yorkshire. In June she held a farewell dinner in her house, but seemed in no hurry to leave. She stayed at the vicarage for most of August and was planning to live in London.

A further leaving party was held. 'The house to be stripped of its tasteful decorations and will descend to the class of a farmhouse' (30/8/60). In October she sold her furniture, except what she would use in lodgings, and Armstrong write that 'she will be rescued from her lonely life on the Heath' (10/10/60). She was still in Dereham at the end of the year, lodging at the bottom of Church Street, next to the church, with Philo, the parish clerk. On Christmas evening she organised the choir to sing carols on the vicarage lawn, to the delight of the family, and afterwards Armstrong escorted her home in the bright moonlight on one of the coldest nights ever recorded (25/12/60). A few days later Mary had a fall on the ice and was in bed at the vicarage. 'Doctor fears it may be a long affair' (28/12/60). One senses a degree of frustration in Armstrong's tone. The months went by. She resigned from the District Visiting Society and by March she was able to get to church in a wheelchair. It is not clear how long she remained in the vicarage, but by census night in April 1861 she was back in lodgings next to the vicarage with a nurse to look after her. Armstrong described her as 'very weak and low' (14/4/61). By June she had moved to London and gave him a prayer book when he visited. In the summer she was back in Dereham and in December was finally winding up her affairs there before going on a two-month visit to Yorkshire. She was obviously in a very unsettled state and Armstrong was beginning to feel somewhat irritated by her. 'I shall lose an active helper, but perhaps too active. The poor girl's generosity and zeal sometimes outruns her discretion, the consequences of which do more harm than good' (19/12/61). By June she had moved to London, where he and Helen called upon her. 'London agrees with her. She is far less lame but very feeble' (6/5/62). Anxious that she should be kept busy, the next day he went to the neighbouring All Saints' church to recommend her to the incumbent and suggest he should give her 'some useful work'. However, she was still restless and came several times to stay in Dereham. In February 1862 she was back in London and 'took rooms near the church. I fear she will be very lonely after 6 months visiting friends and relations' (26/2/62). Little more is recorded in the diary about Mary until the following year, when she went to Brighton for her health. In 1864 she went to Cannes for several months because 'of an infection of the lungs' (16/2/64) but was back with her sister in Whinburgh by September, her health said to be 'not good'.

It was at this time that Mary seems to have shown an interest in joining a religious order and Armstrong took her to Ditchingham to visit the sisters there (20/10/62). Nearly all such sisterhoods were urban creations, but All Hallows, Ditchingham, founded in 1854, was in the depths of the country on the Norfolk–Suffolk border. Armstrong was a supporter and on its council (7/11/61). It provided a home for 'penitents'. In 1864 he took a girl 'that he had rescued from degradation to live there as a penitent' (13/10/64). In the 1860s an orphanage was added for 'the impoverished female children of the better class'. The rector was the warden and Miss Lavinia Cross the superioress.[2] Back in London in 1865 Mary was preparing to be the superior of a home and sisterhood (16/1/65).

This was a period when such sisterhoods were being founded, the earliest being Park Village, Regents Street, founded in 1845, where four ladies taught pauper children and ran an orphanage. Archibald Tait during his time as Bishop of London, before he was elevated as Archbishop of Canterbury in 1868, was active in regulating the many sisterhoods springing up at the time. By 1900 there were over ninety, with over 10,000 women having tried the religious life. They were mostly founded by women of extraordinary character. They came in for a great deal of criticism, being accused of being Roman Catholic orders in disguise and supporters of the Irish nationalist Fenian movement. In a male-dominated world they were accused of giving free range to power-mad, sadistic mother superiors. 'Combining as they did, authority and autonomy for women with Anglo-Catholic theology, there was something in sisterhoods to offend almost all the taboos of this profoundly paternalistic and fiery Protestant culture.'[3] Their members were drawn mainly from the professional and gentry classes, a group in which Mary Hales would have been very much at home. They were attracted to the religious life for three main reasons. They wanted to devote themselves to a life of prayer, they wanted to work with the poor and deprived and they were motivated by the high church desire to return to the medieval ideals of the monastic life.[4] This explosion of interest in a communal life is an indication of a growing pent-up demand for an alternative to marriage that would develop a woman's intellectual, practical and religious potential to its furthest extent. Armstrong saw it rather differently and was very sceptical about the motives of some of the entrants. He wrote of a friend, 'I rather doubt her vocation, but this seems to be the recourse these days for girls who do not marry' (19/3/70). Again, later in life, he wrote of a local lady, 'an exemplary person, always hanging on the fringe of a "sister's" work, but never taking the final plunge. There are a great number of this sort of female about, the best thing to happen to whom is, that they have a family of their own to manage' (1/1/79).

When Armstrong next visited Mary in 1865 she 'looked very well in her sister's habit' and was in a religious house which she had founded, attached to St Mary's in Paddington (3/6/65). Later in the year she was accepted as a probationer at St Peter's House, Brompton, an Anglican community founded in 1861 by Mr and Mrs Benjamin Lancaster, which ran a small convalescent home. 'May this change of life be conducive to her happiness here and hereafter, though I cannot think it is her vocation' (27/9/65). In 1866 he described her as having 'many qualifications for this work, but lacks some' 'More of a Martha than a Mary' (29/5/66). Restless as always, she moved from one sisterhood to another while spending quite some time in Whinburgh. Finally, at the end of 1872 she was living at an orphanage of her own foundation on the Harrow Road where she supported and educated seventeen children. It was paid for by a laundry on the premises. A Miss Hawthorne helped her. 'There is a pretty little chapel furnished with an altar' (14/10/72). We hear little more of her, although Armstrong occasionally called on 'Sister Mary'. In 1877, she was at St Agnes's orphanage in Chiswick and Armstrong delivered to her care a small child from Dereham who had been looked after by her grandmother, but who, on her death, would be homeless (16/12/77). The following July he visited the orphanage where she had 'forty little unfortunates' and where the Dereham child was doing well (17/7/78). In May 1879, when he was in London 'picking up several lost stitches in the web of one's acquaintances', he visited Sister Mary, who had now 'become very grey and fat, but looks well and is as energetic as ever'. 'Like so many of our acquaintances, she has become a total abstainer' (29/5/79). His final visit was in 1882, when he called on Sister Mary at her orphanage, now in Fitzroy Square, and was shocked to see how much she had deteriorated in appearance. 'I fear the institution to which she has given everything, is not in a flourishing state' (1/6/82). There was little glamour in these fledgling sisterhoods, where hard work dominated over the contemplative life. As in Mary Hales's case, they worked mostly with women and children and always the poor.

This sad story shows Mary as the victim of their impossible relationship, which caused firstly her ill health and unsettled state and which then led her to put her energies into a life to which she was not really suited.

His departing friends

The last years covered by Armstrong's diaries, which end in May 1887, record the deaths of many of the people who had been very much part of his life. William Duncombe's death in November 1880 and Dean Bull's in May 1886 were particular blows. In December 1885 Canon Jones of Bradford died. Although not mentioned elsewhere in the diary, Armstrong described him as 'one of my oldest friends and one of the very few left'. He had been a curate at Holborn when Armstrong had been in London (5/11/85). Nellie died in 1888 and it was Helen who looked after him for his last few years. The entry immediately before his own in the Dereham burial register[5] is that of Mr Philo, aged 85, who had been his parish clerk for all his thirty-eight years as vicar. Presumably he was the son of the Edward Philo who died in 1829 and is mentioned in George Borrow's *Lavengro*. He is frequently mentioned in the diaries and his down-to-earth understanding of human nature amused Armstrong. After a funeral at which the 'grief of the widow at the grave [was] very affecting to behold', Philo commented that 'such noisy mourners speedily marry again' (13/6/54). He was less astute when it came to his business affairs and Armstrong had to help guarantee loans to his creditors (26 and 27/2/65) to prevent him being ruined. In later life he went blind, but was still a member of the choir and able to entertain them at their annual supper with the comic song 'Johnnie Sands', as he had always done (27/1/85).

The diaries reveal a whole cast of colourful characters who were part of Armstrong's life. Many were acquaintances or colleagues, but among them were some deep and lasting friendships which he greatly valued and which enriched his life and our understanding of him.

Notes

1   T. Pocock, *Rider Haggard and the Lost Empire*, 1993, 2.
2   W. White, *Norfolk Directory*, 1864, 486.
3   Susan Mumm (ed.), *All Saints Sisters of the Poor: An Anglican Sisterhood in the Nineteenth Century*, Church of England Record Society 9, 2001, xii.
4   O. Chadwick, *The Victorian Church*, vol. 1, 1966, 505–6.
5   NRO, PD 86/23, MF704.

IV
Later Life

Ten

The Later Years

Town and church

By 1870 Armstrong felt he had succeeded in most of the reforms he wanted to make in the parish. There were three Sunday services, as well as a daily service and special celebrations at feasts and festivals. There was a weekly Communion, and a surpliced choir using *Hymns Ancient and Modern.* Beyond the regular services there was a branch of the Society for the Propagation of the Gospel, the St Nicholas Guild for young men, a Union of Church Workers, thriving church schools and a Sunday School, both in Dereham and at Etling Green, a library, shoe savings club and work fund. The District Visiting Society was an active support for the vicar and also ran the lending linen store and clothing club. The church itself had been 'restored', stained-glass windows installed and walls decorated to his satisfaction. When he had come to Dereham his parishioners, except for George Carthew the antiquarian, had been 'evangelical to a man' but by the 1870s they had mostly been won round. A high point had been in 1866, when the parish had presented him with a silver cup filled with 105 sovereigns in recognition of his work in the town and the establishment of the third Sunday service. Carthew spoke of the town's gratitude, explaining that the gift had been a spontaneous one from his parish. There had been no effort to solicit gifts. In his reply, Armstrong expressed his great gratitude to them (27/6/66). Industrial development encouraged by the arrival of the railway meant the town continued to grow and with it the need for a second curate. Permanent missions were set up in Toftwood, a fast-growing hamlet on the edge of Dereham where there were seventy houses by 1881, and also in Etling Green.

Not content with all he had achieved, in 1879 Armstrong embarked

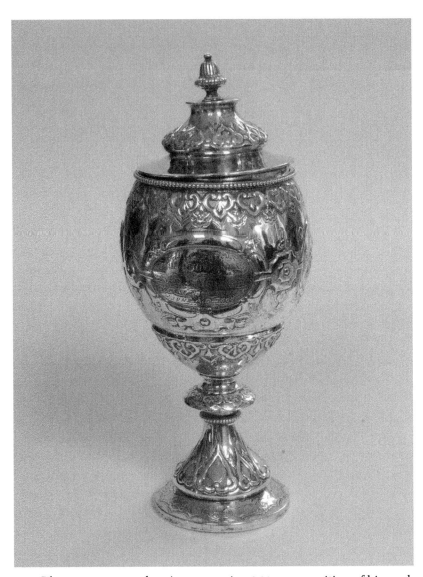

29 Silver cup presented to Armstrong in 1866 as recognition of his work
in the town. The inscription reads, 'Presented with 100 guineas to the Revd.
B.J. Armstrong, vicar of East Dereham. June A.D.1866.'

on a project to build a mission church on the Norwich Road out of Dereham to serve the rapidly expanding town in this direction. It occupied much of his time, until in March 1880 the new church was consecrated by the bishop and dedicated to St Withburga. An opening service was held on 4 April. Later that month Armstrong wrote in his diary that he had been in Dereham thirty years and would not attempt any more changes (20/4/80). In spite of his obvious hard and dedicated work in his large and growing parish he always felt that because of his high church practices, he was looked over for promotion by the low church bishops of Norwich; something that his wife may well have felt more acutely than him.

Two new religious movements reached Dereham in the later years of Armstrong's ministry. In 1862 the Church of England Temperance Society was founded, and reconstituted in 1873 on the American model. Various local societies were set up in the north of England and support for the movement increased. Its first tea party in Dereham, arranged by Mr Watt, Armstrong's curate, was held at the Corn Hall in September 1878, when '150 poor sat down in the Corn Hall, some ladies assisting'. This was followed by a concert (11/9/78). A further concert with readings was held in December. The coffee tavern was opened in 1879. Watt's enthusiasm for the movement was described by Armstrong as fanatical and in December 1880 he announced he would be retiring as curate to become the Society's secretary. Watt encouraged total abstinence, something Armstrong could not support, but towards which the Society was moving. If the society goes that way, 'I will have to retire as it would prevent me conducting our establishment in a liberal manner' (9/1/82). Regular meetings continued. A concert in the Assembly Rooms with Armstrong presiding attracted a large audience, 'including leading residents of the town'. There were solo vocal, piano and oboe pieces, 'many of which were encored'.[1] Later in the month Dr Russell gave a talk 'from the medical point of view' (20/1/80), and in September 1883 Mr Horsley, the chaplain at Clerkenwell prison, preached at the Temperance Society's choral service: 'having so much to do with criminals his evidence is valuable as to drunkenness being the cause of so much rural crime. He is a singular looking man with long hair behind and a red beard down to his waist' (11/9/83). The 1884 annual mission of the Temperance Society was not well attended. Armstrong felt the

30 St Withburga's chapel, opened in 1880, now converted into a house.

subject had been overdone. The non-total abstainers were regarded with 'indifference' by the abstainers (26/11/84). By this date his son John had taken over the position of secretary and vice-president from his father. However, the Society was still going strong in Dereham in 1891, when the *Norfolk Chronicle* reported on the annual Christmas tea, for which Dr Vincent lent his lantern for the lantern slides.[2]

A second movement, linked very much to temperance, was the Salvation Army. Founded in 1864 under its leader General Booth, it very soon gained support amongst the urban poor and spread more slowly in the countryside, where it had to compete with Primitive Methodism. Armstrong described 'the triumphal entry' of Booth as he travelled from the railway station into Norwich in 1885:

> He drove in a carriage with a pair of grays and stood on the seat waiving his handkerchief whenever there was a lull in the cheering. Two alleluia lasses followed in a waggonette dressed in scarlet and looking and behaving like anything but respectable females. There was brass band, of course. The whole accompanied by a body of roughs extending from the houses to the opposite side of the street. There was something absolutely painful in such a travesty of religion. None of the respectable tradesmen with whom I had occasion to converse had anything but misgivings about the whole movement. (23/4/83)

Later in the year the Army sent a 'detachment' to Dereham to carry out an 'assault and bombardment against the citadel of sin'. Armstrong wrote somewhat sardonically that 'the bombardment was of a quiet character'. He did not believe that the instantaneous conversions claimed by the movement were likely to be long lasting, but grudgingly admitted that 'if any were to turn to the right way through this movement, I would truly rejoice', and he purchased a copy of the *War Cry* from a 'alleluia lass' for a halfpenny (25/7/83). Over the winter of 1883/4 numbers at church were somewhat diminished because of the attraction of the Salvation Army meetings, but by March they were returning to the church. Armstrong was told by a parishioner he visited that conversions could indeed be long lasting, and that four railway workers who had been drunkards were now reformed. 'I sincerely hope such a change may be permanent' (11/3/84). The Salvation Army band usually played in the Market Place on a Sunday afternoon, which would attract the crowds, but in January they stopped banging drums as there were complaints from householders that they were too noisy.[3] In June 1884 the Burial Board agreed that there were to be no bands or other music in the cemetery and that this decision should be passed on to the Salvation Army.[4] Armstrong noted with approval that on the day of the church parade of the Rifle Volunteers, the band was not there and so did not play in competition with the Volunteers (30/9/84). Open-air meetings, such as those on the Market Place, were a feature of the movement and they also hired the old theatre (St Nicholas Hall). It was not until Armstrong was retiring that the foundation stone of the Army's tabernacle in St Nicholas Street was laid by Colonel Nicol on 22 May 1888.

A third movement which the clergy could hardly ignore was caused by the agricultural depression which began in the 1870s and was felt by landowners, farmers and their labourers alike. The long series of bad harvests which began in 1865 did not create the scarcities and thus high prices which had happened in the past. Instead, particularly after the end of the American Civil War in 1869, cereal prices actually fell as American grain began to reach the British market. As Norfolk was mainly an arable county, farmers there suffered more than others, with prices falling by 40 per cent between 1873 and 1896.[5] They could not pay their rents or tithes and the income received by landlords and parsons fell. Farm labourers also suffered as harvest pay was reduced. In 1868 real wages fell drastically and after a temporary rise in 1870 they continued to fall. Early spring was the traditional month for an increase in wages as the new season of farm work began.

Farm labourers were beginning to look at the example set by their urban industrial counterparts, who were founding trades unions. When wages fell further in February 1872, a meeting in Wellesbourne (Warwickshire) led to the founding of National Agricultural Workers' Union under the charismatic leadership of Joseph Arch. A few weeks later the first strike was called. News of these events spread rapidly to East Anglia through the pages of the radical *Eastern Weekly Press* and Arch travelled the country recruiting members. In April 1872 farm labourers met at Elsing, near Dereham, and a Dereham-based union was founded. Its leaders were a group of men, most of whom had learnt their leadership skills in the Primitive Methodist chapels and were drawn from a class of self-educated, independent small traders. A strike was called in December 1872 which was not settled until February 1873 and was claimed as a success. Although there was a fiercely local element in the early unions, gradually they joined Arch's national movement and in 1873 the branch became the East Dereham District of the National Agricultural Workers' Union.[6] In April 1875 Armstrong attended a meeting addressed by Arch in Dereham Corn Hall where he was

> haranguing a vast concourse of labouring men to join the union. A thickset coarse sort of man. He is decidedly revolutionary. He let off the church better than I expected. Very hot. I felt green all evening from the steam rising from so many with whom cleanliness was not next to godliness. (6/4/75)

The following year, when he went to Hoe to take a service, Armstrong found that 'the countryside' had gone to Swanton Morley to hear Mr Arch. The leader of the Dereham branch was George Rix, a smallholder and grocer in the parish. Only one person was in church, to whom Armstrong gave 1s for his steadfastness. Mr Lombe, rector at Swanton, was furious that Arch had stolen his congregation (2/4/76). In December Arch was in Dereham again and this time the church came in for more criticism over education, but the meeting is not referred to by Armstrong.[7] Peak membership of the Dereham branch was in 1877, with 1,800 members drawn from a wide area within a 10-mile radius of the town. However, agricultural depression and with it declining farm incomes meant that strikes were less likely to be successful and membership gradually declined. There was still grumbling resentment and Armstrong records the setting fire to stacks in Toftwood by 'incendiaries' in 1881 (7/4/81). Despite a resurgence in 1892, by 1897 the Dereham branch ceased to exist.

The links between unionism and Primitive Methodism were strong, with many of the leaders being preachers in their local chapels. It is not surprising, therefore that there was resentment among union men of the parson's control of church schools, which were often the only means of education in the villages.[8] Most were teetotallers with a strong sense of independence and desire for self-improvement. They hardly deserved the description of 'roughs' which Armstrong gave them.

When relationships between farmers and their labourers became so heated that they resulted in the formation of an agricultural union and strike action, the church had to take notice. In November 1873 the Parochial Work Association chose as the subject of its meeting 'The Labour Question'. The clergy were increasingly identified with the landed interest, which is not surprising as many came from gentry families and derived much of their income from farming their glebe and from tithes. One of the speakers was the Revd Maynard Wodehouse Currie, a member of the Wodehouse family of Kimberley, rector of Barnham Broom and vicar of Kimberley. He echoed Armstrong's view that labourers were heavy and dull, criticising their 'passive acceptance' of the 'practical serfdom' in which they lived, which was a 'sad proof of the class's degradation' (a view also expressed by Augustus Jessopp).[9] He therefore welcomed the 'way the Union had woken them up; 'At last the sluggish waters are stirred'.[10] A second paper was by an equally well-connected parson, the Revd Frederick Blackett de Chair, who was both rector and patron of Morley, near Wymondham. He also deplored the poor living conditions of the labourers and pointed out that 'every village had been affected by the labour movement'. However, he was keen to blame the union press for whipping up anti-clerical feeling with phrases such as 'a serf clergy can never properly train a free people' and 'labourers know that the clergy are their worst enemies'.[11] While all this would probably have been well known to their audience, what was more important was their view as to how the clergy should react. Both speakers suggested that the clergy should not interfere. Currie said the labourers 'should know the clergy are their friends', whilst encouraging prudence and self-denial, and at the same time discouraging their more well-to-do parishioners from indulging in 'luxury and extravagance'. De Chair also emphasised the neutral position they should take. They should not preach on the subject or lend the schoolroom for union meetings. Neither should they farm on their own behalf, as this would put them on the side of the farmers. Instead they should teach and preach 'the grand old truths of the Christian Faith'. The impression that Armstrong took away from the meeting was that 'the debate, in which I took no part, was feeble, the general feeling being that the clergy had better let it alone, and that the question would, in time, rectify itself after the law of demand and supply' (6/11/73). This rather limp response did nothing to endear the rural clergy to the rural poor. By the 1880s Edward King, Bishop of Lincoln, was concerned by what he saw as his clergy's contempt for 'rustic spirituality', summoning them to 'a higher conception of pastoral work'. Lincolnshire villagers might become 'models of what English agricultural poor can be when they have been made intelligent members of the Church. We do not know yet what spiritual capacity and beauty there is in our people.'

Armstrong's concern for the affairs of the town never diminished. In 1878 a new society, described as the Athenaeum, is mentioned in his diary. He gave a lecture to it with the title 'Duties of Young Men to Themselves' – a repeat of one given to a similar group in Watton twenty years before (29/1/78). In 1880 he presided over a well-attended meeting at the Assembly Rooms to found a Literary Society connected to the Athenaeum. It was to meet weekly for readings and monthly for a musical evening. The president was to be Captain Bulwer and the Armstrongs, father and son, were vice-presidents.[12] At its annual meeting in 1886 Armstrong senior spoke, encouraging the reading of history, biography and travel rather than novels, 'Advice which I do not in the least believe they will follow' (6/1/86). The Society was still going strong in 1891, after his death, when there were 240 members and a library of 2,500 books.[13] In 1879 he bought shares in the Coffee Tavern, supported by the Temperance Society, which he then visited and found the 'bar very comfortable, good meat dinners and sleeping rooms'. Although it was all very clean, the coffee was 'execrable' (21/2/79).

The year 1875 saw the passing of a Local Government Act, which created Local Boards for both rural and urban areas responsible for public health, including sewerage and drainage. In 1879 Armstrong was elected a member for Dereham, 'which hitherto has been in the wrong hands, the members doing nothing but quarrel and abuse one another till at length half resigned' (3/3/79). At the first meeting he attended a case of smallpox was reported (20/4/79). Its main task, however, was the provision of a water supply, drainage and a sewerage system, and in 1881 Armstrong was complaining that the town was dug up for the provision of drains. At the September meeting the question of connecting private houses to the system and the carting of stone to mend the roads was discussed, but Armstrong took no part in the discussion.[14] He noted in his diary a population increase for the town shown in the 1881 census from 5,107 in 1871 to 5,563 in 1881 and pointed out that much of this was due to the number of itinerant navvies working on the sewers and piped-water supply system (20/4/81). Its completion in 1882 saw a new landmark on the town's skyline in the form of an ornate brick water tower on the hill beyond the town's cemetery. By 1882 the main subject for discussion was the paving of streets, and Armstrong was adamant that the paving or concreting of Baxter Row should come before the kerbing of Cowper and Norwich roads on the edge of town.[15] The arrival of piped water meant that there was the opportunity to open public baths as a commercial venture. In June 1887 both Dr Vincent and Armstrong attended the opening by Colonel Bulwer of public baths in Norwich Road. They were owned by 'Mr Mayes' (probably Richard Mayes, joiner and builder of 8 Norwich Street). How successful the venture was or how long the baths lasted is not known.[16]

Although already handing some of his parish work to his son John, who became one of his curates in 1880, Armstrong was still active in the town. As well as the Local Government Board he supported the new town fire brigade and in 1881 took the chair at their public dinner in lieu of Colonel Bulwer. He presided over the Oddfellows' dinner the same year (29/5 and 1/7/81). The autumn flower show was later held in the vicarage garden (8/9/81).

Armstrong would have seen many changes to Dereham during his long period as vicar. The population had risen to over 5,000 from the figure of 4,000 when he had arrived. He took an interest in the new industries that were developing. In 1874 he went to see the new leather factory near the station which employed a hundred men working machines powered by steam (15/5/74). Four years later he visited a boot and shoe factory in Church Street: 'Quite a new feature in our town, as we have no other factories except one for leather and two for agricultural machinery.' Fifty people were employed. A pair of boots could be made from the uncut skin to completion in two hours. 'All the different parts of the boot, the cutting out the soles, making uppers and heels to toecaps are done in separate rooms' (20/9/78). Factory work was attracting a new sort of person to the town, 'part dissenting and part antagonistic to any form of Christianity and is a most serious and difficult problem to solve' (16/5/74).

The town was spreading out from its core around the market. Rows of terraced workers' houses were built along narrow streets and professional families were moving out from the Georgian houses in the centre to Victorian villas on the outskirts. Between 1861 and 1871 Armstrong's friend George Carthew, solicitor and antiquarian, moved from the crowded Quebec Street to a villa on the newly developed Quebec Road. When John became his curate, Armstrong complained that there were no suitable houses 'in town' (5/2/80), but 'a gentlemanly little place in Quebec Road, the healthiest and most picturesque part of the parish' was found (3/3/80). John's neighbours in 1881 included several retired farmers and ladies of private means, solicitors, a bank manager, the manager of the gas works and several tradesmen, moving out from living over their premises around the market.

An event that appears in the pages of the later journals is the 'farmers' tea'. Armstrong first attended in 1883 when the new landlord of the King's Arms, 'a churchman', invited him. He explains in his diary that this was not in fact a tea but 'a really good cold dinner'. It could go on late and was of 'a slightly political and agricultural nature interspersed with songs and music'. In 1883 it was attended by a hundred people; the Norfolk tenant farmer MP C.S. Read was in the chair and made a speech (16/11/83). In 1885 and again in 1886, at a time of great agricultural and local distress, Armstrong himself took the chair (23/1/85 and 19/2/86). In 1885 Read had spoken complaining about the level of taxes farmers paid and also about the Parliamentary Reform Act allowing the vote for the first time to farm labourers.[17] Farmers generally resented the clergy, probably because of arguments over the payment of tithes, and Armstrong's farmer friend Mr Everington told him that on the train to the Saturday market in Norwich it was all that the farmers talked about, 'although the interests of the two are so interwoven' (16/11/83). At the tea in 1887 Read was again in the chair and compared the dull church services when he was a boy with the bright and cheerful ones introduced by Armstrong, who was 'a powerful preacher well aided by his son'.[18]

The 'teas' continued into the 1890s, and at the event shortly before Armstrong's death in 1890 Mr Everington recalled with affection

31 Dereham as shown on the Ordnance Survey map of 1882 (Norfolk XLIX 13). The town has spread out along the roads and industries have developed along the railway, but there are still plenty of orchards and market gardens on the outskirts.

Armstrong's time as vicar. 'He was a man of great ability and piety and endowed with great common sense and a kind and genial friend. The parish, according to the Bishop, was one of the best organised in the diocese.' He also commented on the 'good feeling that existed between the late vicar and the ministers of other denominations in the parish'.[19]

A highlight for Armstrong was being chosen by his friend Colonel Bulwer of Quebec Hall to be his chaplain during his time as High Sheriff in 1883. This involved attending the Assizes in Norwich and giving the Assize Sermon in the cathedral, which was bound to attract a lot of publicity. Together they went to the city, and, dressed in his 'new canonicals', he accompanied Colonel Bulwer in a state carriage to the judges' lodgings in St Giles to escort the judges to the cathedral, where trumpeters set up a fanfare. His topic for the sermon was 'Which is the Great Commandment of the Law?' There was an 'excellent luncheon' and 'grand dinner' at the court house to begin the week. After all the pomp and circumstance they returned to Dereham, 'after a novel and interesting week of which however I was beginning to get somewhat tired' (6/8/83). The whole thing was repeated when the assizes were held again and a further sermon was preached. In his sermon of February 1884, Armstrong stressed that punishment would not stop crime. Instead it was necessary to look to religion.[20]

In 1884 the Third Reform Act was passed by William Gladstone's Liberal government, giving farm labourers the vote. Armstrong records a meeting about the franchise bill in the Corn Hall organised by the Conservatives which was disturbed by 'roughs' (3/10/84). The first election under the new law was in 1886 and 'to judge from the specimens exhibited in Dereham, however, it seems a perilous thing to extend the franchise to roughs, many of whom cannot read or write'. The result in Norfolk was that 'Mr Arch the demagogue and agitator and deceiver of labourers has gone from the plough to the senate' (9/12/86), replacing C.S. Read.

Although Armstrong had largely refused to become involved in political debate, thinking it unwise for a clergyman's name to be linked with any particular party, the next generation was not so cautious. In 1883 the Conservative Primrose League was founded, so called because the primrose had been Disraeli's favourite flower. It encouraged the membership of women, although they did not as yet have the vote;

the press noted that at the League's meeting in Dereham in June 1886, Armstrong's curate's wife (his daughter-in-law) was in the audience. The main theme of the evening was opposition to home rule for Ireland, while bemoaning the fact that 'an avowed atheist was in the legislative assembly of our Christian Land'.[21]

With many of his local friends dead (George Carthew, the antiquarian and Armstrong's churchwarden of nearly twenty-five years, with whom he had frequently smoked a pipe, had died in 1882), and changes in society with which he could not agree, Armstrong's final years in Dereham were those of retirement from public life, but there is no doubt that he had taken his duties as a prominent member of Dereham society very seriously during the nearly thirty-eight years that he was its vicar. The opposition which he had encountered to his church reforms from such influential people in the town as Dr Vincent and the lawyer Halcott Cooper had disappeared. His efforts to involve a wider section of the population, particularly the younger men, in church life had paid off. His relationship with the non-conformists was sometimes cool and he thought there would always be resentment amongst the radicals, but in both the church and town he had made a real difference in many ways.

Family

Armstrong celebrated his fiftieth birthday in 1867 and soon began to feel that his responsibilities were changing. His mother died in 1869, aged 75, his father was becoming increasingly fragile and the ill feeling between him and his sister was increasing. He now needed to wear spectacles when reading in the evening (1/1/70) and later in the year went to see a London doctor who diagnosed a depression resulting from thirty years of work (13/8/70). He was spending an increasing amount of time in London with his father, who was no longer able to manage his financial affairs, at the same time allowing himself visits to art exhibitions and attending the opening of Bethnal Green Museum (26/6/72). In May 1873 his father had a stroke which left him paralysed and speechless. He had let much of his London property fall into bad repair and Armstrong had to organise the necessary repair work, which meant that he was spending more than his income (23/8/73). Much of the summer was spent about his father's business and finally on 29 December came the news that his father had died, aged 80. Armstrong now felt the responsibility of being head of the family. Sorting his father's affairs took much of his time through the early part of 1874. His father had never thrown any papers away and Armstrong came across his weekly letters to him going back thirty-five years. His death left a great gap in his life. As well as corresponding regularly all their lives, they had always enjoyed their jaunts together. Now Helen began to take his place as a companion. Together they went to the National Gallery. She 'is as fond of these things as I am' (9/12/74).

Like all parents, anxiety over his children's future continued for Armstrong as they grew up. By the 1870s it was no longer their education that worried him but the careers of his sons and the long-term prospects for his daughters. Helen was always his favourite and was destined to remain at home with her parents and look after her nieces and father in his old age. Unlike her younger sister, Lilly, 'she never gave her parents displeasure, living the purest and most useful life' (6/9/73).

32   The Armstrong children in the vicarage garden, 1872.

All was going according to his father's plan for his eldest son's career in the church, until in August 1873, he heard that John had 'formed an attachment to Mary, a clergyman's daughter [the Revd George Bell, curate for the absentee rector of Snoring] who has not a sixpence'. This was not the only bad news he received that week. Arthur Nelson, the son of another penniless parson, was courting Lilly. 'Then I found the sympathy of my wife enlisted on her children's behalf, giving Lilly permission to correspond with Arthur Nelson, and consenting to chaperon Miss Bell, whom I have not seen, and both without my knowledge' (23/8/73). In spite of their father's objections, John and Lilly became engaged to their respective partners in July 1874. 'This is a great trial in a parent's life' (10/7/74). In August Lilly went to stay with the Nelsons, and 'brought her lover back with her' (24/8/74). Armstrong was still unhappy, particularly about the financial arrangements. However, at the beginning of September he went to London to see a lawyer about Lilly's marriage settlement (1/9/74). The young couple intended to farm and Armstrong was led to understand that Arthur's father would provide them with the money to start up. However, it turned out that it would only be a loan with interest. 'To start on borrowed capital would be ruinous and consent must be withheld' (15/9/74). The resulting tears and resentment can be imagined, and finally Nellie took Lilly to Brighton as 'she needed a change after her recent disappointment' (1/11/74). Within three weeks Arthur had followed them to Brighton, called on Lilly at 8.30 a.m. while her mother was at morning service, taken her to a church, and they were married by 9.30 a.m. 'Grief and indignation knew no bounds' and Nellie felt guilty (26/11/74). She went straight away to stay with John in Thatcham, where he was curate. They then met up with Armstrong at St Pancras and decided to stay in London, calling on Annie, who 'was pleased to regard the matter in a romantic and cheerful point of view' (28/11/74). After all, the elopement could have come straight out of one of her novels. A couple of days later a letter of repentance came from Lilly.

Thus 1874 ended with all Armstrong's children, except the exemplary Helen, a worry to their parents. Soldier Herbert was in Bermuda overspending his allowance with not enough to do, and the deceitful behaviour of Lilly and Arthur over their secret marriage was still an open wound. John preferred to spend the time with the Bells in the impressive, but inconvenient, sixteenth-century rectory at Snoring. 'Sad that he prefers to spend time there rather than with his family after all the sacrifices they made for him' (20/12/74). Christmas that year was therefore a lonely time with only Helen at home.

The beginning of 1875 was no better, with the death of Armstrong's sister Annie, who had become a recluse in her final years. The Wimpole Street house was then sold and 'Dereham was now the headquarters of the family' (13/3/75). In April Armstrong had the pleasure of hearing John preach for the first time in Dereham, and by May he was able to write in his diary that life was far less stressful. His father's affairs were sorted, his sons settled, Lilly married, the worry over his sister was over and his bank balance was better (13/5/75). Now that he had two curates he was able to take longer holidays, and in August he set out with Nellie and Helen for a month on the continent, visiting the Netherlands, Belgium and Germany. In November Lilly and her husband came to stay. They had not been seen since their marriage and the visit must have been awkward to begin with. However, they seemed happy and prosperous, but Armstrong was pleased that there were as yet no children (18/11/75).

John was now anxious that his marriage should take place, and in January 1876 Armstrong met the Revd Robley Bell to discuss the prospects for the couple. There would certainly be a shortage of money. 'The dear boy indulges in the "Love in a cottage dream".' The engagement has been for two years and 'he could have done so much better' (28/1/75). A month later John was getting impatient. 'I replied that the pecuniary difficulty was in no way solved ... if he deliberately chose to make a poor man of himself for life the responsibility was with him' (21/2/76). In May a curacy that would allow him to be married was found for him at Brome, just over the border, in Suffolk. They would be living in a former rectory. Armstrong was still worried about money but hoped 'the young couple would be happy' (16/4/76). On the day of the wedding he was still fretting that 'John could have done better', but wished him well (18/4/76). It was not long before Armstrong was reconciled to the marriage and John's 'bonnie little wife', buying them a cart, strong cob pony and a new harness. On 1 July he took his 'dear daughter-in-law, whose good qualities become more apparent, to Norwich, to effect some business in the plate line and to furnish them with a hamper of port'.

The month following John and Mary's wedding saw Armstrong and his wife staying in London, where Lilly and Arthur joined them before they all went to the Nelsons' Berkshire farm in Sulhampstead, in wooded countryside not far from the river Kennet and 10 miles south of Reading. The house was 'very bright, pretty and happy, but still not the sort of home we could have hoped for our child'. There was plenty of stock, 'which alone can pay the farmer these days, all in good order' (25/5/76). The mid-1870s were difficult times for farmers and even livestock could not be guaranteed to make a profit. It is unlikely that Arthur Nelson as the son of a clergyman had much farming experience, and so it is not surprising that by the end of the year Lilly was writing to her father saying that the farm was a losing affair and they were thinking of giving up (28/11/76). The following February Nelson was declared bankrupt, a fate not uncommon amongst small, undercapitalised farmers at the time. He had not admitted how bad things really were and Armstrong could not forget that their marriage 'had begun in deceit'. Nelson attributed his failure to bad land and the fact that he had invested too much in setting up the farm. Armstrong's main concern was that 'our poor child is without a home of her own' (7/4/77).

The next year began on a more cheerful note. All the family were home in the New Year and in February John announced that a baby was on the way. Armstrong was still worried about their finances and when the young couple went back to Brome via Norwich, he travelled that far with them and bought them a small stock of wine to take with them on the train to Diss. 'I don't know how they manage' (on John's income) (26/7/78). A grandson was born on 15 October and baptised on the 27th.

Meanwhile Armstrong's younger son, Herbert (Bertie), was making his way in the army. His first regimental appointment was as a sub-lieutenant in the 97th Foot. In 1881, when county regiments were established, the 97th Foot became part of the West Kent Regiment, with which Herbert served for the rest of his career.

The period following the Crimean War, which had ended in 1856, was a time when Britain had kept aloof from European conflicts. Armstrong and his compatriots watched with horror the Franco-Prussian war and the fall of Napoleon III, but there was no British involvement. Instead concerns were more with the expanding British Empire. Troops were stationed in India, where numbers had increased since the Indian Mutiny of 1857. In 1858 the Crown took over control from the East India Company and appointed a viceroy. Soldiers were also sent to the West Indies, where they were more likely to die of disease than in combat. It was therefore no surprise to Bertie's parents to learn that after a spell in Colchester and Sandhurst, Bertie would be going to Jamaica. On 5 April 1874, Armstrong went to Liverpool to see his younger son off on the boat for Halifax (Canada), from where he would sail to Bermuda. Once in Bermuda, Bertie's letters described a life of ease with his fellow officers, and Armstrong was concerned that he did 'not have enough to do', which could easily result in overspending (13/7/74). The following year Armstrong heard that Bertie had in fact overspent and he was worried that his son was gambling, which proved not to be the case (7/7/75). In September he was promoted to lieutenant. Overspending continued into the following year, and at the end of July Armstrong increased his allowance. At the end of 1877 he came home after three and a half years abroad, and in spite of all his worries and family troubles, Armstrong could write that he was proud of his soldier and parson sons (7/12/77).

After a family Christmas Herbert enjoyed five months' leave before sailing for Halifax in May. He was back again in October to qualify as an adjutant and then to return to Halifax to train troops in musketry. In December he distributed prizes to the Volunteers, 'looking very fine in his uniform' (9/12/78). His course was over in April and he returned to Halifax. Armstrong described him in July as 'Thoroughly honourable, but thoughtless and vain with an absence of resources within himself. These defects of character are full of danger' (3/7/79). He was frequently overspent 'but claimed to be reformed', and so Armstrong agreed to pay his debts (2/11/79). In November he returned to the depot in Maidstone.

Meanwhile Arthur Nelson had found himself work at the Paris Exhibition and he and Lilly moved there: 'Quite a new era for Lilly' (22/3/78). Armstrong, with his wife and Helen, visited them in June. The Nelsons were home by December and stayed in Dereham until February, when they went to Arthur's parents: 'Their future depresses me' (18/2/79). By late summer they were living in Chippenham and 'Lilly, I am sorry to say, is to become a mother. How they can support a family on such small means I know not' (9/9/79). In November he and Nellie went to Chippenham to see her. Armstrong was impressed by the picturesque town with its cheese market and was pleased to see the 'comfortable apartments in which they were living' (11/12/79). Arthur's father called to visit and a couple of days later they went to call on him in his parish of Biddestone, 6 miles from Chippenham. To Armstrong's prejudiced eyes it was 'an out of the way dilapidated place of 400 inhabitants'. The church he described as a 'beautiful new one built by the local MP', although in reality it was mostly thirteenth century, and had been restored rather than rebuilt. The vicarage, described as a 'very poor affair', was in fact a fine, large stone house, but it may well have been in poor condition at the time (15/11/79).

The year 1880 began with Helen going to stay with her sister, to be with her for the birth of her child, and a daughter, Helen, was born on 19 February. Armstrong wrote rather unkindly, 'in the present state of their finances they would be better without children' (19/2/80). Meanwhile, in May, with the departure of the senior curate at Dereham, John took the position and moved to a house in Quebec Road with his wife, Mary, and their baby, Herbert Benjamin. Gradually he took on more of the parish duties from his father. In July Lilly came to stay for six weeks with her baby and a nurse. Her husband managed to get 'a situation in some factory' in the Yorkshire town of Ripley. Armstrong hoped it would 'lead to something better', but meanwhile they were to live in lodgings and Lilly left to join him (16/8/80). Armstrong did not know the area and he took his wife and Helen on a visit. Ripley turned out to be an unpleasant town dominated by coal furnaces and they soon moved to an inn in Matlock. They thought Lilly's lodgings were poor and that she looked pale (5/10/80). They enjoyed visits to Haddon Hall and Chatsworth before returning to Dereham. By the end of the year Herbert was again home having a long leave before sailing to Gibraltar: 'The army is an easy life and well paid' (16/11/80).

The army could certainly be an easy life so long as there was no enemy to engage. So far, Herbert had been on garrison duty in Bermuda and training duties in Halifax. However, the long period in which Britain had avoided military action was about to change, as was the theatre of war. From the 1870s attention was turning to the colonies, particularly Africa and India. In Africa the competition between European nations to establish colonial rule was intensifying, and in South Africa there were clashes between the native Zulus, the Dutch settlers, or Boers, and the British. The discovery of diamonds in the Dutch Orange Free State in 1869 resulted in a rush of prospectors to the Kimberley region, and the disorder that ensued provided the British army with an excuse to move in and administer the area. In 1877 the British annexed the Boer colony of Transvaal to forestall a Zulu advance. By 1879 the British settlers were in danger from two directions. The Boers were threatening revolt and the Zulus were amassing an army under their leader Cetawayo, who inspired as many as 40,000 followers, superbly trained in tactics that could easily out-manoeuvre the lumbering columns of British soldiers led by their smartly dressed officers, all in highly visible red tunics. The shock back at home was immense when news came through that a British force had been slaughtered by Zulus at Isandhlwana in 1879.

Rider Haggard, the son of Armstrong's friend, Captain Haggard, who was in South Africa at the time, reported the details and that many of his friends were killed. He wrote home to Bradenham announcing that he would be joining a volunteer troop because the 'emergency was too great ... to hang back now'.[22] More British troops were sent to the area and the Zulus were finally defeated outside Cetawayo's capital Ulundi in the northern part of what is now Kwazulu-Natal in August 1879. In October Armstrong had dinner with the Bulwers at Quebec Hall, where he met a party from South Africa who reported that the Zulu War was an 'absolute necessity' as the colony of Natal was at the Zulu's mercy and without a victory over him, 'every white would have been murdered. Information from such near sources is always interesting' (1/10/79).

With victory over the Zulus secured, many of the British troops were sent home. But this, and the loss of a common enemy encouraged, the Boers to declare war on the British. British troops were again needed and Gibraltar would be the port of embarkation for the war zone. It looked as if Herbert might see some action as he set sail for Durban on 19 February 1881. He did not wish his parents to come and see him off. The casualty lists of Norfolk officers had been long and it was with heavy hearts that they said their farewells. News of the defeat of British troops by the Boers at the battle of Majuba in Transvaal on 27 February reached Armstrong the next day. 'Thankful Herbert not there, being not quite half way' (28/2/81). The scale of the slaughter and defeat caused consternation in the British government, which determined to send ten more regiments, but also to try and agree terms of peace. Meanwhile a letter arrived from Herbert, sent from Madeira, assuring his father that he could now live within his army pay, 'particularly as one has to live on Government rations which one gets free' (7/3/81). At this time Rider Haggard was writing home with the news that morale amongst the settlers in Natal was low, especially as it seemed that the British government was inclined to make peace with the Boers at almost any price. By the time Herbert arrived in Newcastle, near the border with Orange Free State and Transvaal, at the beginning of August, the Pretoria Convention was almost ready to be signed. His letter home explains that he was now training soldiers in the use of muskets, and that he was on a captain's pay, but other than this the only news is of a deal he had made over the purchase of a horse. There is nothing about the negotiations with the Boers and the fact that the Pretoria Convention ending the war had been signed on the third of the month (8/8/81). This granted the Boers self-government in the Transvaal, while Britain retained nominal suzerainty and control over foreign affairs. We do not know whether Herbert met his Norfolk contemporary from Bradenham, Rider Haggard, while in Newcastle. Like other disillusioned settlers, he was planning his return to Britain. The farm and his household goods were sold by auction on 25 August, after which he went with his family to Newcastle for a few days before traveling on to Durban and sailing for Britain on 1 first September 1881.[23] After the signing of the Pretoria Convention, the army presence in South Africa could be reduced, and Herbert was on his way home in the New Year, reaching Dereham at the end of March, by which time his captaincy had been confirmed (27/3/82). A month later he was garrisoned in Aldershot, where he remained until August.

In Dereham, meanwhile, John was settling into his responsibilities as senior curate and Lilly was dividing her time between Malmesbury and Dereham. Arthur Nelson was making little effort to find a job and seemed happy to live off Lilly's allowance.

The other major British possession was India, and keeping the trade routes open to India was a major concern. The opening of the Suez Canal in 1869 was of crucial importance in this respect. The shares in the canal were divided equally between Egypt and France. By 1875 the Egyptian government, whose rule also extended into Sudan, was bankrupt and Disraeli immediately bought its shares on behalf of the British government, thus preventing the French from increasing their influence. The weak and corrupt Egyptian government was soon faced by a rebellion led by the Egyptian nationalist Arabi Pasha, and in order to increase its influence in the area and protect its interests in the Canal, Britain sent an expeditionary force to support the government. On 3 August Herbert wrote from Aldershot that his battalion had been ordered to go to Portsmouth the following day to embark the same evening for Egypt to be part of the expeditionary force. This sudden news was a shock to his parents: 'God knows when the poor fellow will be home

33   Queen Victoria sees Herbert's regiment off as it sails to Egypt in August 1882. Illustration from *The Graphic*, 12 August 1882.

again if ever! Daily the Egyptian crisis becomes more intricate' (5/8/82). Many Norfolk officers had gone with the force and Egypt was the main topic of conversation at the garden parties that summer. By the end of the month action was imminent. Alexandria was bombarded by the British and Herbert described its destruction as 'complete' (28/8/82). There followed land engagements with the enemy, 'but our dear Herbert was not in either of them. This war occupies everyone's attention and everyone seems to have some relation in it' (30/8/82). There followed a week or so of stalemate with no information in Herbert's letters, except of heat, flies, sand and filthy water (7/9/82). Finally on 13 September came reports of the great victory at the battle at Tel-el-Kebir, 60 miles from Cairo. Herbert, though, had been left with a portion of his regiment to guard the camp. The telegram with news of the battle arrived only hours after the battle had been won. 'The actual fight which took place in Egypt <u>this very morning</u> and we knew of it in Norfolk <u>before luncheon</u> whereas in 1798 the news of the Battle of the Nile took <u>six weeks</u> before it arrived in England' (13/9/82). The following day Armstrong wrote, 'Thank God the name of our dear boy is not among the casualties' (14/9/82). The surrender of Cairo followed swiftly and the British occupation of Egypt, securing the Suez Canal and the route to the east, began. As Egypt also ruled much of Sudan, British control extended south into this tribal area. Christmas at the Dereham vicarage was enlivened by the news that Herbert had landed from Egypt, and on 1 January he arrived in Dereham, bringing a copy of the Qur'an for his father which he had looted from an enemy tent. The whole family was at home and Herbert was to remain for eleven months on leave, most of it spent at the vicarage.

Lilly remained in Dereham after Christmas to await the birth of her second child. A baby girl was born on 27 March and all went well for some days. However, she soon began to seem unwell and Dr Hastings was called. He recognised that there was a problem, but could find no cause. The following day, 'I was convinced that the hand of death was upon the dear child.' A Norwich doctor was telegraphed who came and diagnosed an embolism, 'deranging the whole arterial system and inevitably ending in death', and Lilly died on the evening of 8 April. All three children were at home. Helen 'behaved like a heroine, John was of the utmost use and poor Herbert was sadly overcome' (8/4/83). Arthur had been summoned, but did not arrive before she died. Such was the local degree of sympathy expressed that prayers for the family were offered up by the dissenters in the 'Cowper memorial Meeting House' (11/4/83). The funeral was on the 12th. Arthur Nelson left again on the 16th, leaving his two children to be brought up in the vicarage. Helen was godmother to Lilly's older child, now 2 and 'an engaging little thing', and she became responsible for her upbringing as well as that of baby Margaret, 'so the nursery is started again with a new generation' (15/4/83).

Meanwhile the situation in Egypt and Sudan was by no means settled. It was important to British imperial interests that the route to India via the Suez Canal should be secure and this meant stable government in Egypt. There was a British military presence in Egypt as well as Egyptian-held Khartoum. In 1881 Muhammad Ahmad proclaimed to the Sudanese that he was the Mahdi, a leader many Sudanese expected to appear to restore justice to the oppressed. He appealed to a people subjected to their corrupt Egyptian rulers and his army swept through the country. The British feared that he might reach Egypt and immediately sent the army back to Alexandria, so on 26 November 1883 Herbert set sail again. Gladstone's government was reluctant to get involved in a war in the Sudan and wanted to limit British involvement to protecting Egypt, so General Gordon was sent to evacuate the Egyptian garrison from the city of Khartoum. Instead of ordering an evacuation, Gordon prepared the city for a siege, which began on 13 March. Later in the month the British won a decisive battle at a strategic point on the road, at Tamiya, some 40 miles south of Cairo, and the Mahdi's triumphant progress was halted. Gradually the war was changing from a defensive to an attacking one, very much supported by public opinion at home. Armstrong was relieved to hear that Herbert was still in Alexandria, and later heard that he was enjoying sumptuous living in a palace near the sea. 'The officers have a boat on which they disport themselves' (1/5/84). In July Gladstone, in response to public opinion, reluctantly agreed to send a force to relieve Gordon and in August Herbert moved to Cairo to join the expedition up the Nile. 'The enterprise will be full of difficulty and danger' (1/11/84). By the end of the year Herbert had only reached Luxor, where he was enjoying the sites, but Armstrong caught the jingoistic atmosphere of the time and wrote, 'this is the greatest undertaking of the age' (30/12/84).

Back in Dereham there were other things to occupy the family. In February Arthur Nelson came to stay to see his daughters. Armstrong was pleased that he took an interest in them, though he still had no work — Armstrong described him as 'lazy and good natured' (13/2/84). In June John's second child, Dorothy, was born. This made Armstrong even more anxious that John should have his own living. However, the next month Armstrong suffered a fall in which he dislocated his shoulder. It took him some time to recover and he began to feel his age (66). 'It is not to be wondered at my time of life this accident should have thrown me a good deal out of health. It is a time of life when most people do meet with a bad accident which often proves to be the beginning of the end' (4/8/84). He came to rely very much on John's support in parish work.

In January 1885, the main British force entered Sudan and Herbert's letters record the towing of their boats up the Nile and marches through difficult terrain. However, on 5 February the shocking news reached home that Khartoum had fallen on 26 January and Gordon, along with all the Egyptian troops and most of the inhabitants, had been slaughtered. Armstrong was relieved that Herbert had not yet reached the town. A letter received on the 8th had been written near Korti, about 150 miles north of Khartoum, describing his beautiful camping spot in a jungle. The inhabitants had probably never seen a white man, 'and were amused at his washing and astonished at his washing his teeth' (8/2/85). Now that Khartoum had fallen, the point of continuing the campaign was unclear and Armstrong was now referring to it as 'this wretched campaign' (15/2/85). By the beginning of March the troops were retreating and assembling at Korti. At the end of April the troops were being recalled from the Sudan. The Mahdi had 'vanished and there is no "enemy" to be found and no further object in the expedition'. In August came news that the Mahdi was dead and on the 17th a letter from Herbert arrived to say he had been suffering from a fever and was being sent home on three months' sick leave. On the 26th came the news that he had been promoted to Major and that 'He is also honourably mentioned in dispatches ... considering he is only 32 or 33 years old, I consider he has been most fortunate' (26/8/85). In 1886 Armstrong wrote, 'The army is a great profession for getting on' (15/2/86). Congratulations flowed into the vicarage from friends, although those whose sons had not been mentioned, such as the Edwards, Bulwers and Haggards, were more reticent. 'I fancy Herbert's promotion is due to his having conducted his boats so far up the Nile and bringing them safely back to Wadi Halfa' (31/8/85). Herbert arrived in Dereham on 26 September 'looking pale and thin, but will soon rally no doubt' (26/9/85). By the end of the year he was safely at Colchester barracks and from March the following year was to be stationed at Shereness. Herbert had been in the army eleven years, and although he had been promoted to Major, had not fired a single shot in combat. We know little about the later years of his career, but when he retired in the early 1890s he had reached the rank of colonel. Armstrong's remark that an army career was one in which one could 'get on' may well have reflected his own lack of promotion under his low church bishop.

The new regime in the vicarage was settling down. By 1885 Helen was mostly in charge of Lilly's children, but went for a short holiday to Lagley. In September the Nelson grandparents came to visit. Nellie was afraid that they might want to take the children away, but this fear was fortunately unfounded. 'Arthur as usual doing nothing and seeming to lose what little "nous" he ever had' (22/9/85).

For the first time, 1886 saw far fewer entries in his diary and Armstrong was clearly feeling old. 'Though able to do my work, I am not so well as I used to be' (13/3/86), and again a month later, 'old age is now on the threshold' (26/4/86). A few days later he did not attend the diocesan conference, 'too much out of health to attend' (29/4/86). The family did not go for their annual visit to London in May because Armstrong was not feeling up to it, but instead went to Yarmouth. The quiet and the sea air did him some good: 'I had kept at home too long' (30/6/86). In October Herbert was home from Chatham on leave, much to the pleasure of his proud father. At Christmas he wrote, 'I have not been able to do as much over the last three months as I used to.' John was doing more (25/12/86), taking services and presiding over the many clubs and societies with which his father had been involved. He took the choir on their annual outing to Yarmouth (16/9/86). John's particular project was the Churchman's Society, designed to attract younger men like himself. Meeting weekly, in 1884 its numbers were said to be 'steadily increasing' and it 'offered a pleasant and instructive evening for all'.[24] Subjects ranged from John Armstrong himself talking on the first chapter of St John's gospel, 'Why Should We Have an Established Church?', 'Purity and Impurity' ('for which there was a large attendance') and the Prayer Book, to secular subjects such as 'Life Saving at Sea', Dr Vincent on 'The Digestive Organs' and 'a lecture on electricity accompanied by some capital experiments'.[25]

The last diary entry was on 12 May 1887, when Armstrong recorded that he did not attend the officers' dinner because he did not feel up to it. He preached his last sermon on Good Friday 1887 on the theme, 'Christ Crucified'.[26] In May 1888, Nellie, his wife of forty-eight years, died at the age of 72. Her funeral was marked by deep respect throughout the town, with shops shut and shuttered. The church was full, with all the 'leading ladies, gentry and tradesmen'. However, Armstrong himself, already in poor health, was not there.[27] When later in the year John became rector of Heydon, Norfolk, a parish in the gift of Colonel Bulwer, Armstrong's

34 Armstrong in later life.

time to retire had come. The *Norwich Mercury* commented that 'The loss of both these gentlemen will be felt in the town.'[28] He stayed at the vicarage with Helen and the Nelson grandchildren until they found a house in Elvin Road just off Quebec Road and not far from the Market Place. On his death the *Norwich Mercury* wrote that he retired 'on account of ill health, having given up active duty some time previously. During the later years he had suffered from paralysis and latterly the malady which affected both mental and physical faculties assumed a more acute form.'[29]

It is clear that concern for his children was an important part of Armstrong's life. Herbert was the only one of whom we are given any sort of character analysis by his father. Easygoing and rather lazy seemed to sum him up. Why he could ever have been 'mentioned in dispatches' was a source of wonder, even to his father. Both Helen, always described as 'dearest', and John performed perfectly the roles that had been mapped out for them, while Lilly, always described after her marriage as 'poor', was the rebel.

Armstrong died on 20 December and on 30 December was buried near his wife, Nellie, and his daughters, Gertrude and Louise (Lilly), in Dereham churchyard beside the cross he had erected for his infant daughter in 1856. He had been vicar of Dereham for thirty-eight years. The *Norfolk Chronicle* recorded that his funeral was attended by a large number of his parishioners. 'His long and successful work in the parish endeared all to him by his kind good nature, geniality, uprightness and zeal for his work.'[30] A muffled bell was tolled to signal his departing and the *Dead March* was played on the organ on the Sunday following. 'He was greatly respected by all classes in the community. The poor to whom he was exceedingly kind will long cherish his memory.'[31]

Notes

1 *Norfolk Chronicle*, 17 January 1880.
2 *Norfolk Chronicle*, 10 January 1891.
3 *Norfolk Mercury*, 19 January 1884.
4 *Norfolk Mercury*, 14 June 1884.
5 S. Wade Martins, *Changing Agriculture in Georgian and Victorian Norfolk*, 2002, 89–100; S. Wade Martins and Tom Williamson, *The Countryside of East Anglia*, 2008, 12–14.
6 A. Howkins, *Poor Labouring Men*, 1985, 61–8.

7   *Norfolk News*, 2 February 1876.
8   N. Scotland, *Methodism and the Revolt of the Field 1872–1896: A Study of the Methodist Contribution to Agricultural Trade Unionism in East Anglia, 1872–96*, 1981, passim.
9   For instance, A. Jessopp, *Arcady, for Better or for Worse*, 1887.
10 R. Currie and F. de Chair, 'The Clergy and the Labourers' Movement'. Two papers read to the General Meeting of the Pastoral Work Association, November 1873, 73.
11 Ibid., 89–97.
12 *Norwich Mercury*, 30 October 1880.
13 *Norfolk Chronicle*, 10 January 1891.
14 *Norfolk Chronicle*, 17 October 1881.
15 *Norfolk Chronicle*, 26 August 1882.
16 *Norwich Mercury*, 4 June 1887, W. White, *Norfolk Directory*, 1883, 227.
17 *Norfolk Chronicle*, 31 January 1885.
18 *Norwich Mercury*, 27 February 1886.
19 *Norfolk Chronicle*, 8 January 1890.
20 *Norfolk Chronicle*, 16 February 1884.
21 *Norfolk Chronicle*, 5 June 1886.
22 Quoted in T. Pocock, *Rider Haggard and the Lost Empire*, 1993, 33.
23 Ibid., 53.
24 *Norwich Mercury*, 19 January 1884.
25 *Norwich Mercury*, 15 March 1884; 2 January 1886; 27 March 1886; 22 January 1887; 11 March 1888.
26 NRO, PD86/46.
27 *Norfolk Chronicle*, 5 May 1888.
28 *Norwich Mercury*, 18 February 1888.
29 *Norwich Mercury*, 27 December 1890.
30 *Norfolk Chronicle*, 30 December 1890.
31 *Norwich Mercury*, 27 December 1890.

Eleven

Armstrong: A Man of His Time

A biography can be read on two levels. First, it is a story of an individual life with its moments of joy, worry, emotional turmoil and tragedy, with which we empathise as fellow human beings, and certainly Armstrong's diaries allow us to enter and share his experiences with him. Second, a biography can show how upbringing, education and circumstances have shaped the subject's role and influence on events around him. In this way it is more than simply the story of a life, fascinating though that may be; it is also a contribution to an understanding of the times in which that life was lived and its contribution to the changes and debates of the period. This final chapter attempts to look back over Armstrong's life to discern how far he was an influence for change, both in the town and on the church he loved.

Armstrong's upbringing and early life were very much that of a young man born into a comfortably off family benefiting from the increasing commerce of the early nineteenth century. He took the conventional route through school and university and was as well equipped as any new clergyman of the time to take up a role as parson in his own parish. It was a role he fulfilled for forty-six years until his retirement in 1888.

The years which passed between Armstrong's ordination and his death in 1890 were a period of great change, both within the church and in society as a whole. When he was a child, the family retreat at Southall had been in the countryside, but with the arrival of the railway in 1856 it attracted a new sort of commuter and gradually lost its rural atmosphere. His first curacy was in the slums of Saffron Hill, but by the time of Armstrong's death the area was gradually improving. Changes during his time in Dereham included an increase in population by a third to over 5,600 as, attracted by the railway, more industries arrived. The town became a healthier place to live as a result of the work of local boards on which Armstrong sat. The provision of schooling, over which the church had almost a monopoly until 1870, was now a shared responsibility with the School Board (with which Armstrong was not associated). Three Board Schools had joined the church-controlled National School as providers of elementary education in Dereham. The increasing of the franchise in 1884 to include the labouring class meant a dramatic change in the power structure in Armstrong's part of Norfolk. C.S. Read, a well-to-do farmer and an acquaintance of Armstrong's, was replaced as MP by Joseph Arch, the founding leader of the farmworkers' union. Gradually, the strict social boundaries between classes, which had been such an important foundation of Armstrong's social life, were beginning to crumble.

The period was also one of great change within the church. By the time of Armstrong's death the life of gentlemanly ease which had been typical of the country parson was replaced by one of dedication and care for his parish. Absentee parsons were a thing of the past, and whether they were low church Evangelicals such as Henry Tacey of Swanton Morley or high church ritualists, their time and energy were now devoted to their parishioners. There can be no doubt as to Armstrong's conscientious hard work, but some of his early contemporaries of the old school were only gradually being replaced by more professional new men, sometimes trained in the theological colleges founded mainly in the early years of Victoria's reign.

Armstrong saw his aim as working for the 'Glory of God and the Salvation of Souls', to be achieved through a church building returned to what he perceived to be its pre-Reformation glory in which all the trappings of music and ritual would inspire his congregation. As important was the encouragement of the school and regular visits to the poorer inhabitants of the town. In an age when the only form of social welfare was through the workhouse, the role of the clergyman within his community, supported by a band of local Visitors, could be vital. His control over parish charities meant that it was up to him to distinguish between 'deserving' and 'undeserving' cases and this strengthened his hold over a deferential society. His presence at many death-bed scenes meant that he was more familiar than most of his class with the deprivation to be found in the yards behind Dereham's main streets and in the poor-quality and overcrowded cottages of surrounding hamlets.

However, in spite of his frequent dealings with his poorer parishioners, he had very little understanding of them. He described them as 'heavy and dull' (9/12/53) and difficult to engage with. To him the poor 'all seem alike' (26/11/64). The social divide was too great for any real empathy.

This constant association with the poor and the depressing conditions of their existence could wear him down and he frequently records in his diary his need for change. He described himself as being of an anxious and nervous disposition and not of a strong constitution. Dedicated as he was to his church work, he also complained sometimes of its 'monotony'. He was a man who thrived on new experiences, and especially travel. The growing rail network in Britain and across Europe opened up travel to a newly leisured middle class. He looked forward to his six weeks' holiday a year, which was divided between London, travels with his father and family trips to the seaside.

As well as his clerical duties, Armstrong was deeply involved with the affairs of the town. He was responsible for the setting up of the town Institute with its library and programme of lectures. He took the chair at the annual dinners of local bodies such as the Oddfellows Friendly Society and was active in his encouragement of the local Rifle Volunteers. In all these duties he was ensuring that the church was central to town life. His later involvement with the 'farmers' teas' meant that he also understood something of the agricultural interest of the area, at least from the farmers' point of view.

He saw his role extending to local government. He was on the local Sanitary Committee and later on the Cemetery Committee. He was able to negotiate a settlement in a dispute between the town council and the local gas company, and after the establishment of wider powers for local government he was on the board which was responsible for introducing drainage and piped water to the town. In these roles he had to engage with the tradesmen and professionals within the town, a more independent-minded group than the subservient poor and with whom his relations were not always cordial. Unlike many of his contemporaries, however, he did not think it was right for the clergy to be magistrates. In that role they could not be seen as 'friends of the poor'.

So how effective as a force for good within Dereham was the Revd Benjamin Armstrong over the thirty-eight years of his ministry there?

When he took up his post he found a church which he described as neglected by its sinecure rector and vicar. However, the state of the church before Armstrong arrived must not be exaggerated. His description of the dereliction of the chancel is not supported by a drawing of the church made before Armstrong began his restoration, and much of the work in the chancel was paid for by the sinecure rector. Nevertheless, in the years that followed the church was completely transformed. Stained glass filled the windows, walls were painted and box pews removed. Changes to the building were reflected in the style of worship, which gradually became more elaborate. Many of these changes were not welcomed by his congregation, but it says something for Armstrong's personality that they were finally accepted. When Dereham was visited by reporters from the *Norfolk News*, described by Armstrong as a 'radical' newspaper, he received a far more complimentary portrayal than his high church and unpopular neighbour, the Revd Salisbury Everard of Swaffham.

Ultimately working for the 'salvation of souls', Armstrong's regular involvement with the schools was to ensure that the children were being taught the principles of the Christian faith, while the main purpose of his visits to the poor was to encourage them to have their children baptised and then to send them to school. His presence at death-beds was to give the Last Rites and provide Christian comfort to the dying and bereaved.

In the town as a whole, his service on committees and influence on affairs generally ensured his popularity amongst his own class. He was prepared to work with the dissenters on secular matters such as the running of the Institute, but could never accept their legitimacy, always stubbornly referring to their chapels as 'meeting houses'. His conviction that the Church of England was of divine origin while all dissenting sects were of human creation (3/4/68) led to an intolerant and, at best, patronising attitude to other Christian denominations in the town. His concern with the minutiae of worship, such as the details of ritual, could prevent him seeing the bigger picture.

It would have been easy for a clergyman of a small market town involved in local affairs to have a limited interest in the wider world. However, this was never the case with Armstrong, who needed the stimulation of new experiences and places to counteract the 'physical and nervous debility' of which he frequently complained. He often bemoaned the small talk which dominated the gatherings of the neighbouring gentry. In contrast, he would enjoy an evening of more informed and academic conversation with his antiquarian neighbours, George Carthew and, later, Augustus Jessopp. Towards the end of his active life, when he was feeling tired and depressed, the annual holiday in London was exchanged for a trip to Yarmouth, 'because my health was at a low ebb'. Even this less ambitious break did him good: 'I had kept at home too long' (19/5/86). This passion for new things was something he shared with his father. He never ceased to wonder at the speed of the railway which allowed him to get to London easily. While there, often with his father or other members of his family, he would visit galleries and theatres and attend lectures at a dizzying pace. As well as the annual London trip, there were expeditions further afield, firstly mainly within Britain, but as Thomas Cook introduced cheap excursion tickets, they travelled further afield to Ireland, France and Germany, while Armstrong's last overseas adventure took him to Mont Blanc. On his return from these jaunts he would put together a lecture on his travels to deliver to the Literary Institute.

A reality of Victorian country life was the overwhelming importance of social position, with its many nuances, and in this regard his outlook was as narrow as those around him. He married socially above him and was keen to stress his wife's connection to Lord Feversham, someone whom they never visited and who never featured in the diary. However, the relationship, no matter distant, may well have given him an entrée to local aristocratic society. He felt that his children should have looked to improve their standing by 'good' marriages. Above all else, money and social position mattered. Both John and Lilly married the children of clergy, something one might have expected to be acceptable, but both marriage partners were the children of poor parsons. He frequently bemoaned the fact that John could 'have done better'. Eventually he realised that John's wife was in fact a strong support to her husband and accepted that this was more important than money. Lilly's husband, on the other hand, was a ne'er-do-well who, after her death and much to Armstrong's chagrin, chose to live off her marriage settlement.

Armstrong's attitude to the leisured classes was ambivalent. On the one hand he enjoyed grand dinners, such as those given at Letton Hall, but on the other he 'disapproved of the aristocratic and worldly set' with their idle conversation and small talk. Choosing dinner guests to invite to the vicarage could be a real problem. Mixing town and country did not work well. 'This absurd distinction, having no definite basis, renders it difficult for a town parson to give a party' (17/10/83). There were many in Dereham who 'could not well be asked to dinner' (17/7/67), but instead came with their children to teas or to garden parties. Respectable parishioners could be permitted to walk in the vicarage grounds on Sunday afternoons.

There was far more to Armstrong than his church and public roles, important and time-consuming as these were. His family and his concerns for the welfare of his children were central to his life, and it was the stability centred on house and home which gave him the greatest happiness, one that was cherished by Victorian society. 'The view from my study window is one to fill the heart with thankfulness. The weather lovely, the hay about [ready] my dear father frolicking with his grandchildren, my wife working under the shade of the trees, the bells ringing in memory of the Queen's coronation, myself sermonising and giving directions to my curate' (28/6/56). However, this serenity could sometimes be broken, as on the occasion of a whole series of domestic disasters on one day in November 1855 when the well fell in, the pump broke and the chimney caught fire. The excitement caused when his curate, Mr Watt, proposed to Mary Frazer, William Duncombe's step-daughter, is described with affectionate humour. Watt proposed and was accepted. 'Then of course followed mysterious disappearances on the part of the females, slamming of bedroom doors, brandies and water and the usual concomitants of "declarations"' (9/11/76). The ensuring of domestic stability was paramount, and to this end the 'disciplining of affections' was all-important. It was 'the great secret of happiness of existence and the only safeguard against moral defection' (12/8/54). It was this fundamental principle that governed and limited his relationship with Mary Hales.

Placed as he was securely in the middle class, he faced several family crises. The death of his infant daughter Gertrude followed by that of Lilly after childbirth is a reminder of the fragility of life and the impotence of doctors in the age before modern medicine. The elopement of Lilly shows that such things did not just happen in novels, but in a respectable parson's household. The financial problems of his clerk, Philo, the near-bankruptcy of his brother-in-law and the actual bankruptcy of Lilly's husband indicate how uncertain life could be, even for the apparently well-off.

Although he claimed that his main hobbies were those connected with his profession, he found relaxation in the countryside, fishing and, at certain times in his life, painting, but it was writing that gave him the greatest pleasure. This included the writing of sermons and several books, all except his guide to Little Stanmore of a religious nature. His shrewd eye and ability to create a scene or describe a person in a few carefully chosen words is shown in his diaries and it is in these that his literary abilities are seen at their best. They reveal a man who, for all his snobbery and uncompromising views on church matters, showed a gentle sense of sharp, yet kind humour when describing the foibles of his fellow men. He records the remark of Mr Philo, his 'sententious and matter-of-fact clerk', who noted after a funeral where the widow seemed particularly overcome with grief that 'noisy mourners speedily marry again' (13/7/54). The main object of Mr Wigg, the retiring people's warden, was to 'offend no-one and therefore [do] nothing' (17/4/64). Mr Wright, a respected draper in Dereham, had been entirely devoted to making money, living by the philosophy that you 'must look after yourself' (17/11/64). He enjoyed observing and writing about the various ways others made their living, such as the chemist who provided the travelling quack with a weekly supply of pills made of 'soap and other things which could do no harm' (10/5/54), and his conversation with the gingerbread maker in Castle Acre is also recorded (22/7/53). He included examples of Norfolk dialect and superstitions. Two parishioners believed they were bewitched, 'a notion still widespread in country parishes' (1/4/64).

He also wrote with great feeling about the countryside around him. Born a Londoner, he always looked forward to his visits to the city, but was always glad to return to his rural vicarage. He found the Norfolk landscape more pleasing than 'majestic scenery'.

The grandeur of the Alps could pall, after being long accustomed to regard them, and a level country has the advantage of good roads and consequent facilities to travel. He must have little of the painter

or poet in him who cannot enjoy any district, save only the fens....
The landscape wide-spread before the eye must always be beautiful.
The waiving fields of golden grain, the peaceful pastures, the retired
villages and the rippling stream. (28/9/54)

He described a March evening in 1854 as 'One of those premature
summer evenings on which everyone stands at his door' (27/3/54).
Returning to his newly painted vicarage after a spell in London in 1855
he wrote 'the perfect of cleanliness, the air was buoyant and redolent
with roses, the birds singing in the foliage and when I had washed off
the London dirt I took a deep breath and stood on the lawn and thanked
God my lot was cast in the country' (28/7/55). These quiet enjoyments
are lovingly described amid the busyness of his professional life.

There were many changes that Armstrong witnessed in the thirty
years he was at Dereham. Lawn tennis was replacing croquet as the
fashionable game at garden parties. New parlour games from America,
such as spelling bees, were becoming popular (16/2/76), and the first
'Hansom' cabs arrived in Norwich. In 1883 Helen had teeth extracted
using chloroform (7/11/83). Some old superstitions hung on, however.
Armstrong described in 1880 an old woman who had recited the Lord's
Prayer backwards to be cured of an affliction that had been 'put' on her.
'She promises me to say it <u>forwards</u>, thrice daily – but added "unless the
trouble come back and then I say it backards again"' (30/9/80). Nationally, too, society was changing. Ladies such as the Plumer girls lived in
'flats' in London and a farm labourer could become an MP.

Assessing how far Armstrong can be seen as 'typical' of the Victorian
clergy as a whole is difficult because there is little detailed evidence about
individuals with which to compare him. Nationally, the church reforms
beginning in the 1830s, along with the influence of a body of reforming
bishops, made the church less attractive to those simply seeking an
easy life of leisure. Men such as Armstrong's friend Henry Collinson of
Bilney were being replaced by a more conscientious generation. The life
of a hard-working priest in the slums of a great industrial city was very
different from that of a country parson. The sort of person who chose
the priesthood and the motives that attracted him to the life of a clergyman were thus as varied as they have ever been, but Armstrong was
one of an increasingly numerous group within the church who shared

the desire to give their parishioners an uplifting Sunday service and through regular visiting and support of the school and local charities, to improve their material as well as spiritual lives. Services could range from ones dominated by a rousing sermon, such as at Swanton Morley in the days of Henry Tacey, to those where music and ritual were more prominent, as in Dereham, but the motive of 'the salvation of souls' was always the same.

Armstrong's diaries reveal a man very much of his time, with the prejudices of his class and period. He was cultured and had a love of travel and new experiences, his descriptions of which show his clear-sighted observation and intellectual curiosity. But he was at his happiest within his own family circle. He took an interest in foreign affairs, particularly when they impinged upon the safety of his soldier son, while at the same time keeping abreast of changes in Dereham, visiting the new factories that were opening. His main concern was always the well-being of his family and of his parishioners. Relaxation involved the simple pleasures of fishing, reading and smoking a pipe, or sometimes cigars, with a friend. He also enjoyed painting, but undoubtedly his greatest talent was as an observer of life, recorded with such skill in his diaries, which allow us a window into the life of a typical Victorian country parson in a typical market town.

Bibliography

Allen, D.E. 1976. *The Naturalist in Britain.* London, Allen Lane.

Ambler, R.W. (ed.). 2006. *Lincolnshire Parish Correspondence of John Kaye, Bishop of Lincoln 1827–53.* Lincoln Record Society 94. Woodbridge, Boydell.

Armstrong, B. 1843. *Six Lectures on the Morning Services of the Church.* Doncaster.

—— 1847. *A Little History of Stanmore.* N.p.

—— 1847. *Questions and Answers on the Catechism.* London.

—— 1852. *Holy Catholic Church and the Communion of Saints.* Norwich.

—— 1853. *Sermon on the Advantages of Daily Public Worship.* Norwich.

—— 1856. *Manual of Devotion for Private and Parochial Use*, 5th edn. Norwich.

—— 1858. *A Selection of Psalms and Hymns Used in the Parish Church of East Dereham.* East Dereham.

—— 1861. *Military Life Not Incompatible with Religion: A Sermon Preached before the Officers and Men of the 15th Norfolk Rifle Volunteers in East Dereham Church.* Norwich.

—— n.d. *Short Prayers for the House.* N.p.

Armstrong, C. (ed.). 2012. *Under the Parson's Nose.* Dereham, Larks Press.

Armstrong, H.B.J. (ed.). 1949. *Armstrong's Diary.* London, Hodder & Stoughton.

—— 1963. *Armstrong's Norfolk Diary: Further Passages from the Diary of the Reverend Benjamin John Armstrong, Vicar of East Dereham, 1850–88.* London, Hodder & Stoughton.

Atherton, I., Fernie, E., Harper-Bill, C. and Smith, H. (eds). 1996. *Norwich Cathedral: Church, City and Diocese 1096–1996.* London, Hambledon.

Ayers, J. (ed.). 2003. *Paupers and Pig Killers: The Diary of William Holland, 1799–1818.* Stroud, Sutton.

Barney, J. 2015. 'Scandal at Bracon Ash', *The Annual* 24, Norfolk Historical and Archaeological Research Group.

Barry, F.R. 1970. *Period of My Life*. London, Hodder & Stoughton.

Baty, E. 1987. 'Victorian Church Building and Restoration'. PhD thesis, University of East Anglia.

Bennett, N. 2013. *Lincolnshire Parish Clergy c.1214–1968*, vol. 1. Lincolnshire Record Society 103. Woodbridge, Boydell.

Best, S. 1839. *Parochial Administrations*. London.

Bloom, J.H. 1843. *Castle Acre Priory*. Norwich.

Blunt, J.H. 1899. *The Book of Church Law*, 8th edn. London, Rivingtons.

Boston, N. and Puddy, E. 1962. *Dereham: The Biography of a Country Town*. Dereham, Colby.

Bowen, D. 1968. *The Idea of the Victorian Church*. Montreal, McGill University Press.

Brittain-Catlin, T. 2008. *The English Parsonage in the Early Nineteenth Century*. Reading, Spire Books.

Brontë, S. 1994. *Shirley*. London, Penguin.

Brooks, C. and Saint, A. (eds). 1995. *The Victorian Church, Architecture and Society*. Manchester, Manchester University Press.

Brown, C.K. Francis. 1953. *A History of the English Clergy, 1800–1900*. London, Faith Press.

Carthew, G.A. 1877. *The Hundred of Launditch and the Deanery of Brisley*, 3 vols. Norwich, Miller and Leavins.

Chadwick, O. 1960. *Victorian Miniature*. London, Hodder & Stoughton.

—— 1966, 1971. *The Victorian Church*, 2 vols. London, Black.

Challice, A. 1847. *Village School Fête*. London, John Oliver.

—— 1852. *The Laurel and the Palm*. London, John Oliver.

—— 1857. *Sisters of Charity*. London, Richard Bentley.

—— 1859. *The Wife's Temptation*. London, C. Westerton.

—— 1861. *A History of the Court of France under Louis XV*. London, Hurst and Blackett.

—— 1864. *French authors at home*. London.

—— 1871. *Memoirs of French Palaces*. London, Bradley, Evans and Co.

—— 1873. *Illustrious Women of France*. London, Bradley, Agnew and Co.

Colvin, H. 1995. *Dictionary of British Architects 1600–1840*, 3rd edn. New Haven, CT and London, Yale University Press.

Coombs, H. and Bax, A. 1930. *Journal of a Somerset Rector*. Edinburgh, John Murray.

Cozens-Hardy, B. 1946. 'The Early Days of the Society', *Norfolk Archaeology* **29**, 1–7.

Cresswell, Mrs. 1875. *Norfolk and the Squires, Clergy, Farmers and Labourers*. Norwich.

Crowther, M.A. 1970. *Church Embattled: Religious Controversy in Mid-Victorian England.* Newton Abbot, David and Charles.

Dashwood, G.H., Bulwer, W.E.G.L., Carthew, G.A., Grigson, W. and Jessopp, A. 1878. *The Visitation of Norfolk in the Year 1563*, 2 vols. Norwich, Norfolk and Norwich Archaeological Society.

Dymond, D. (ed.). 2007. *Parson and People in a Suffolk Village: Richard Cobbold's Wortham, 1824–77.* Ipswich, Wortham Research Group and Suffolk Family History Society.

Ede, J. and Virgoe, N. 1998. *Religious Worship in Norfolk: The 1851 Census of Accommodation and Attendance at Worship.* Norfolk Record Society 62. Norwich, Norfolk Record Society.

Farrer, E. 1890. *List of Norfolk Monumental Brasses.* Norwich.

Garrard, J.C. 2004. 'Longley, Charles Thomas, 1794–1868', *Oxford Dictionary of National Biography*, vol. 34, 401. Oxford, Oxford University Press

Gouldstone, T.M. 2005. *The Rise and Decline of Anglican Idealism in the Nineteenth Century.* Basingstoke, Palgrave Macmillan.

Greenwell, W. 1870. 'On the Opening of Grimes Graves'. *Journal of the Ethnological Society* n.s. **2**, 419–39.

Haig, A. 1984. *The Victorian Clergy.* London, Croom Helm.

Hammond, P.C. 1977. *The Parson and the Victorian Parish.* London, Hodder & Stoughton.

Hart, R. 1844. *The Antiquities of Norfolk.* Norwich, Charles Muskett.

Hartley, N. 2017. *Augustus Jessopp, Norfolk's Antiquary.* Kidderminster, Torre Books.

Hart-Raven, W. n.d. *Guide to the Roman Saxon Shore Fort of Burgh Castle.* N.p.

Hassall, W.O. (ed.). 1956. *Wheatley Records, 956–1956.* Oxfordshire Record Society 37. Oxford, Oxfordshire Record Society.

Heeney, B. 1976. *A Different Kind of Gentleman: Parish Clergy as Professional Men in Early and Mid-Victorian England.* Hamden, CT, Archon books.

Heitland, W.E. 1927. *After Many Years.* Cambridge, Cambridge University Press.

Henslowe, W.H. 1876. *The Accepted Rejection.* Norwich.

Howkins, A. 1985. *Poor Labouring Men.* London, Hodder & Stoughton.

Iremonger, R. 1813. *Suggestions to the Promoters of Dr Bell's System of Tuition.* Winchester, William Jones.

James, M.R. 1926. *Eton and King's* London, William & Norgate.

Jefferies, R. 1992. 'The Parson's Wife' (1880), in *Hodge and His Masters.* Stroud, Alan Sutton.

Jessopp, A. 1879. 'Gilbert Haultoft's Will', 'Bowthore Hall' and 'Notes on the History of Breccles Hall', *Norfolk Archaeology* **8**, 171–82; 273–81; 303–18.

—— 1884. 'On Married Clergy in the Thirteenth Century', *Norfolk Archaeology* **9**, 187–200.

—— 1887. *Arcady, for Better or for Worse.* London, T. Fisher Unwin.

—— 1892. *Studies by a Recluse in Cloister, Town and Country.* London, T. Fisher Unwin.

—— 1894. *Trials of a Country Parson.* London, T. Fisher Unwin.

—— 1901. *Before the Great Pillage.* London, T. Fisher Unwin.

—— 1998. *The Phantom Ghost and Other Ghost Stories of an Antiquarian,* ed. J.A. Salmonson. Uncasville, CT, Richard H. Fawcett.

Kelly's Directory. 1916. *Cambridgeshire, Norfolk, Suffolk.* London, Kelly's Directories.

King, D. 1996. 'The Panel Paintings and Stained Glass', in I. Atherton, E. Fernie, C. Harper-Bill and H. Smith (eds), *Norwich Cathedral: Church, City and Diocese 1096–1996.* London, Hambledon.

Knight, F. 1995. *The Nineteenth-Century Church and English Society.* Cambridge, Cambridge University Press.

Lee, R. 2002. 'Paternalism, Distance and Dignity', *Norfolk Archaeology* **44**, 1–14.

—— 2006. *Rural Society and the Anglican Clergy, 1815–1914: Encountering and Managing the Poor.* Woodbridge, Boydell.

Legge, A. 1891. *Ancient Churchwardens' Accounts in the Parish of North Elmham, from A.D. 1539 to A.D. 1577.* Norwich.

Lentin, A. 1988. 'Anglicanism, Parliament and the Courts', in G. Parsons (ed.), *Religion in Victorian Britain*, vol. 2, *Controversies*. Manchester, Manchester University Press.

Liddon, H.P. 1895. *Clerical Life and Work.* London, Longman.

Longcroft, A. and Wade Martins, S. (eds). 2013. *Building an Education: An Historical and Architectural Study of Rural Schools and Schooling in Norfolk, c.1800–1944.* Norwich, Norfolk Historic Buildings Group.

Loudon, J.C. 1822. *Magazine of Natural History.* London.

Machin, G.I.T. 1987. *Politics and Churches in Great Britain.* Oxford, Clarendon Press.

Manning, C.R. 1872. 'Grimes Graves, Weeting', *Norfolk Archaeology* **7**, 168–77.

Manual of Clerical Life by Various Authors 1888. London.

Marcon, W.H. 1927. *Reminiscences of a Norfolk Parson.* Holt, Rounce & Wortley.

Maurice, P. 1851. *Postscript to the Popery of Oxford: The Number of the Name of the Beast.* London.

McClatchey, D. 1960. *Oxfordshire Clergy, 1777–1869.* Oxford, Oxford University Press.

Moore, N. and Matthew, H.C.G. 2004. 'Elwin, Whitwell, 1816–1900'. *Oxford Dictionary of National Biography*, vol. 18, 373–4. Oxford, Oxford University Press.

Morris's Commercial Directory. 1868. *Suffolk.* N.p.

Mumm, S. (ed.). 2001. *All Saints Sisters of the Poor: An Anglican Sisterhood in the Nineteenth Century.* Church of England Record Society 9. Woodbridge, Boydell.

Muthesius, S. 2012. 'Provinciality and the Victorians: Church Design in Nineteenth-Century East Anglia', in T.A. Heslop, E. Mellings and M. Thøfner (eds), *Art, Faith and Place in East Anglia.* Woodbridge, Boydell.

Neave, D. 1986. *Armstrong's Crowle Journal 1842–1844.* Crowle Parochial Church Council.

Obelkevich, J. 1976. *Religion and Rural Society.* Oxford, Oxford University Press.

O'Day, R. 1988. 'The Clerical Renaissance in Victorian England', in G. Parsons (ed.), *Religion in Victorian Britain*, vol. 1, *Traditions.* Manchester, Manchester University Press.

Owen, D. 1996. 'The Cathedral 1840–1945', in I. Atherton, E. Fernie, C. Harper-Bill and H. Smith (eds), *Norwich Cathedral: Church, City and Diocese 1096–1996.* London, Hambledon.

Oxenden A. 1857. *The Pastoral Office: Its Duties, Difficulties, Privileges and Prospects.* London.

Parsons, G. 1988. 'Reform, Revival and Realignment: The Experience of Victorian Anglicanism', in G. Parsons, (ed.), *Religion in Victorian Britain*, vol. 1, *Traditions.* Manchester, Manchester University Press.

—— 1988. 'Victorian Roman Catholicism', in G. Parsons, (ed.), *Religion in Victorian Britain*, vol. 1, *Traditions.* Manchester, Manchester University Press

Pevsner, N. 1951. *The Buildings of England: Middlesex.* Harmondsworth, Penguin.

Pevsner, N. and Wilson, B. 1997, 1999. *The Buildings of England: Norfolk*, 2 vols. London, Penguin.

Plomer, W. (ed.). 1980. *Kilvert's Diary, 1870–1879.* London, Jonathan Cape.

Pocock, Tom 1993. *Rider Haggard and the Lost Empire.* London, Weidenfeld and Nicholson.

Russell, A. 1980. *The Clerical Profession.* London, SPCK.

Scotland, N. 1981. *Methodism and the Revolt of the Field: A Study of the Methodist Contribution to Agricultural Trade Unionism in East Anglia, 1872–96.* Stroud, Alan Sutton.

—— 2004. 'Sumner, John Bird, 1780–1862', *Oxford Dictionary of National Biography*, vol. 53, 330–2. Oxford, Oxford University Press.

Sisam, K. and Brewer, C. 2004. 'Skeat, Walter William', in *Oxford Dictionary of National Biography*, vol. 50, 817–18. Oxford, Oxford University Press.

Skinner, J 1984. *Journal of a Somerset Rector, 1803–1834.*Oxford, Oxford University Press.

Thistlethwaite, J. 1977. 'The Etchings of Edward Thomas Daniell (1804–1842)', *Norfolk Archaeology* **36**, 1–22.

Tiller, K. 2016. *Parsonages.* Oxford, Shire Publications.

Trollope, A. 1996. *Framley Parsonage.* London, Trollope Society.

Turner, B. 2015. *The Victorian Parson.* Stroud, Amberley.

Verey, D. (ed.). 1979. *The Diary of a Cotswold Parson, 1783–1854.* Stroud, Alan Sutton.

Virgin, P. 1989. *The Church in the Age of Negligence.* Cambridge, James Clarke.

Wade Martins, S. 1980. *A Great Estate at Work: Holkham and Its Inhabitants in the Nineteenth Century.* Cambridge, Cambridge University Press.

—— 2002. *Changing Agriculture in Georgian and Victorian Norfolk.* Cromer, Poppyland.

—— 2010. 'The County School Movement', *Rural History Today* **18**, January, 4–5.

Wade Martins, S. and Williamson, T. 2008. *The Countryside of East Anglia.* Woodbridge, Boydell.

Weaver, J.R.H. and Curthoys, M.C. 2004. 'Jessopp, Augustus, 1823–1914', *Oxford Dictionary of National Biography*, vol. 30, 94–5. Oxford, Oxford University Press.

Wells, R. (ed.). 1992. *Victorian Village: The Diaries of the Reverend John Coker Egerton of Burwash, 1857–1888.* Stroud, Alan Sutton.

White, W. 1845. *Norfolk Directory.* Sheffield: Robert Leader.

—— 1864. *Norfolk Directory.* London, Simpkin, Marshall and Co.

—— 1872 *Lincolnshire Directory*, 3rd edn. Sheffield, William White.

—— 1883. *Norfolk Directory.* London, Simpkin, Marshall and Co.

Wilson, R.G. 1996. 'The Cathedral in the Georgian Period', in I. Atherton, E. Fernie, C. Harper-Bill and H. Smith (eds), *Norwich Cathedral: Church, City and Diocese 1096–1996.* London, Hambledon.

Winstanley, R.L., James, P. and Richards, H. (eds). 1981–2000. *The Diaries of James Woodforde*, 17 vols. Chinley, The Parson Woodforde Society.

Woodward, L. 1962. *Age of Reform 1815–1870*, 2nd edn. Oxford, Oxford University Press.

Yates, N. 1991. *Buildings, Faith and Worship*. Oxford, Oxford University Press.

Timeline

Significant national (N), local (L) and family (F) events during the lifetime of Benjamin Armstrong, 1817–1890

1817 (F) Birth of Benjamin Armstrong.

1820 (F) Birth of Benjamin's sister Ann Armstrong (Challice).

1828 (N) Repeal of the Test and Corporation Acts.

1829 (N) Passing of the Catholic Emancipation Act.

1832 (N) Passing of the Great Reform Act.

1833 (N) John Keeble's Assize Sermon at Oxford and the formation of the 'Association of Friends of the Church'.

(N) John Henry Newman began publishing *Tracts for the Times* and the 'Oxford' high church movement began.

(L) Dereham gasworks erected.

1834 (N) Passing of the Poor Law Amendment Act leading to the reorganisation of Gresenhall House of Industry as a Union Workhouse.

1835 (N) Report of the Ecclesiastical Commission.

1836 (N) Laws introduced to limit the holding of parishes in plurality, enforcing residency and tithes to be paid in money rather than kind.

1837 (N) Accession of Queen Victoria.

(L) Death of Bishop Bathurst, replaced as Bishop of Norwich by the reformer, John Stanley.

(F) Armstrong entered Caius College, Cambridge.

1841 (L) Dereham National School rebuilt to replace that set up in 1814.

(L) The British School founded.

(F) Armstrong ordained as a deacon by the Bishop of London.

(F) Marriage of Anne Armstrong to John Challice.

1842 (N) John Henry Newman resigned from his Oxford college and withdrew with his followers to his parish of Littlemore.

(F) Armstrong ordained as a priest.

(F) Marriage of Armstrong to Anne (Nellie) Duncombe.

(F) Armstrong and Nellie move to Crowle, Lincolnshire.

1844 (F) Birth of Helen Armstrong; family move to Little Stanmore-with-Whitchurch.

1845 (N) Newman joined the Roman Catholic Church.

(N) Samuel Wilberforce becomes Bishop of Oxford.

1846 (L) The railway reaches Dereham, linking it to Norwich, London, Cambridge and the east coast.

1848 (N) Establishment of a Central Board of Health with powers to set up local health boards.

(F) Birth of Louisa.

1849 (N) Publication of John Ruskin's *The Seven Lamps of Architecture*.

(L) Samuel Hinds becomes Bishop of Norwich.

1850 (N) Pope Pius IX creates hierarchy of Roman Catholic bishops in England.

(N) Privy Council's rejection of the Bishop of Exeter's refusal to institute Gorham to his living increases the rift between the high and low church parties and was the first of many such cases.

(F) Armstrong moves to Dereham. Birth of John.

1851 (N) Great Exhibition in London.

(N) Religious census of Great Britain.

(L) First phase of 'restoration' of the chancel of Dereham church, including a stained-glass east window, completed.

1852 (F) Armstrong enlarges Dereham vicarage.

1853 (L) Dereham Institute founded.

(L) Dereham Health Board set up.

(F) Birth of Herbert (Bertie).

1854 (N) Beginning of the Crimean War.

(N) Samuel Wilberforce founds Cuddesdon College, Oxford.

1855 (F) Birth of Gertrude (dies at 11 months).

1856 (N) Treaty of Paris ends Crimean War.

(L) Dereham Corn Hall opened.

(F) Erection of memorial cross to Gertrude.

1857 (L) John Pelham replaces Samuel Hinds as Bishop of Norwich.

1858 (L) De Narde gravestone erected in memory of French prisoner of war soldier shot near Dereham in 1799.

1859 (N) Publication of Darwin's *Origin of Species*.

(L) Gas lighting installed in Dereham church.

1860 (N) Publication of controversial *Essays and Reviews*.

(L) Founding of the Dereham Rifle Volunteers.

1861 (N) First edition of *Hymns Ancient and Modern* published.

1862 (N) Newcastle Commission report published, leading to the establishment of 'payments by results' system in schools.

1864 (N) Founding of the Salvation Army.

1867 (N) Second Reform Act extends parliamentary franchise.

1869 (L) Dereham Burial Board set up and new cemetery established.

1870 (N) Forster Education Act allows for the establishment of School Boards and thus secular elementary education.

1871 (L) Final gilding and painting of chancel of Dereham church completed.

1872 (N) Founding of Joseph Arch's Agricultural Labourers' Union.

1873 (N) Founding of the reconstituted Church of England Temperance Society.

(L) Dereham British School becomes a Board School.

(F) Death of Armstrong's father.

1874 (N) Archbishop Tait's Public Worship Regulation Act, designed to limit high church ritual, becomes law.

(F) Louisa marries Arthur Nelson.

(F) Herbert leaves for West Indies with 97th Foot (later part of the West Kent Regiment).

1875 (N) Local Government Act creating Local Boards (forerunner to elected local councils).

(L) Founding of Toftwood and Etling Green Board schools.

(F) Death of Anne Challice.

1876 (F) John Armstrong marries Mary Bell.

1877 (N) Founding of the Society for the Preservation of Ancient Buildings (SPAB) by William Morris.

1878 (L) Founding of the Dereham branch of the Temperance Society.

(F) Birth of son, Herbert Benjamin, to John and Mary, Armstrong's first grandson.

1879 (N) Zulu War, January to June

(L) Armstrong elected to Dereham Local Board.

1880 (L) Consecrating of St Withburga's chapel, Norwich Road, Dereham.

(F) Birth of Louisa's first child, Helen.

(F) John Armstrong becomes his father's curate.

1881 (N) Boer War December 1880 to March 1881.

(L) Founding of Dereham Fire Brigade.

1882 (N) War in Egypt and Sudan against the Mahdi.

(L) Completion of piped water supply to Dereham.

1883 (F) Death of Louisa after the birth of her second child, Margaret.

1884 (N) Third Reform Act, giving farm labourers a parliamentary vote.

1885 (N) Fall of Khartoum and death of General Gordon.

(L) Removal of galleries and installation of a heating system in Dereham church.

1887 (F) Last diary entry in May.

1888 (F) Death of Armstrong's wife, Nellie.

(F) John becomes rector of Heydon.

(F) Armstrong resigns his living.

1890 Death of Armstrong in December.

Index